Old Lerwick
Lanes and Lodberries

Old Lerwick
Lanes and Lodberries

Douglas M. Sinclair

The Shetland Times Ltd.
Lerwick
2021

Old Lerwick - Lanes and Lodberries

First published 2021.

ISBN 978-1-910997-39-0

© Douglas M. Sinclair

Front cover photograph: The North Lodberry and Lerwick waterfront from below Fort Charlotte. c.1880

Douglas M. Sinclair has asserted his right under the Copyright, Designs and Patents Act 1988, to be identified as Author of this work.

All rights reserved. No part of this publication may be reproduced, stored in a retrieval system, or transmitted, in any form, by any means, electronic, mechanical, photocopying, recording or otherwise, without the prior written permission of the publishers.

A CIP catalogue record for this book is available from the British Library.
British Library Cataloguing-in-Publication Data

Printed and published by
The Shetland Times Ltd,
Gremista, Lerwick, Shetland, ZE1 0PX.

To Margaret

for all her valuable help and encouragement
that ensured this book came to fruition

Contents

Acknowledgements viii
Introduction ix
Perspective View of Lerwick xi
Naming Lerwick's Lanes, Closes, Courts, Places and Piers xvi

Chapter 1: From Twageos Road to Scottshall Court
    Twageos Road and Lovers Loan 1
    Leog 3
    Copland's Pier 7
    Miss Chalmers Stair and Murray's Lodberry 9
    Stout's Pier and Stout's Court 14
    Nice Court, now Hayfield Court 16
    Ross Court and Steamers' Store 19
    Craigie's Court and the Craigie Stane 25
    The Lodberrie 27
    Sands' Court, Raven's Court and Water Lane 29
    Chromate Lane 33
    Seafield Court 35
    Scottshall Court 37
    Lodberries and Piers at the South End 39

Chapter 2: From Church Road to Charlotte Street
    Church Lane and Queens Lane 42
    Spence's Court 45
    Crooked Lane 47
    Norna's Court 49
    Gardie Court 52
    Gardie Lane 55
    Heddell's Court 56
    Heddell's Park 59
    The Market Cross 61
    Mounthooly Street 64
    Navy Lane, Baker's Court and Wren Court 68
    Law Lane 72
    Albert Court 74
    Pirate Lane 76
    Hangcliff Lane 78
    Swallow Lane later Bank Lane 81
    Mariners' Court 83
    Reform Lane 86
    Park Lane 87

    Pitt Lane 90
    Kelday's Court 92
    Quendale Lane 94
    Fox Lane 96
    Pilot Place now Pilot Lane 98
    Burns Lane 99
    Hill Lane 102
    Back Charlotte Lane 104
    Charlotte Street 105

Chapter 3: From Tolbooth Quay to the Esplanade
    Tolbooth Quay, Hay's Corner and the Towbooth Walk 108
    Mouat's Lodberry 111
    Clark's Court 113
    Sinclair's Steps and Greig's Pier 120
    Leask's Lodberry 122
    Taylor's Steps and Taylor's Pier 123
    Victoria Wharf 125
    Trance Closs 130
    Irvine Closs 133
    Harrison Square 136
    Lower Tait's Closs, now Reform Lane 138
    Angus Pier and Angus Closs 140
    Mullay's Steps 142
    Peterson's Closs 143
    Grierson's Lodberry 144
    Greig's Closs 146
    Campbell's Lane, now Campbell's Closs 149
    Nicolson's Closs 150
    Merran Moad's Steps 152
    Tait's Lodberry 154
    Muir's Steps and Osy Anderson's Pier 158
    Charlotte Place 160
    The North Lodberry 162
    Tod's Steps 166
    The Esplanade 170

Chapter 4:
    Other Names Agreed in 1845 182
    Gullet's Brae 183
    Whisky Lane 186
    References 197
    Index 219

Acknowledgements

I would like to recognise the valuable contribution made by Lerwegians past and present who, by sharing their knowledge and enthusiasm, inspired me to write this book. The photographs that are not acknowledged are from my own collection or taken by my wife Margaret or myself.

A special thank you is extended to Brian Smith, Angus Johnson and Mark Smith at Shetland Archives for their continued help and patience during my frequent visits, and Linda Sutherland for her input. Also Charlotte Black, Kenneth Shearer and the staff of The Shetland Times Ltd for the production of an excellent publication.

Introduction

Gordon Stevenson replacing signs in May 1993 after repainting (Courtesy of Malcolm Younger)

Visitors and locals alike often ask "Why do most signs in Lerwick's lanes, closses and courts have more than one name?" It is hoped that this book may provide the answer.

In 1845 the lanes, closses, courts, places and piers of Lerwick existing at that time were officially named by a sub-committee of the Commissioners of Police of the Burgh of Lerwick. Some retained the name they were known by but others received a completely different designation. It transpired that many of these were not popular and consequently Lerwegians continued to refer to the original name for many years afterwards. Therefore, to ensure that the original names are not forgotten, previous names are now signposted as are those introduced at a later date. However, some names continue to be used which have never been signposted, e.g. Gillie's Pier, Heddell's Park and Gullet's Brae.

As far as possible I have researched the origin of the previous names and identified the various people associated with them. It is not known why the names of some individuals were retained and others were not, or in many cases how or why the new names were chosen.

Lodberries were built by merchants and were referred to by their names as they were privately owned. In early legal documents, in particular sasines, the term *Loadberry* was used, but later changed to *lodberry*. Consequently lodberry is the spelling I have used throughout this publication with the exception of "The Lodberrie", which was the name Tammie Moncrieff gave to his property. It was previously Robertson's Lodberry. The piers were removed or built over when the Esplanade was created between 1883 and 1886. Although they lost their original use many of the lodberries still exist, such as Greig's Lodberry which is now the Peerie Shop and the Peerie Shop Café. The piers and lodberries are worthy of documentation as are the many courts and buildings that were demolished in the 1960s.

Following my retirement I began writing articles about Lerwick for *Shetland Life* magazines under the heading "The Past in Pictures" and have included some of these where appropriate.

It is hoped that this publication will bring these aspects of Old Lerwick to life and encourage the reader to notice the signs when walking along Commercial Street and the Esplanade. Take a moment to stop and look upwards and view the wide range of architectural styles of the buildings too.

A wander through the numerous lanes and closses will reveal many hidden gems that still exist of Old Lerwick.

Douglas M. Sinclair

PERSPECTIVE VIEW OF LERWICK
from the North End by William Aberdeen in 1766

The first significant reference to market activity in Bressay Sound was in 1615 when an edict was issued from Scalloway, the capital at that time, whereby due to theft and prostitution women were forbidden to trade with the Dutch in the Sound and booths were ordered to be burned to the ground.

The first mention of Lerwick in a trade connection was in 1625 when trade was prohibited due to lawlessness in which drunkenness, theft, prostitution, assault and murder were all alleged and again buildings were destroyed.[1]

However, by the 1640s the merchants had built the first substantial houses along the shoreline.

In the 1700s a path along the water's edge was referred to as The Shore and it eventually formed the line of Commercial Street as we know it. William Aberdeen's *Perspective View of Lerwick* in 1766 shows that there were about 90 properties along the shore from Lower Leog to the fort that existed at that time. William Aberdeen was an excise man stationed in Scalloway when the plan was drawn.[2]

From Leog to the Market Cross area, where two boats can be seen, was mainly rock banks with sandy sections, while from there towards the fort was a stretch of sandy beach. In the mid-17th century the Dutch referred to Lerwick as Sand Bay.[3]

The first fort was built between 1652 and 1653 during the First Anglo-Dutch War (1652-1654) to protect from the Dutch, but no trace remains. The building of the second was started by Charles II's master builder, Robert Milne, at the beginning of the Second Anglo-Dutch War in 1665, but the walls were still not finished in 1667 when the war ended and the fort was subsequently abandoned. In 1673, during the Third Anglo-Dutch War (1672-1674), the Dutch landed unopposed and burned the barracks.

Three companies of the Sutherland Fencibles arrived in 1781, commanded by Major James Sutherland, to start on the extensive repair of the fort under the direction of Captain Fraser, chief engineer for Scotland.[4] The intention was to protect the town from French and American privateers including the renegade Scotsman John Paul Jones.[5] This was during the American War of Independence when Britain was at war with France, Spain and the Netherlands. That same year Fort Charlotte was named after Queen Charlotte, the wife of King George III who was the reigning monarch at the time.[6]

Fort Charlotte from the air. c.1950

Replica 18th century 18-pound cannons were installed by Historic Scotland in April 1995.[7]

Many early properties can be seen on the 1766 map. The Old Manse is believed to be the oldest continually inhabited house, dating from around 1683.[8] [9]

Unfortunately, many of these buildings at the south end of Lerwick, such as Ross Court, Craigie's Court, Sands' Court, Raven's Court and Water Lane were demolished in the 1960s to make way for housing. Thankfully, some old houses still exist at the south end, such as 10 Commercial Street, Lochend House, Seawinds, Scottshall Court, Seafield Court, and also current shop buildings along Commercial Street including The Shetland Times, Jamieson's Knitwear, Island Larder Ltd and Outdoor Trek/Outdoor4Kids to mention but a few.

In 1766 there were three rows of buildings extending across the thoroughfare and on to the beach with "trances", or openings in the middle, to allow access to pedestrians and very narrow carts. These are shown on the map.

The South Trance, known as Yorston's Trance[10] and also as the Dark Trance,[11] stretched across the space between what is now the Wine Shop at 113 Commercial Street and Santander, opposite, at 66 Commercial Street. James Yorston was a merchant who bought the houses from Andrew Heddell in 1793. The trance house was removed in either 1836 or 1837[12] and the street was widened.

The Middle Trance is believed to have been between what was until recent years S. & R. Swanson, but since 2020 Nordsterna Shetland Crystal Boutique at 141 Commercial Street, and opposite, presently R.A.M. Knitwear, at 84 Commercial Street.[13] The date of its removal is not known, but it still existed in 1773 when stated as an address in a document.[14] However, John Robertson, who was born in 1826 and lived in the South Trance, made no mention of any other trance when he gave evidence in the Lerwick Paving Case. This fact was reinforced by J.K. Galloway, procurator fiscal, who also mentioned the existence of only one trance in Commercial Street in 1834.[15]

An illustration by Davy Cooper showing how the trances may have looked

The location of the North Trance was in the vicinity of where Boots UK Ltd is now, at 173 Commercial Street. Part of the building and the arch were removed in April 1781 following a petition by Major James Sutherland. He had complained that the trance house was in a dangerous condition and hazardous to inhabitants and his troops. They were billeted at Fort Charlotte and regularly had to pass back and forth through the arch. An inspection was carried out and as a result the sheriff ordered that the northeast part of the gable and part of the north wall of this building, owned by Mrs Elizabeth Yorston and Mrs Jean Redder, née Kelday, be taken down and stones and materials be sold to pay expenses.[16]

Between 1834 and 1837 what remained of this former trance house was removed. It was described as a low dilapidated building that extended 3m to 5m into the street.[17] Robert Linklater, merchant, bought the ruinous buildings, including what was commonly called Jean Kelday's House, and waste ground opposite on the lower side, in 1844 from the sequestrated estate of William Hay and Charles Ogilvy, merchants and bankers.[18] He built a dwelling house and shop on the landward side. An upper storey was added in 1868 and it became the Royal Hotel.[19] This building now houses Boots UK Ltd. On the waste ground opposite he built a house and shop, which is now Universal Stores, and moved his business there. This was his residence until his death in 1874.

Modern day examples of trances can be found at Norna's Court (between Island Larder Ltd and Outdoor Trek/Outdoor4Kids at 97 & 99 Commercial Street respectively) and also in the Heddell's Park housing scheme. Another example is at the foot of Burns Lane between Tooth & Nail Barber Surgeons and Burns Lane Clothing.

Several structures obstructed the street before improvements were made in about 1840. In front of the shop that is now Loose Ends, at 96 Commercial Street, there was a curious wall jutting out. It started from the north side and extended along for some little distance to the south, then took a curve towards the house leaving a narrow opening between it and the opposite building.

Mr Magnus Burns's house was on the site of the present M&Co and the entrance to the kitchen was by a flight of steps that came out right into the middle of the street. There was a parapet wall at the side with an iron railing to prevent people from falling to the beach below. The shop opposite (for many years Dennis Coutts but since 2020 Boo-Stanes) protruded several feet beyond its present line resulting in the width of the street being no more than 2m.[20]

The trance at the foot of Burns Lane. 1950s (Courtesy of Elizabeth Angus)

Perspective View of Lerwick

Below Fort Charlotte with the North Lodberry and Charlotte Place on the right. c.1880

The steps at the foot of Sooth Kirk Closs had been taken away in 1818.[21] With the removal of the South Trance, then Miss Chalmers' Stair in about 1847,[22] this allowed a thoroughfare from Commercial Street to Twageos.

Miss Chalmers' Stair had crossed the street at Stout's Court, restricting carts at the south end, while at the north end below Fort Charlotte there was a dangerous steep rock drop to the sea with a narrow sheep path which could be accessed on foot and possibly by a pony with a very narrow cart. The narrowest part of the path was at the corner of the fort and from there towards the north it became wider.[23]

The Esplanade. c.1900

In 1838 construction work began by cutting into the solid rock cliff face to create a narrow roadway below the fort.[24] Doing so resulted in a steep embankment without protection down to the beach below.

In fact it was only after the mail gig had fallen over the embankment that it was thought necessary to erect a safety barrier, but it was not until about 1880 that a simple wooden fence was erected. By 1896 several of the posts required to be renewed.

In 1904-05 the road was widened and a considerable amount of stone from the rock face was used for infill in the construction of Alexandra Wharf. Debris was used to construct the high retaining wall that replaced the wooden fence and a wide pavement was created.[25]

Commercial Road was named in 1845.

Naming Lerwick's Lanes, Closses, Courts, Places and Piers

Lerwick's South End. Late 1880s

By the middle of the 19th century Lerwick had rapidly grown from Leog to Fort Charlotte. Rows of tenement type houses had been built from the Hillhead with gables facing Commercial Street. Buildings and lodberries had also been constructed on the lower side of the street.

Lodberries were an integral part of Old Lerwick's waterfront. The word lodberry derives from Old Norse, *hladberg* – a landing rock,[1] but in the Lerwick context it applies to a courtyard built into the sea, with a strong sea wall with a door through which goods could be unloaded from or loaded into a boat. In the courtyard there was usually a store, and in some few instances the store itself was built into the sea, with a courtyard behind.[2] Merchants had them built as a convenient means of unloading supplies and goods, which had been transported by sea in the days before piers were built.

From left: Lodberries stretching from Anderson & Company, built on the site of Innes's Lodberry, to Charlotte Place and the North Lodberry on the right. c.1880

Lodberries had another purpose too – namely to facilitate the covert practice of smuggling Dutch gin, tobacco and tea. The merchants who lived on the landward side of the street had tunnels built from their lodberries to exit either in their house or a skilfully concealed outlet in a convenient garden.

There was by now an escalation of lanes, closses and courts with a diverse assortment of names. Some bore the name of residents while others reflected the profession or activity of the inhabitants. Others simply related to topography.

An agreement was reached in 1815 whereby the heritors of Sound disponed to the feuars and heritors of Lerwick certain waste grounds and quarries on the Lerwick side of a line stretching approximately from the Sletts to Freefield.[3] This line formed the Burgh Road. On 10th February, 1818, the town of Lerwick became a free and independent burgh of barony.[4]

As a result of legislation the Commissioners of Police were elected in 1833 with the power to levy rates. The income raised was used to clean and pave the streets and lanes, also to maintain and improve water supplies, i.e. wells.

In 1845 the commissioners set up a small sub-committee to officially name and number the streets, lanes and houses in the burgh of Lerwick.[5] Burgh Road was officially named, also Commercial Street. The original path along the foreshore from Leog to Fort Charlotte was commonly called The Shore, and in very early documents it was mentioned as the King's Street.[6] It was later referred to as Main Street before becoming Commercial Street.

Although the location of some thoroughfares had been dramatically changed by development, an attempt was made to keep the old names as far as was possible. However, it could be argued that some of the new names adopted lacked imagination.

Reform Lane, formerly Gilbert Tait's Closs. c.1910

In particular those being attributed to earlier politicians and reference to the Scottish Reform Act, as in Gilbert Tait's Closs being renamed Reform Lane.

Houses and shops were numbered from Leog north along Commercial Street with the odd numbers on the upper or landward side and the even numbers on the lower or seaward side. Some courts were given numbers but the name remained in general use. Houses in the lanes and closses were given odd numbers on the south side and even numbers on the north.

On 20th April, 1882, Lerwick's coat of arms was granted. The Viking warship recalls the link with the Nordic countries and Lerwick's reliance on the sea. The battle-axe is a symbol of the Norse warriors. The crest shows a raven, which is an important bird in Norse mythology.

In 1883 work commenced on creating the Esplanade and it was completed by 1886.[7] As a consequence the small piers were no more and although most lodberry

Lerwick's coat of arms. 1882

The Esplanade. c.1903

buildings were retained their contact with the sea was lost. A good example is at the Peerie Shop where an inscription on the wall to the left of the entrance states Greig's Pier.

Lerwick Town Council and Zetland County Council agreed in February 1936 that the boundary be extended. This took place on 15th May, 1938, and included an area from approximately Seafield,

Greig's Pier carved into stone provides evidence that the Peerie Shop was once a lodberry

around the back of Clickimin Loch, along the old Staney Hill road, then by the side of the Gremista burn and on to and including Green Head.[8]

Lerwick Community Council received a coat of arms on 23rd February, 1983. It was basically the same as the old burgh arms, only the helmet was replaced by a crown, common to community councils.

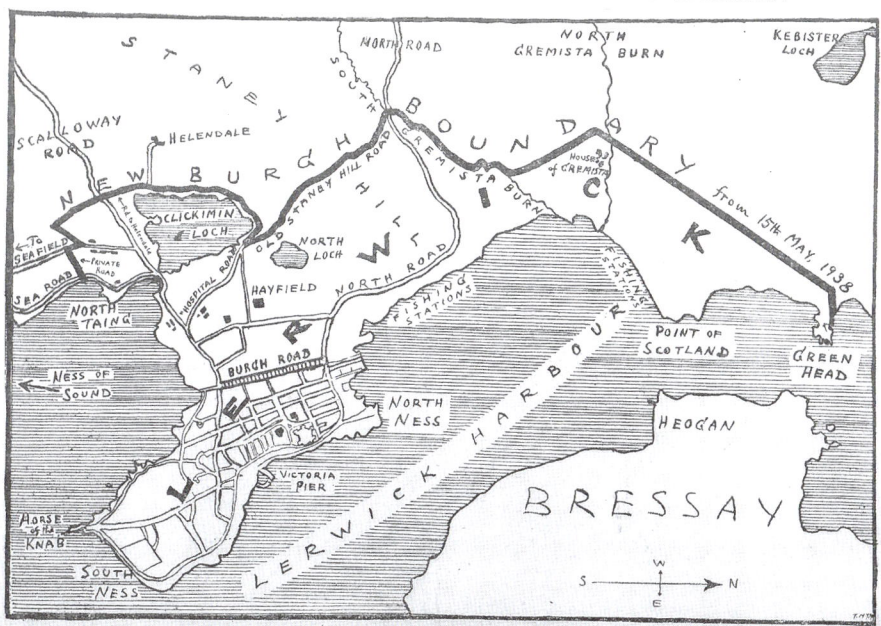

The burgh boundary in 1938

Lerwick Community Council's coat of arms. 1983

CHAPTER 1

FROM TWAGEOS ROAD TO SCOTTSHALL COURT

Twageos Road and Lovers Loan

Twageos from the sea showing, from left: Jeannie Bult's Hoose, Strong's House, Twageos House, the Widows' Asylum, The Knowe, Anderson Educational Institute, Lower and Upper Leog. Late 1880s

From Twageos House north to the Tirl Grind was named Twageos Road in 1845 and The Lovers Lane was renamed Lovers Lane.

The Tirl Grind, or gate, marked the boundary between Lerwick and Twageos and was described as having three pillars.[1] It opened on to a road and Twageos parks.

The gate was at the foot of Lovers Lane, now Lovers Loan, between there and towards the south end of the Widows' Asylum, which was constructed in 1865. The name was changed to Widows' Homes in 1912 and renamed Anderson Homes in 1971.

Twageos House was built at the beginning of the 18th century for the Earl of Morton to house his personnel.[2] The large, imposing and allegedly haunted building was

Lovers Loan. c.1910

Twageos House. It was demolished in 1961

Twageos and Lerwick. c.1900

situated near the foot of what is now Gressy Loan on the south side. It was demolished in 1961.

The word Twageos is reputed to have been derived from the two geos that are in the vicinity: Scottish *twa* – two, and Old Norse *gjá* – a cleft in the landscape.[3]

Twageos. c.1967 (Courtesy of Dennis Coutts)

LEOG

Leog is derived from Old Norse *ljog* – a low flat marshy place.[1] The area was originally referred to as "the Mires o Leog".[2]

Leog Place, officially named in 1845, was from the foot of what is now Lovers Loan to Leog, including the houses that later became known as Lower Leog.

Lower Leog prior to demolition in early 1958. (Courtesy of Elizabeth Angus)

The first mention of a house at Leog is found in a sasine by James Laurenson to John Mitchell of Berry dated 1684. It refers to the new house of Leog being built by William Craigie, merchant, who had obtained a piece of waste ground from James Laurenson two years earlier.[3]

At this time the local prominent families often intermarried, or were connected through marriage, and property frequently changed hands.

William Dick of Wormadale, who incidentally was married to Janet Mitchell of Berry, obtained the house at Leog in 1687.[4] The property ultimately passed to his grandson and heir, Andrew Dick of Wormadale. In 1741 he disponed to William Irvine the large house in Leog, "now waste", which had belonged to his grandfather, and the new house immediately below which had been built by William Dick.[5]

The property passed from William Irvine to William Nicolson of Lochend in 1756,[6] whom it is said built, or repaired, the house at Leog that later became known as Lower

Leog.[7] Following his death, his cousin Arthur Nicolson of Lochend became his heir. He was married to Margaret, William Irvine's daughter. Arthur died in 1793.[8] Their son and heir, also Arthur, sold the house, garden and parks of Leog to Robert Deans in 1815.[9] Arthur died in 1819.

Robert Deans, merchant, came to Shetland on 24th March 1781 for the repair of Fort Charlotte and two years later he married Barbara Torrie,[10] daughter of Patrick Torrie, 10 Commercial Street.

In 1829 Robert passed the property in favour of his son John Deans, formerly of the East Indies, then resident in Ayrshire. This was finalised following Robert's death on 24th April 1834.[11] On his marriage John became John Deans-Campbell of Curreath.[12]

John did not live in Leog as the Lerwick census for 1841 and 1851 reveals that instead it was occupied by James Greig and his wife Ann, who was Robert Dean's daughter and John's sister.

A map in Shetland Archives, which was drawn in 1850, shows Leog House with a court in front and adjacent small house. A path at the back, separating two gardens, led up to a larger garden. The park of Leog covered an area from the street in front of Leog House to the wall bordering Lovers Loan, up to what is now part of Breiwick Road and then down to join the upper corner of the large garden.

This Leog House was renovated in 1864-65 and was later to be called Lower Leog.

At the same time the present Leog House was under construction in the large upper garden[13] and, by 1867, the new "Mansion House of Leog", owned by John Deans-Campbell, was occupied by Charles G. Duncan, procurator fiscal and chief magistrate of Lerwick.[14]

William B. Tulloch and his wife Jane I. Laurenson were the next tenants. William died there in 1874. Jane's unmarried brother, Arthur, resided with her until his death there in 1890. He is remembered for being instrumental in the introduction of the stained glass windows and roof shields in Lerwick Town Hall, and the design of the county seal with the Old Norse motto "*Með lǫgum skal land byggja*" (By laws shall a country be established). He is commemorated in the Town Hall by a brass tablet in the form of a pointed shield with Norse runes round the edges.[15]

The gardens behind Lower Leog. c.1908

Lower Leog Houses on the left with Leog House in the centre. Late 1880s

In 1897 the trustees of the late John Deans-Campbell sold the Mansion House of Leog and the Old House of Leog, or Lower Leog, to William and Jane's son, William A.A. Tulloch.[16]

His daughter, Catherine L. Tulloch (Kate), inherited the properties and lived in the upper Leog House. Following her death, her trustees sold both houses to Zetland County Council in 1953.[17] Her will stipulated that Leog House was to be used as an eventide home.[18]

Leog House, the former Mansion House, then became Leog Eventide Home. Elderly people were cared for there including patients from Brevik Hospital who were transferred to the home during hospital renovations in 1959.[19] Towards the end of 1978 the thirteen residents were the first to occupy the newly opened Kantersted Eventide Home.[20]

Leog housing scheme under construction. c.1959 (Courtesy of Elizabeth Angus)

The grass track to the south of Leog House. Lower Leog is partly obscured by trees. 1957 (Courtesy of Elizabeth Angus)

Leog House immediately became a children's home[21] and remained so until 2012. In 2013 it was offered for sale by Shetland Islands Council. Leog House underwent renovation and conversion into five private flats which were sold during 2019.

Several tenants lived at Lower Leog over the years. It has proved difficult to ascertain if the property actually dates back to the 17th century, or the mid-18th century. However, the building depicted on the *Perspective View of Lerwick*, drawn in 1766, clearly resembles that which was frequently photographed.

The house was demolished to provide a site for the Leog housing scheme in 1958. By this action yet another historic part of the south end was lost forever.

Leog Lane

The lane at the south side of Leog House, provides access to Commercial Street for residents of the house and those living nearby. It was transformed from a grass track to the road we see today.

Leog Lane in 2021

Copland's Pier

Copland's Pier was officially named in 1845. It is currently erroneously signposted as Copeland's Pier, but continues to be referred to by locals as Gillie's Pier.

James Copland, an Orcadian, was a tacksman on the island of Noss and had accumulated wealth.[1] In 1815, when he was about 64 years old, he bought a tenement of houses on the lower side of the street from William Henderson of Gloup, with kailyards and garden ground opposite.[2]. On this land he built a smithy, shed and yard, and two houses – 11 and 13 Commercial Street. The latter was a small two-roomed cottage attached to Stout's property at 15 Commercial Street. These buildings were demolished in the mid 1960s and the site is now part of the Stout's Court housing scheme.

James Copland extended his tenement, 2-8 Commercial Street, by including wings on each end and building the pier to the south, referred to as Gillie's Pier.[3] George Gillie was the first resident of what became, until 2018, the Lerwick Sea Scouts' building. He was a blacksmith at the previously mentioned smithy.[4]

Copland also built a lodberry yard with stores at the rear of the block. Incidentally, James Stout Angus later lived at number

Copland's or Gillie's Pier. 1880s

Copland's Pier sign. 2021

The Old Manse is on the left. Copland's Pier and Lodberry is in the foreground with the lodberry at 10 Commercial Street on the right. c.1966 (Courtesy of Dennis Coutts)

Copland's Walk was in front of the property. 2021

A high tide at Copland's or Gillie's Pier. 2021

6 and carried on business as a joiner and contractor here. Angus wrote and published several books when he was over 80 years old, namely *A Glossary of Shetland Place-names*, *A Glossary of the Shetland Dialect* and a volume of verse entitled *Echoes from Klingrahool*.[5] It was in this publication that the lodberry was highlighted in "Da Kokkilurie" – his poem for the daisy that grew alongside it.[6] He died in 1923.

The street in front of the housing block between Copland's Pier and Stout's Pier was commonly known as Copland's Walk.[7]

Copland's premises passed to his son,[8] who sold to John H. Johnson in 1857.[9] Johnson's widow was the last remaining trustee of his property which then passed down through the family to Mrs Theodora Howell, his granddaughter, who lived in New Zealand.[10] In 1951 she sold the property at Gillie's Pier and 2, 4, 6, 11 and 13 Commercial Street to Lerwick Town Council.[11] In 1964-65 the council completely renovated the block to provide four flats while 11 and 13 Commercial Street opposite were demolished. Mr Gillie's former home, which had been used as a store for many years, was leased to the sea scouts in 1964.[12]

In 2018 the south wing of the lodberry was put up for sale by the owners, Shetland Islands Council. Unable to raise the necessary funds to purchase the property the sea scouts were told to find a new permanent home.

In 2019 an application was submitted by a Canadian couple to change the use of the building to a one-bedroom house. However, in 2020 the premises were put back on the market by Shetland Islands Council following rejection of the prospective buyers' planning application on safety grounds.[13] In November 2020 the premises was bought by the local engineering company Ocean Kinetics to be used for training staff, especially in marine works. An extensive restoration of the building, courtyard and pier, including flood prevention measures, was undertaken the following year.

In 1951 Mrs Howell had also sold the small dwelling house at 8 Commercial Street – the lodberry wing on the north end of the block bordering Stout's Pier – to Albert E.R. Bowie[14] who used it as his photographic studio. He in turn sold the property to Peter Smith[15] who sold to Lerwick Town Council in 1966.[16] The building was vacant until 1971 when it was repaired and let to Lerwick Boating Club. Members undertook interior renovation and by 1972 there was a clubroom and bar upstairs with kitchen and toilets below, at street level.[17] After the boating club vacated in 1983 the Shetland Country Music Club moved in and was there until 1993 when the club moved to premises at Grantfield. The next occupant was Shetland Football Club, until 1999. Shetland Link Up has been based there since then.[18]

MISS CHALMERS STAIR
AND MURRAY'S LODBERRY

The location of Miss Chalmers Stair. The corner of 1 Hayfield Court is on the left with 12 Commercial Street opposite. Part of 10 Commercial Street is on the right. 2021

Miss Chalmers Stair was not named in 1845 as these five steps were earmarked for removal and this took place in 1847.[1] They extended right across, and obstructed the street at "da Roost", a very narrow part between the corner gable of the house at 17 Commercial Street, which protruded into the street and was part of Stout's Court at that time, and the house opposite at 10 Commercial Street, which still exists.

It was at 10 Commercial Street that Miss Margaret Chalmers, the poetess, lived with her mother, as tenants, after they moved from Twageos House following the death of her father in 1772. He was William Chalmers, collector of customs and factor for the Earl of Morton.[2] Miss Chalmers wrote only one book, through the necessity to generate income, which was published by subscription in 1813.[3,4] She died in Lerwick in 1827 when she was 69 years old.

Although it has been written that the house at 10 Commercial Street was built in 1730, along with the first lodberry, this may be so, but not by Patrick Scollay as stated by William Sandison.[5] Robert Scollay bought land in 1724[6] and presumably built the house in 1730, and possibly the lodberry too, but this is uncertain. It would appear that the names Robert Scollay and Patrick Torrie were mixed up at some point. Robert Scollay's sons, Arthur and Samuel, inherited the property in 1754. It was sold to Patrick Torrie, shipmaster and merchant, in 1758.[7]

10 Commercial Street. 2021

The inaugural meeting of Morton Lodge took place in this house in 1764 but was not given No.89 until 1826.[8]

Number 10 Commercial Street is often referred to as Patrick Torrie's house but he owned it for only seven years, until 1765, when it was sold to Samuel Scollay, Robert's son.[9]

The house and lodberry are clearly shown on the *Perspective View of Lerwick 1766*.

Number 10 Commercial Street had several owners over the years until bought and restored by Richard Gibson in 1987.

Da Roost Hoose

In 1847 James Sinclair undertook the work to remove Miss Chalmers Stair.[10] He and his wife Barbara, née Stout, inherited the lower part of her father's property at 17 Commercial Street, known as "da Roost Hoose".[11]

The removal of the five steps opened up a cart passage at the south end of Commercial Street to and from Twageos. Previously, cart access to Commercial Street was mainly via Baker's Closs (later Mountholy Street), as North Kirk Closs (later Queens Lane) was said to have had steps at one time.[12] Steps crossing the street at the foot of South Kirk Closs, later Church Lane (now part of Church Road), were removed in 1818.[13] Below Fort Charlotte was a sheep path, wide enough to accommodate a pony with a very narrow cart but with a steep drop down to the sea. The rock was blasted to form

Da Roost Hoose, 17 Commercial Street, is extending into the street. To its right is Nice Court (now Hayfield Court) and garden wall. The space on the left is where Lerwick Boating Club is now, then 12 Commercial Street, and in the centre is 2-8 Commercial Street. 1950s. (Courtesy of Elizabeth Angus)

The same location today

a narrow road in 1839 or 1840.[14] Bank Lane, Hangcliff Lane, Chromate Lane and Church Lane did not have steps but were either too steep or too narrow for carts.

Although the proposal to demolish 17 Commercial Street in order to widen the street had been discussed by Lerwick Town Council in 1954,[15] it was not pulled down until the early 1960s. Before then a small car could navigate through the space at "da Roost" with care.

Murray's Lodberry

William Sinclair, James and Barbara's son and grandson of Robert Stout, entered into partnership with John Hardie as Messrs Sinclair & Hardie, joiners, in about 1860, after they had completed work on the Anderson Educational Institute,[16] which opened on the 4th August 1862. The partners bought a small house at 12 Commercial Street in 1868[17] and used Murray's Lodberry, and the workshop built on top of an old store, for their business.

The lodberry had been used by Robert Davidson, joiner, and his partner John Mullay,[18] and previously by John (Jock) Murray, also a joiner, who is believed to have built it some time after 1790. That year his uncle John Murray and his wife Elizabeth Scott had bought a ruinous house on the site and also property opposite called the "Meeting House".[19] It had been built by William Tyrie in 1670,[20] and was said to have been used as a place of worship by troops who were based at Fort Charlotte. There is an article dated 1862, looking back 100 years, which mentions that the house opposite "Robert Davidson's workshop" at the south end of the town was once an Episcopal Church.[21] There is also the suggestion that there was a small chapel in that area referred to as St Barnaby's or St Barnabas.[22] However, this fact is refuted by Gilbert Goudie, local antiquarian, and Francis J. Grant, Lord Lyon and King of Arms, who is of the opinion that the chapel was situated in Dunrossness[23] and R.G. Cant confirms the possible site of the chapel as at Toab.[24]

The first reference to the building being referred to as the Meeting House was in a document dated 1733. The house was on three levels and a substantial staircase led from Nice Court to the middle floor. By the 1750s the house had been divided into three flats. At that time James Vance had a schoolroom on the top floor, the middle floor was occupied by Margaret Bourmaster, and ground floors by George Corner and Bretta Jamieson.[25] The stairs were removed in 1776.[26]

A house on the site of 12 Commercial Street dates from 1678 when John Andersone and Christiane Bult are mentioned in a document.[27] Jock Murray renovated the little house which was attached to the lodberry. He apparently frowned on people smuggling and, while doing so himself, he erroneously announced that he was a "customs man" and so avoided any punishment.[28]

The house, which was below street level, was rebuilt by John Hardie using stones from the now ruinous Meeting House[29] which was situated in what is now the Hayfield Court garden. John – who was firstly married to William's sister Margaret – and his large family lived in the rebuilt house;[30] the one we see today.

Messrs Sinclair & Hardie were good tradesmen and for many years were the principal contractors in Lerwick.[31]

William Sinclair died in 1892 at his home, 4 Albany Street, while John Hardie died at 12 Commercial Street in 1902.[32]

10 Commercial Street is on the left with lodberry behind. The adjacent house is number 12 with Murray's Lodberry next to the yard and pier. Opposite 12 Commercial Street is Hayfield Court, with trees at Kveldsro Gardens. c.1966 (Courtesy of Dennis Coutts)

This area had been a renowned spot for smuggling contraband cargo. It was said that the entrance to a smuggler's tunnel existed under the wooden pier at Murray's Lodberry,[33] which was adjacent to the yard on which the present Lerwick Boating Club was built in 1983 (not to be confused with the lodberry at the Queens Hotel with the same name).

Apparently, when part of the premises had been altered, subterranean passages about four feet (1.25m) in height were discovered and were said to lead to green fields.[34] This was possibly in 1847 as the street was set back 5 or 6 feet (1.5-1.8m) at the lodberry about the same time as Miss Chalmers Stair was removed.[35]

Number 12 Commercial Street, along with adjoining wood yard shed and lodberry, was sold to John M. Aitken, contractor, in 1903.[36] In 1906, despite objections from Lerwick Harbour Trustees and 125 proprietors and residents in the south end of the town, he built a pier at Scarfa Taing[37][38] and a herring curing yard which was on the site of the present Lerwick Boating Club.[39] The yard was initially occupied by an Aberdeen curer then by J. & M. Shearer for two years from the summer of 1919.[40] It was later used for a time by Robbie Sinclair, acting as agent for Russian Oil Products.[41]

John M. Aitken's grandson, Stephen V. Mouat, ultimately inherited the property which in 1943 he sold to John W. Robertson[42] of Robertsons (Lerwick) Ltd. The pier was virtually rebuilt as a base for their contract with the Ministry of Aircraft Production to service seaplane moorings. After the war the pier was occasionally used by the firm as a loading station for the converted drifter *Lord Curzon* and later the *Gossawater*.

In subsequent years the pier again deteriorated and was sold to the Lerwick Harbour Trust in 1979, who leased it to Lerwick Boating Club. The pier was partially re-decked and had other repairs carried out. In 1992 a survey again revealed deterioration and consequently a new pier was constructed and opened by Lerwick Boating Club in 1995.[43] The club had met at 8 Commercial Street until the new Lerwick Boating Club was built. It opened in 1983.

The property at 12 Commercial Street remained in the Robertson family until the lodberry, workshop and shed were bought by Alexander W. Fox, the present owner, in 1986.

The house was sold to Mr & Mrs I. Horne in 1997. They in turn sold it in January 2017.[44]

The yard adjacent to Murray's Lodberry being prepared for the construction of Lerwick Boating Club in 1982.

Stout's Pier and Stout's Court

Stout's Pier. 2021

The New Pier was officially renamed Stout's Wharf in 1845, now Stout's Pier.
   In 1819 Robert Stout purchased ground with houses and yard opposite 10 Commercial Street, from Charles Ogilvy, merchant and chief magistrate of Lerwick.[1] This property, including 17 Commercial Street or "da Roost Hoose", had previously belonged to various occupants of 10 Commercial Street.

Stout filled in the space between 8 Commercial Street and the lodberry at 10 Commercial Street to create what became known as the New Pier.[2]

In the mid-1830s Stout, a mason to trade, erected a new house – 15 Commercial Street – with gable facing the street.

Stout's Court was an open square with the original house at the upper end. Access could be gained from Commercial Street by a narrow passage between the houses at numbers 15 and 17 and another between number 17 and Nice Court (now Hayfield Court).[3]

All the various buildings at Stout's Court were bought by Zetland County Council in 1938 and passed to Lerwick Town Council in 1962. They were then all demolished and the site was cleared for work to commence on the Stout's Court housing scheme in 1966.

Houses at Kveldsro Gardens were built at the same time.

A small plaque on a wall at Stout's Court indicates that it was the birthplace of Sir Robert Stout, Robert Stout's grandson, who became the prime minister of New Zealand in 1884 and chief justice in 1889.[4]

The passage between Hayfield Court on the left and the now demolished 17 Commercial Street. 1962. (Courtesy of Elizabeth Angus)

The block of flats at Stout's Court. 2021

The commemorative plaque for Sir Robert Stout. 2021

The upper part of Stout's Court. 2021

Nice Court, now Hayfield Court

1 and 2 Hayfield Court 2021

Nice Court was officially named in 1845. It was renamed Hayfield Court about 1960, prior to Capt. John (Jock) Westwood Hay of Hayfield selling the main house and upper small adjoining uninhabited building.

Although it could be described as a "nice" court with plants and trees that was not how it got its original name.

The first mention of property on this site was in 1678, following charter by Laurence Williamson, merchant, Bressay, of ground and property to William Richan and his wife Issobel (sic) Scollay.[1] William died in 1687 but in 1733 a tenement of houses occupied by Mathew Smith was referred to as William Richan's house.[2]

James Nice and Arthur Nice, both slaters, are documented in 1717, and James Nice in 1754, and it is believed that the court is named after these people.[3] Thomas Nice and his wife Catherine Yorston, who married in 1758, were tenants in William Richan's upper house in 1793, while Laurence Mouat and his wife Janet lived in the lower house. At this time the proprietor was Mrs Ann Innes, daughter of Samuel Scollay, who also owned 10 Commercial Street.[4]

When Thomas Nice applied in 1769 to be admitted as an apprentice to Morton Lodge (then at 10 Commercial Street), he was described as a slater and good musician. It was agreed that he should be immediately admitted, without the usual dues payable, knowing him to be a very honest, though poor man. A few months later there is reference to him carrying out the traditional Tyler's duty of summoning the brethren to a meeting. Morton Lodge moved to the Old Tolbooth in 1770. However, in 1771 the eagerness for the brethren to have Thomas admitted to the Lodge became apparent when a decision was made to hold monthly dances and, in addition to tyling the Lodge, he was expected to be the musician. It was said that these monthly assemblies held in the building became a popular event in the life of the town. Thomas was paid a salary of £2 sterling per annum for his duties.[5] He was later to receive a monthly allowance and when he died in 1814 the Lodge paid for his funeral.[6] He had a surviving daughter, Barbara Ann, who died in 1824 in Lerwick but it is not known if she lived in Nice Court.

Over the years the dwellings changed hands and became dilapidated but were still inhabited and tenants were numerous.

It has been thought that the larger house presently in the Court may have been built in the early 1800s.[7] There is no evidence to support this but in fact there is a summons of removing, dated 1856, against Thomas Anderson who was tenant of "a ruinous house" in Nice Court[8] and the 1851 Census confirms that he lived there. Only six people are listed at Nice Court in 1861 but in 1871 there are three families listed at 1 Nice Court and two families at number 2 – a total of twelve people, obviously tenants. This would indicate that the house we see today was built during this decade and is confirmed in a disposition dated June 1863 to Henry Cheyne, by James Ross Spence, which refers to a new house above the street opposite 12 Commercial Street.[9]

Arthur James Hay obtained the property from his sister Barbara, wife of Henry Cheyne in 1869.[10] On his death in 1896, Hay's daughter Margaret E. Hay inherited Nice Court which was ultimately passed on to her first cousin's son, Col. Westwood Norman Hay, who in turn passed it on to his son, Capt. John (Jock) W. Hay in 1943.[11]

In 1924 the author's grandmother moved from Kveldsro Cottage to Nice Court where, in fact, he was born in 1943, following his parents' return to Shetland having lived for a short time in Edinburgh. He remembers as a young boy accompanying his grandmother to a small shed in Seafield Court, lit only by a candle, to pay rent to Jock Hay. In

1 and 2 Hayfield Court. 2021

1954 Capt. Hay offered to sell the house, attached coal store and garden to Lerwick Town Council to provide a site for council housing but, after prolonged negotiations over the next four years, this never took place. The author's relations were evicted and rehoused in the new Heddell's Park housing scheme in 1958.[12]

Capt. Hay was the owner of the 600-year-old Delgatie Castle, near Turriff, which he spent 40 years rebuilding using his talents as a mason. Over the years he sold the estate he had in Shetland to pay for the castle renovations.[13] In 1961 he sold the recently renamed Hayfield Court to John Wills[14] who later renovated the derelict attached store on the upper end of the house. In 1964 he in turn sold it as Hayfield Court Cottage to Miss Hilda Clark.[15]

Hayfield Court sign. 2021

It was later sold to Derick Herning, the well-known Anderson High School teacher and polyglot of Europe, who extended the cottage on his marriage. It would appear that his Russian bride Nina, from the city of Kazan in the Republic of Tatarstan, agreed to the marriage on the condition that her residence would be in Kazan. Derick duly obliged but Nina found that her new home address was not Kazan in Russia but instead Kazan, 2 Hayfield Court, Lerwick, Shetland. It is still Mrs Herning's home, following Derick's death in 2019.[16]

Hayfield Court House was also sold in 1964 and has had numerous owners since then with the address 1 Hayfield Court.

Jock Hay died at Delgatie Castle on 6th September, 1997, aged 91 years. He had no surviving family.[17]

1 Hayfield Court viewed from Kveldsro Gardens. 2021

Ross Court and Steamers' Store

Ross Court was opposite the house presently known as "The Sea Door" at 14 Commercial Street. It was not officially named in 1845.

The original buildings were erected prior to 1669 as George Johnston and William McKinlay were documented as tenants there at that time.[1]

The open courtyard at Ross Court was entered from Commercial Street through a narrow opening between a building on the left side – which was 1, 2 and 3 Ross Court – and 25 Commercial Street on the right. Adjoining this house was a building larger than the Ross Court houses, which is 27 and 29 Commercial Street which still exists. The court could also be accessed via a passage at the upper end of number 29.[2]

Ross Court. 27 and 29 Commercial Street is on the left but the remaining houses were demolished during 1963. c.1900

Around about 1781 William Ross, or "Bombardier Ross" as he became known, came to Lerwick and was stationed at Fort Charlotte. He married Janet Gray and then acquired property from his father-in-law William in 1790,[3] commonly called William Gray's House. It subsequently became known as Ross Court. William Ross's son, John, was drowned while swimming at the Sletts and, as William had no heirs, he left his share of the property to William Mouat of Garth in gratitude to him for making him barrack master sergeant.[4]

In 1829 William Mouat obtained, with the consent of William Ross's late wife's sister Elizabeth and trustees of the late Margaret Gray, the house at Ross Court with outhouses, garden and park, and also another house on the lower side of the street with William Ross's north lodberry and adjoining warehouses and cellars.[5]

Ownership of Ross Court passed down through the Mouat and Cameron family, with many families being tenants there over the years, until it was ultimately sold by Norman O.M. Cameron in 1949 to Mrs Jessie Goudie.[6] Two years later it was resold to Lerwick Town Council.[7] Mr Cameron also sold 25, 27 and 29 Commercial Street to Lerwick Town Council and, while number 25 was subsequently demolished,[8] numbers 27 and 29 were renovated. The building containing 1 and 2 Ross Court was partly demolished during 1963 and in December of that year the council agreed that the site be cleared.[9] It became a car parking area.

27 and 29 Commercial Street is on the left and "The Sea Door" is in the centre. The space in front is the site of Ross Court and the trees are in the Hayfield Court garden. 2021

The site of Ross Court is now a car parking area. 2021

William Ross's south lodberry, adjoining cellars and a house on the lower side of the street were obtained by the late Mrs Ross's sister Elizabeth and trustees of the late Margaret Gray.[10] The property was sold to Andrew Mcbeath in 1839.[11] A document dated 1843 refers to his new dwelling house[12] on the northwest side of the lodberry, later to become known as Mcbeath's Lodberry. This house became "The Sea Door", 14 Commercial Street. At a later date the lodberry was built over with the basement blocked up.[13]

Andrew Mcbeath was a boot and shoemaker. As agent for Greenland ships he had a grocery business in the house, a mail service and owned the brig *Amelia*. He was also a gig hirer and was the first, or among the first, to have a gig in Lerwick.[14] He rented grazing where the County Buildings now are and was often seen there stabling his horses.[15] He also had use of the lodberry at 10 Commercial Street where he stabled a horse and two cows that grazed in a park where Kveldsro House was later built.[16] Andrew died in 1882.

The yard is the site of Lerwick Boating Club. "The Sea Door" is to its right and visible is the extension that was built over the lodberry which was originally known as William Ross's south lodberry and then as Mcbeath's Lodberry. The site of Ross Court is in front of "The Sea Door". c.1966 (Courtesy of Dennis Coutts)

Smuggling did take place in the vicinity of "The Sea Door". A tunnel extended from this house under Commercial Street and Ross Court opposite. The walls of the tunnel were built of stone and lime with a whale-bone roof and clay floor and it exited through an old well, surrounded by a high wall[17] in the Court's garden. In about 1918 some of the flagstones were seen to be sinking and during excavations a sunken area was discovered showing a door and a window, possibly a storage space for smuggled goods.[18] Shortly before the houses in Ross Court were demolished the tunnel could only be partially accessed as the middle

William Ross's north lodberry became the first steamers' store

contained rubble almost to the roof.[19] As a consequence of increased traffic it was subsequently filled in for safety reasons.

In recent years "The Sea Door" was acquired by Colin Spence who then let it to Schlumberger staff. He later sold it to Stuart Leask who completely gutted the interior and carried out extensive restoration including blocking up the basement. The exterior walls were untouched, however a new roof was added which entailed demolishing a gable. This is now the property of Mr & Mrs Peter McKenzie.

William Ross's north lodberry became the first "steamers' store". In the early to mid-19th century, before the very small Morrison's Pier to the east of the Market Cross was extended in 1866 to become Victoria Wharf,[20] and then further extended 20 years later to create Victoria Pier, the "nort boats" had to anchor in the harbour. Cargo, livestock and passengers were transported by flit boats. It was an alarming prospect for travellers, especially female passengers, to discover that after a long and uncomfortable journey to Bressay Sound, they had an even more uncomfortable and frequently dangerous journey in an open boat before they were landed at Morrison's Pier. However, luggage was landed at one of the numerous little piers and travellers had to undertake a search for their belongings. Cargo was unloaded and loaded at the lodberry which was used as a store by the Aberdeen, Leith, Clyde and Tay Shipping Company.[21] The shipping office was situated in an adjacent building which was on the site of the current house at 16 Commercial Street.

Many of the flit-boat men lived in a row of houses which was demolished to make way for the building of Ellesmere House in 1906[22] (now D.G. Leslie at ground level).

The outward appearance of the lodberry is virtually unchanged since its heyday. Depending on tides and weather, cargo was landed at either the double door opening near the Craigie Stane, which led on to an open courtyard, or through the door in the sea-facing wall on the east side. The cargo was then stored in the lodberry.

Following the building of Victoria Pier and its formal opening on 23rd June 1886,[23] a store was built on the pier and the use of William Ross's north lodberry was no longer required.

However, ownership of the lodberry, cellars, warehouses and former office, later a house, remained in the Mouat and Cameron family until sold in 1961 to Laurence (Sonny) Goudie, David (Davie) Carfrae, Laurence (Lollie) Smith and John (Jacky) Tait.[24]

The ruinous house was sold in about 1970 and was later renovated while the lodberry buildings were, and still are, used as a boatshed and workshop.[25]

The Steamers' Store

In 1838 the Aberdeen, Leith, Clyde and Tay Shipping Company was awarded a government contract to carry mail to Orkney and Shetland by steamer once a week between April and October. Initially paddle steamers and schooners carried the mail but these were either unsuitable for winter conditions or proved to be unreliable. Only when the S.S. *Queen* arrived in 1861 was a reliable weekly winter service begun. Following the expansion of the fleet the tradition began of naming the vessels after saints. The S.S. *St Magnus* appeared in 1867, the S.S. *St Clair* in 1868 and the S.S. *St Nicholas* in 1871.[26]

In 1875 the company moved its office from 16 Commercial Street to larger premises at 90 Commercial Street (now part of J.G. Rae Ltd) and that same year it was renamed the North of Scotland & Orkney & Shetland Steam Navigation Company.[27]

In 1897 the shipping company purchased nearby ground and property extending to the Esplanade which included cellars, warehouses and Grierson's Lodberry.[28] In 1899 the lodberry site was cleared and premises were built at the Esplanade which opened the following year.[29] This is now part of the LHD Marine Supplies Ltd shop.

The new pier soon became a hub of activity. A store, or transit shed to give it its proper title, was erected not long after the pier opened in 1886 to enable unloaded goods to be held prior to delivery or collection.

A congested Victoria Pier. c.1900

The store with the Earl of Zetland and the St Clair. 1960s

Folk regularly met the "north boats" and it became a tradition to watch them depart, even though folk may or may not have a friend or relative involved, and a huge crowd was a common sight. Unlike today, scant attention was paid to health and safety measures as there was no separation of the general public from the activities on the pier.

By 1903 it had become clear that more storage space was required and, rather than build a new store, the Lerwick Harbour Trust (renamed Lerwick Port Authority in 1999) arranged for the steamers' store to be extended by 15 feet (4.5m.) on the east side.

In 1956 a major harbour works improvement scheme commenced. Included in the scheme was the construction of a new steel-framed store on the steamers' pier and this was completed in November 1957.

While the work was being undertaken activities normally carried out on Victoria Pier moved to Alexandra Wharf where the firm, renamed The North of Scotland, Orkney & Shetland Shipping Co Ltd in 1953, was given the use of a store in the new Alexandra Building. Unfortunately, berthing at Alexandra Wharf proved difficult due to exposure and after a few months the steamers returned to Victoria Pier after specially constructed fenders were introduced to protect the concrete from damage.[30]

It took three years to complete the widening of the pier and the construction of the arm. On 10th August 1960 the new harbour scheme was officially opened by Her Majesty Queen Elizabeth II.

It must be remembered that back then all cargo was unloaded from the boats by crane and dockers using barrows manually transported much of it to the store to await delivery or collection. A tally of everything coming in and leaving the store was the responsibility of the squad of checkers.

Signs around the store identified either shops – such as Home Furnishing, Hay & Co, the Co-op – or country districts. The North Isles section was naturally on the north side (nearest to the *Earl of Zetland*'s berth), next came the "drinks cage", then the scales, with North Roe, Reawick, Skeld, Voe and Nesting on the northeast side. Along the far end of the store on the east side was Bressay, Sandwick, Quarff, Cunningsburgh, Dunrossness, and the checkers' desk, with a hatch from the shipping office where casual dockers received their pay. Upstairs was the office where a clerk was responsible for completion of the cargo books, detailing all inward deliveries. Around the southeast corner was Aith, Walls, Girlsta, then Tingwall and Scalloway. South and North Commercial Street were opposite the North Isles.

Interspersed with districts were firms now no longer in business such as Ganson, Willie Fraser, Pearson & Tawse, T.L. Arcus, Hughson Bros., Walter Brown, W.C. Bain, Tod's, Aitken & Wright, Davie Shearer; then space for Clarkson's tyres and Grantfield Stores (Pete's). Mail order or "club book" parcels filled a large area and those who couldn't wait for the "North of Scotland" to make a delivery called along the store to collect their items and probably annoyed the checker.[31]

In 1961 the "North of Scotland" was taken over by Coast Lines then, in 1975, by P. & O. Ferries, Orkney & Shetland Services.

Following the construction of the Holmsgarth Road and terminal during 1976, roll-on/roll-off ferries were introduced in April 1977. For a short time cargo was transported from Holmsgarth to "da Steamers' Store" but gradually the store became redundant.

Work began on demolishing the store on Victoria Pier during the week beginning 12th January, 1987, and the site is now a car park.

The entrance to the Small Boat Harbour and Victoria Pier. 2021

CRAIGIE'S COURT AND THE CRAIGIE STANE

Craigie's Court was officially named in 1845.

In the 18th century, on the site of the present Quendale House at 31 Commercial Street, stood the town house of Bailie James Craigie.[1] The court was entered by an archway and on the top was carved the date 1737.[2] The stone also included the Craigie coat of arms bearing the initials JC and EH – James Craigie and his wife Elizabeth Henderson.[3] James Craigie was thought to have died in 1741 and his grand-nephew, also called James, ultimately inherited the property. When he passed it to his son, Captain John Craigie[4] who lived in the Old Manse, the property was referred to as Miss Craigie's House and she is believed to have been Bailie Craigie's daughter, Catherine.

Quendale House

Following John's death in 1855 it passed to his niece, Elizabeth Craigie,[5] who married James Grierson. In 1864-65 their son, Andrew John Grierson of Quendale, built a new house on the site which was named Quendale House.[6] During the demolition of Craigie's Court the family coat of arms was saved and when the construction of the Town Hall began in 1881 the stone was incorporated into the north gable of the building, above the rose window.[7] It remained there until 1996 when it was removed to prevent further erosion and is now stored in the Shetland Museum.

Over the years the house had several owners and tenants, including during the Second World War when it was requisitioned by the Admiralty and provided accommodation for a number of Wrens (Women's Royal Naval Reserve). In 1946 it was sold to the Postmaster General.[8] Plans were in place to relocate the telephone exchange from Market Street in 1949 and it opened in Quendale House on 10th May, 1950.[9] It remained there until 26th March, 1975, when the new automatic exchange opened nearby.[10]

The house became a Category B listed building on 18th October, 1977.[11]

In May 1982 the next owner was Shetland Leasing and Property (SLAP) who leased the building to Shetland Islands Council and they in turn bought the property in 2008. In 2012, when it

Quendale House. 2021

was no longer required as council offices, it was offered for lease the following year.[12] After Shetland FM vacated in 2020 it was then sold into private ownership later that year.

The Craigie Stane

The Craigie name remains, as the large slanting solid rock known as The Craigie Stane can be seen opposite Quendale House on the shore, below the wall.

To the south of the Craigie Stane stands the former steamers' store lodberry which was at one time William Ross's north lodberry.

The Craigie Stane. 2021

The Lodberrie

The Lodberrie. 2021

The walls of The Lodberrie are virtually unchanged since its construction about 1772 by a merchant named James Linklater, who had property on the opposite side of the street. The Lodberrie, still surrounded by the sea on three sides, stands between the Craigie Stane and Bain's Beach.

The Lodberrie was described as having steps down to boat noosts at the Craigie Stane, with an entrance leading to a kitchen and office, a store for boats and gear, a wet fish store, a cellar, and also an area for storing masts and spars. North, east and south facing sea doors allowed the transfer of cargo to and from vessels at all times, depending on the tides. At Commercial Street level there was a shop above the cellar, and a parlour, bedroom, a sail loft with dry goods store, and a skeo for drying fish and meat.[1]

The property was ultimately sold to Bailie John Robertson in 1859[2] and thereafter became known as Robertson's Lodberry.[3]

The shop part of The Lodberrie was destroyed by fire in 1925[4] but the house was unaffected. The whole building was vacant by the mid-1930s.

The property lay in a derelict condition until 1956 when Mr Thomas Moncrieff, commonly known as Tammie, leased the premises and then bought it. He undertook a restoration programme and succeeded in reinstating the old building[5] at a time when many of the historic houses at the south end were demolished to make way for modern flats. He resided there with his wife until his death in 2005 and it is now the home of their son, Erik.

Bain's Beach and The Lodberrie. 2021

Over the years The Lodberrie has become a well-photographed landmark and is now a Class A listed building. At the present time it is a popular tourist attraction following the screening of the *Shetland* crime series on television. The Lodberrie is portrayed as the fictional home of Jimmy Perez, the main character.[6]

In 2021 a Hollywood-style plaque was awarded to actor Douglas Henshall in recognition of the success of the TV series and the boost it has given to tourism. The plaque, inserted in the street adjacent to the steps leading to The Lodberrie, was unveiled by him on 5th October.

Sands' Court, Raven's Court and Water Lane

From left – part of The Lodberrie, 27-29 Commercial Street, Bain's Court, Raven's Court and Water Lane. 1950s

Sands' Court, Raven's Court and Water Lane were all officially named in 1845. The name Sands' Court most likely arose from the fact that the Rev. James Sands and family members had property in the court.[1] He was the fourth minister of the Parish of Lerwick from 1767 until 1793.

It later became Bain's Court after James Bain, joiner and auctioneer, who bought the run down property and carried out renovations. He was the father of Gilbert Bain whose sisters donated a hospital in his name[2] (now Goudies Funeral Directors Ltd). The Bain family resided in Lochend House, built or rebuilt in about 1760, which had been purchased from Arthur Nicolson of Lochend in 1818. The beach opposite is still called Bain's Beach.

Over the trance entrance to Bain's Court was a motto carved in Latin with the words "*Pro deo, pro rege, et patria*", translated as "For God, for King and Country".[3] The house built over the trance had, as a joist, the helm taken from an old Dutch vessel. This was retrieved by Tammie Moncrieff when the building was being demolished[4] and it is

Bain's Beach sign and steps.

Bain's Beach. 2021

Raven's Court and Irvinesgord. 1969

currently displayed in Shetland Museum and Archives. In January 1958 demolition of this, by now derelict, property at Bain's Court began and the stones were used to build garden walls at the Heddell's Park Housing Scheme,[5] i.e. Gardie Lane, Mounthooly Place, Haldane Place, Queens Place and Chapel Place.

Raven's Court was to the north of Bain's Court. The name is said to have

Da Draa-well Closs and Water Lane. 1950s

The houses in Water Lane. 2021

originated from the fact that the Misses Campbell, who lived in the house at the upper part of the court, had a pet raven.[6] In the early 1800s the Campbell family lived there and sisters Dorothea Primrose and Eliza Matilda ran a private school for the education of daughters of the local gentry. Dorothea published a book of poems in 1811, also a revised edition, and a novel entitled *Harley Radington* in 1821.[7]

The upper part of Raven's Court and Irvinesgord were demolished in 1970

The next opening was Water Lane and between the row of houses there and the courtyard wall of Lochend House was Da Draa-well Closs, a very narrow trinkie or passage. Dutch fishermen used to come ashore to obtain drinking water from the draw well that was at one time situated at the top of the closs. Barrels were filled then rolled down to The Lodberrie from where the fishermen loaded them on to their vessels.[8]

All the houses and buildings at Bain's Court, lower Raven's Court, Water Lane and Da Draa-well Closs were demolished in the late 1950s and early 1960s to make way for the new housing scheme which was named Water Lane in 1965.

The demolition of the upper part of Raven's Court and the adjoining Irvinesgord took place in 1970. It was reported that these two roomy and strongly-built old houses were in good condition with modern conveniences. Their destruction was not due to any deterioration, or an over provision of houses in Lerwick, but was carried out in order to provide additional space for the construction of and access to a new telephone exchange.[9]

Quendale House continued as the telephone exchange until 26th March, 1975, when a reduced number of switchboard operators moved to the new building. In 1987 the telephone exchange closed when operator services were transferred to Aberdeen.

A car parking area is now on the site of Bain's Court, lower Raven's Court and Water Lane. 2021

Chromate Lane

The foot of Chromate Lane. Seafield Court is on the left and Seawinds is on the right. The Lochend House garden is beyond the wall on the right. 2021

Chromate Lane was officially named in 1845. It had previously been called Yates's Closs after Francis Yates who had lived in Seafield Court, the house to the north of the lane.

The lane today is signposted as Chromate Lane formerly Lochend's Closs, as part of it borders the garden of Lochend House. Between it and the lane is the house known as Sea Winds, which was built about 1760.[1]

Significant developments took place in the 1960s when many old houses were demolished in order to provide sites for new housing. The original lane turned to the

Lochend House is on the left, then Sea Winds, the entrance to Chromate Lane and Seafield Court. 2021

The Commercial Street entrance to Chromate Lane. 2021

right near the top to join South Kirk Closs and today it joins Church Road at the same location. The houses situated between the lane and South Kirk Closs were demolished to facilitate the construction of Church Road.

Why was it called Chromate Lane? In the 1820s Dr William Spence crushed chromate ore using a mill being turned by a horse in the large garden behind his home, Greenfield House at Greenfield Place. Part of the resulting washings from the mill worked its way down to Bain's Beach via a drain in the closs.[2] His daughter Jane was married to Gilbert Spence of Hammer, a proprietor of chromate quarries in Unst.

The closs had always been referred to as "da dirty closs". In fact "dirty" could be attributed to most if not all the lanes at that time.

Lerwick was teeming with life and the 1851 Census recorded the large number of people crammed into very small areas. For example, Church Lane had 179 residents and Chromate Lane had 45; 120 lived in Mounthooly Street, 48 in Navy Lane and 88 in Law Lane; Hangcliff Lane housed 146 people, Reform Lane 100, Pitt Lane 107, Fox Lane and Quendale Lane had 126 residents and Burns Lane had 189.

Da Auld Kirkyard, as it was known, was cleared in 1966 and the site is now the Church Road car park. The two houses on the right were demolished to enable Church Road to be built. Chromate Lane is in the background. c.1965 (Courtesy of Dennis Coutts)

SEAFIELD COURT

Seafield Court. 2021

Seafield Court was officially named in 1845. The address of the court is 49 Commercial Street.

Before the various buildings comprising the Queens Hotel existed the property at Seafield Court, commonly called Stebbagrinds House, would have enjoyed an open view of Bressay Sound.[1]

The property consisted of a house with an adjoining house at the upper end, also a ruinous house. It was passed by Robert Craigie to James Craigie in 1778.[2]

The next owner was Francis Yates, cooper and slate merchant, in 1787.[3] Yates's Closs (now Chromate Lane) was to the south of his property.

A house and shop was built above Yates's Lodberry in the 1840s

An extension in 1910 provided the hotel with ten extra rooms.

Yates's Court was a small court up Yates's Closs on the north side. Yates's Lodberry and bulwark was opposite his house, on the north side of Bain's Beach. Yates's son, also Francis, inherited the property and he sold the lodberry to William Hay in 1836.[4]

In 1845 it was bought from William's estate by John Henry, a boot, shoe and leather merchant.[5] He built a house and shop over the lodberry, with an entrance from a balcony overlooking Bain's Beach.[6]

In the early 1850s John emigrated to Australia, where he died in 1856, and his wife followed with some of her family in 1857.[7] Robert Henry, John's son and heir, sold the property to George H.B. Hay in 1866[8] who incorporated it into his property to create the Queens Hotel.

Francis Jnr sold the house to Charles Ogilvy, also in 1836.[9]

Charles was the son of Charles Ogilvy and Barbara Ross and he changed the name to Seafield Court after the Ogilvy property at Seafield, Lower Sound.[10] He and his family used Seafield Court as their town house. He died in 1844.

Seafield Court was purchased by John Stout of Graven in 1845 from the sequestrated estate of Charles Ogilvy.[11] John's relatives inherited the property in 1863[12] and they sold to Joseph Leask of Uyea a month later.[13] On Leask's death in 1866 it passed to his heirs[14] until it was sold to Bruce Sinclair in 1935.[15] Ownership remains in the Sinclair family.

It was in this house that a smugglers' tunnel led from the kitchen, in a southerly direction under Chromate Lane, and is said to exit in the vicinity of Lochend House. Part of this tunnel still exists.[16]

The entrance to the tunnel at Seafield Court. 2010

Scottshall Court

Scottshall Court was officially named in 1845.

The present building dates from about 1760, possibly earlier. There were several owners until Robert Scott of Scotshall acquired it in 1770. It passed to his son Walter in 1784 and then to John Murray in 1790.[1] John married Elizabeth Scott, Walter's sister, in 1781.[2]

An alternative name was Murray's Closs. John also owned the lodberry opposite (now part of the Queens Hotel) that contained what was known as Murray's Hol – a passage with an arched roof leading from the sea. It was a convenient place for landing smuggled tobacco, gin, cigars, etc. A tunnel under

Scottshall Court. 2021

Low tide at the Queens Hotel. The former Murray's Lodberry is in the centre with Murray's Hol to its right, now blocked off. 2020

a part of the hotel and under Scottshall Court, on the opposite side of Commercial Street, exited in Sooth Kirk Closs[3] (now part of Church Road).

The original entrance to Seafield Court and Scottshall Court was via two twin stone arches with the names carved above. These structures were demolished by Lerwick Town Council in September 1967. In an irate response Dr T. Mortimer Y. Manson wrote that in his opinion the action was quite unnecessary. He encouraged the public to demand their restoration and then to vote in the local elections the following May to replace the entire council.[4] Replica arches were erected in the early 1990s.

The replica arches at Seafield Court and Scottshall Court. The names are carved into the stone above each arch but are now in poor condition and require repair. 2021

Lodberries and Piers at the South End

Identifying south end piers and lodberries

1. Copland's Lodberry
2. Stout's Pier
3. Torrie's Lodberry
4. Murray's Lodberry
5. William Ross's South Lodberry, later Mcbeath's Lodberry
6. William Ross's North Lodberry, later the Steamers' Store
7. "The Lodberrie"
8. Part of Yates's Lodberry
9. Murray's Lodberry
10. Hay's Lodberry
11. Hay's Pier

The lodberries stand in the sea as they have always done.

CHAPTER 2

FROM CHURCH LANE AND QUEENS LANE TO BACK CHARLOTTE LANE AND CHARLOTTE STREET

CHURCH LANE AND QUEENS LANE

The Old Tolbooth is on the left with steps leading to Commercial Street. The shop, Economy Corner, can be partly seen next to Church Lane. On the upper right is a house in Church Lane and Jamieson's Knitwear shop is in the foreground. Late 1950s (Courtesy of Elizabeth Angus)

Looking down Church Lane. Buildings at the foot were demolished to allow Church Road to be constructed. (Courtesy of Jim Anderson)

South Kirk Closs

South Kirk Closs was changed to Church Lane in 1845. The narrow lane stretched from Commercial Street to opposite the bottom of Knab Road. The upper part bordered the wall of what became known as Da Auld Kirkyard. The cemetery had been in use from the 1680s until 1841 when the last burial took place.

The steps crossing the street at the foot of the closs were removed in 1818 to allow a thoroughfare from below Fort Charlotte to Miss Chalmers Stair at the south end.[1]

Thomas Strong, who was a boot and shoemaker, bought premises at 65 Commercial Street in 1852 from the estate of William Hay of Hayfield. His property was on the south side of Church Lane. The purchase consisted of a shop, two dwelling houses

Looking up Church Road from alongside the Old Tolbooth. The pavement in front of the house with the three windows in vertical line is part of the original Church Lane. On the right is currently the Antique and Collectible Shop. 2020

with shed and back closs which became known as Strong's Court.[2] In 1935 the shop became the Economy Corner.

In the mid-1960s several houses between Church Lane and Chromate Lane were demolished along with Da Auld Kirkyard to enable Church Road and the car parking areas to be constructed. The demolition of Economy Corner in 1966 enabled the "new road", as it became known, to connect with Commercial Street.

With the demolition of Seaview House, Seaview Stores and the Seaman's Home, the road continued to join the south Esplanade. Church Road opened in 1968.

Nort Kirk Closs

The closs became Queens Lane in 1845 and it was said that the closs at one time had steps.[3][4]

Queens Lane with cassies to provide a grip for horses. Late 1950s (Courtesy of Elizabeth Angus)

The Auld Parish Kirk (now part of the Masonic Hall) was, and is still, situated between the two former closses, now Queens Lane and Church Road.

Da Auld Kirkyard was enclosed by drystone walls and there was a piece of waste ground at the top. Cars initially used Queens Lane as a route to and from Commercial Street before a one-way system was introduced.

Da Auld Kirkyard and the Masonic Lodge. c.1965 (Courtesy of Dennis Coutts)

The top of Queens Lane and Church Lane. Late 1950s (Courtesy of Elizabeth Angus)

The same view in 2021

Spence's Court

Spence's Court is on the far left next to Gifford & Smith's shop, which is now Jamieson's Knitwear. 1950s. (Courtesy of Elizabeth Angus)

A large old house on Commercial Street, believed to have been built about 1671,[1] was situated between what is now the Royal Bank of Scotland and Jamieson's Knitwear. It became known as Spence's Court but was not officially named so by the Commissioners in 1845.

The Commercial Bank (now The Royal Bank of Scotland) was completed in 1871[2] on the site of houses dating from before 1680.[3] James Ross Spence, son of Balfour Spence and Charlotte Ogilvy, had set up in business in buildings here as a ship agent, broker and general merchant in 1839, when he was 23 years old. His father had been a well known merchant and shipping agent and on his death, in 1843, James succeeded him as consul for the Netherlands, a post he held for ten years. Afterwards he was also consul for the Hanseatic towns. He took a great interest in all aspects relating to Dutch fishermen. Dutch clogs graced the shop windows, and with his phenomenal memory he was a fount of knowledge about ships, shipping, cargo and seamen.[4]

The Shetland Book Shop. Late 1950s (Courtesy of Elizabeth Angus)

The space between the bookshop and Gifford & Smith. Late 1950s. (Courtesy of Elizabeth Angus)

James and his sister Elizabeth lived in the adjacent house, known as Spence's Court, but had the address 85 Commercial Street. At some point he moved his business there as, in 1862, he advertised that Fair Isle Hosiery was available at that address.[5]

Numerous families lived in Spence's Court over the years but the property may be remembered as Peter L. Angus's bookshop. Peter had tragically lost both his legs in a shell explosion a few days after the Armistice in 1918. He was a nephew of the well-known poet James Stout Angus. In about 1924 Peter opened The Shetland Book Shop at 87 Commercial Street, in the rooms on ground level facing the street. In addition to Shetland books he sold Typhoo tea, cleaning cloths and other goods. (It is difficult to confirm whether or not James Spence was in business in this premises as the shop numbers along Commercial Street changed in 1885.[6])

The Angus family lived in Windhouse, 14 Law Lane (recently renamed Ortolan House) and, following Peter's death in 1955, the business was carried on for a time by his sister Chrissie, who had retired after a lifetime of teaching in Lerwick Infant School.[7]

This very old building in the court, which had housed many families and contained the bookshop, was demolished in the late 1950s and the site subsequently became a car parking area.

Cars parked in the vicinity of Spence's Court. 2021

Crooked Lane

Betty Mann's Closs became Crooked Lane in 1845. The lane is between Jamieson's Knitwear at 93-95 Commercial Street and number 97, which was Smiths of Lerwick until February 2020 when it became Island Larder. The original building housing Jamieson's Knitwear dates back to 1667.[1]

These steps lead to the path that joins with the top of Norna's Court and also Gardie Lane. 2021

The bottom of Crooked Lane. 2021

This upper part of the lane follows the line of Betty Mann's Closs. 2021

Crooked Lane now ends at the Queens Place trance. 2021

Near the foot of the lane looking down towards Commercial Street

Betty Mann's Closs was originally long and narrow, old and tumble-down in places with dangerous steps at the bottom. At the top of the steps a path to the right led across to what became Norna's Court.

At the top of the closs it turned to join North Kirk Closs,[2] later to become Queens Lane. This changed when houses were built there in the early 1880s and these were named Queens Place in 1885.[3] The narrow, long and renamed Crooked Lane now stretches from Commercial Street to Queens Place.

It is recorded that Betty Mann occupied a house in the closs in 1825 but unfortunately nothing is known about her.[4] It can be guessed that she probably had some notoriety before her name was used to identify the closs. Although it was renamed in 1845 it was still being referred to as Betty Mann's Closs in 1881. At that time a report mentioned that the lower steps were no longer there and that a rail should be provided to prevent "a stranger on a dark night from sustaining a serious injury".[5]

The bottom of Crooked Lane on the right. The top of Taylor's Steps is opposite. Early 1950s

Norna's Court

The entrance to Norna's Court. 2021

Nicol's Court was renamed Norna's Court in 1845. Alexander Nicol, sheriff clerk depute and merchant (1767-1837), lived at the foot of the court in a house above what is, since May 2021, Outdoor4Kids/Outdoor Trek at 99 Commercial Street. He had his business premises at 78 Commercial Street (now the part of Conochies nearest to Ninian).[1]

Who was Norna and how did she manage to get a court named after her? She actually did not exist except in the imagination of Sir Walter Scott, the renowned Scottish author. One of the characters in his novel *The Pirate*, published in 1821, is Ulla Troil, also known as "Norna of Fitful Head", who was said to have been in league with the fairies and possessed supernatural powers. Her character was seemingly based on the Orkney witch Bessie Millie, whom Sir Walter Scott met.

Looking down into Norna's Court. 2021

A scene from The Pirate whereby Norna is performing her curative spell on Minna Troil

Legend has it that Bessie, a resident of Stromness, sold favourable winds to sailors for sixpence.[2]

Scott visited Shetland in 1814 along with Northern Lighthouse Commissioners. One of them was his friend Robert Stevenson, civil engineer, who designed Sumburgh Lighthouse, built in 1821. He spent six days visiting Lerwick and the surrounding area. In his journal he described walking to Twageos (which he called Twaggers) and to Cleikhimin (sic). He stayed at Sinclair's Inn (at 59 Commercial Street, opposite the Queens Hotel), where he slept on a straw couch, and later dined with "notables of the town" in the Tolbooth across the street (the town hall at that time). He also visited Noss and Bressay, staying overnight as a guest of Mr Mouat at Gardie House. On the Sunday he rode on a Shetland pony to the Tingwall Manse where he had breakfast with the Rev. Turnbull then, after attending church, travelled on to Scalloway and was entertained by John Scott and his two daughters at his home.[3] That house dates from 1750 and is now the renovated Auld Haa Apartments in New Street, which provide self-catering accommodation.

Following Scott's visit to the South Mainland, including Mousa, his imagination ran riot. He had seen the ruins of "the old house of Sumburgh", built by Earl Patrick Stewart in 1604, and consequently incorporated it into his novel *The Pirate*, naming the fictional house "Jarlshof". Scott would have been totally unaware of the wealth of archaeology later to be discovered in the area. However, it is possible that he did see the broch at Sumburgh Head, which was totally removed to make way for the lighthouse.

The Commissioners of Police were evidently keen to exploit Shetland's newfound fame and were apparently very impressed with Scott's novel and, in particular,

Norna and her son, the shipwrecked Captain Clement Cleveland. Pirate Lane was consequently named in his honour.

Although aspects of the novel were widely inaccurate, it was well received and attracted people to Shetland in the way that the Ann Cleeves's novels set in Shetland and the subsequent TV series *Shetland* do today.

A busy cruise ship day on Commercial Street at the foot of Norna's Court. 2018

Gardie Court

Gardie Court. 2021

Gardie Court was named in 1885 and was originally known as Gilbertson's Closs or Court due to earlier residents with that surname. It is situated at the bottom of Gardie Lane between 99 and 101 Commercial Street.

Thomas Gilbertson is recorded as a merchant tailor 1854.[1] He was also an agent for the firm Cassell & Co which was founded by Englishman John Cassell and was famous for its educational books and periodicals. John campaigned for the temperance movement in Britain so it comes as no surprise that Thomas Gilbertson provided lodgings and a temperance coffee house at 101 Commercial Street. He died in 1868.

Thomas's son, Robert P. Gilbertson, was a wealthy businessman abroad who amassed a fortune as a West African merchant.[2] He bought land to the west of the Burgh Road and was the donor of the Gilbertson Public Park.³ Gilbertson Road was also named after him.

Incidentally, a later occupant of 101 Commercial Street was the firm A.L. Laing, chemist, who traded from 1885⁴ until 2018. The following year Love from Shetland moved into the shop but then moved back to 177 Commercial Street early in 2021.

In 1879 William Robertson, who had been born in Unst and was an auctioneer, purchased the whole block from the trustees of the deceased Thomas Gilbertson.⁵ It consisted of the shop and house bordering Commercial Street dating back to the mid part of the 18th century,⁶ an adjoining building to the south that Thomas had built, and the little house at the upper end, still known to this day as the "Candle Hoose". Around about 1816 a merchant, Andrew Smith, commenced a candle making business there.⁷ Almost every shop in town was stocked with "Smith's celebrated mould candles".⁸

In 1885 William Robertson changed Gilbertson's Court to Gardie Court.⁹ However, Mr Robertson and his family continued to live at 99 Commercial Street above what is presently Outdoor4Kids/Outdoor Trek. This shop for many years was J.R. White & Company.

Until 17th October, 1958, a broad, two-way flight of stone steps, surmounted with a cope and panelled pedestal, was attached to the side of 99 Commercial Street. This old building, which may have been in existence in 1656,¹⁰ and its steps were listed in the Inventory of Shetland of the Royal Commission of the Ancient Monuments of Scotland, number 1245, in March 1935. The steps were recorded as having possibly been built during the second decade of the 18th century.

It transpired that councillors had met in private on 14th October, 1958, and agreed that the steps should be demolished with the result that neither press nor public had the slightest inkling that it was to take place, far less any time in which to think about it.¹¹ With undue haste it took place three days later. On the morning of demolition a group of local men requested that proceedings be delayed and the action

The stone steps are on the left. 1930s

Looking down Gardie Lane towards Gardie Court. The Candle Hoose is on the left. 2021

be reconsidered, but Lerwick Town Council went ahead and carried out the demolition of a unique part of Old Lerwick.[12]

Gardie Court and the steps had been seen by both locals and visitors as a picturesque part of Old Lerwick. Today it is difficult to comprehend why this action was allowed to take place, even though Lerwick Town Council wanted to widen the court and had reached agreement with Mr J.R. White whose shop adjoined the steps.

However, in the late 1950s and early 1960s there was a trend throughout Great Britain of "out with the old and in with the new" and Lerwick Town Council was an enthusiastic participant with many old buildings being unceremoniously demolished.

The outline of the steps can still be seen, along with blocked up windows, on the side of 99 Commercial Street.

The steps were removed in 1958 but their outline and the door is still visible. 2021

Gardie Lane

Above: Gardie Lane. 2021

Left: Gardie Lane and Chapel Place. 2021

The lane is a long, winding lane that more or less forms the line of the original. The upper end is at Annsbrae Court then continues down through a trance at Chapel Place in the Heddell's Park housing scheme before taking a right turn towards Queens Place. The lane then carries down to end at Gardie Court.

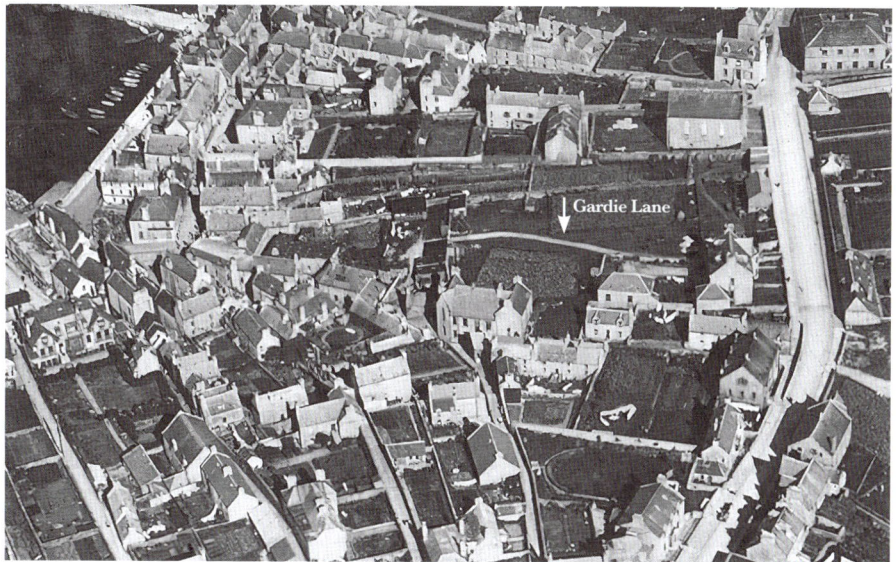

Chapel House can be seen in the centre of the picture with the lane immediately above. St Olaf's Hall and St Columba's Church is at the top right. Early 1950

Heddell's Court

The entrance to Heddell's Court. 2021

Heddell's Court is situated between 103 Commercial Street and the Tourist Centre and gets its name from the family who owned the property at the head of the court. Francis, a dyer by trade, was the first Heddell to settle in Lerwick. He died in 1756.[1]

The shop at 107 Commercial Street, now the Tourist Centre, was owned by members of the Heddell family over the years until Francis's great-great-grandson, James J.G. Heddell,[2] grocer and wine merchant, died in 1888.[3]

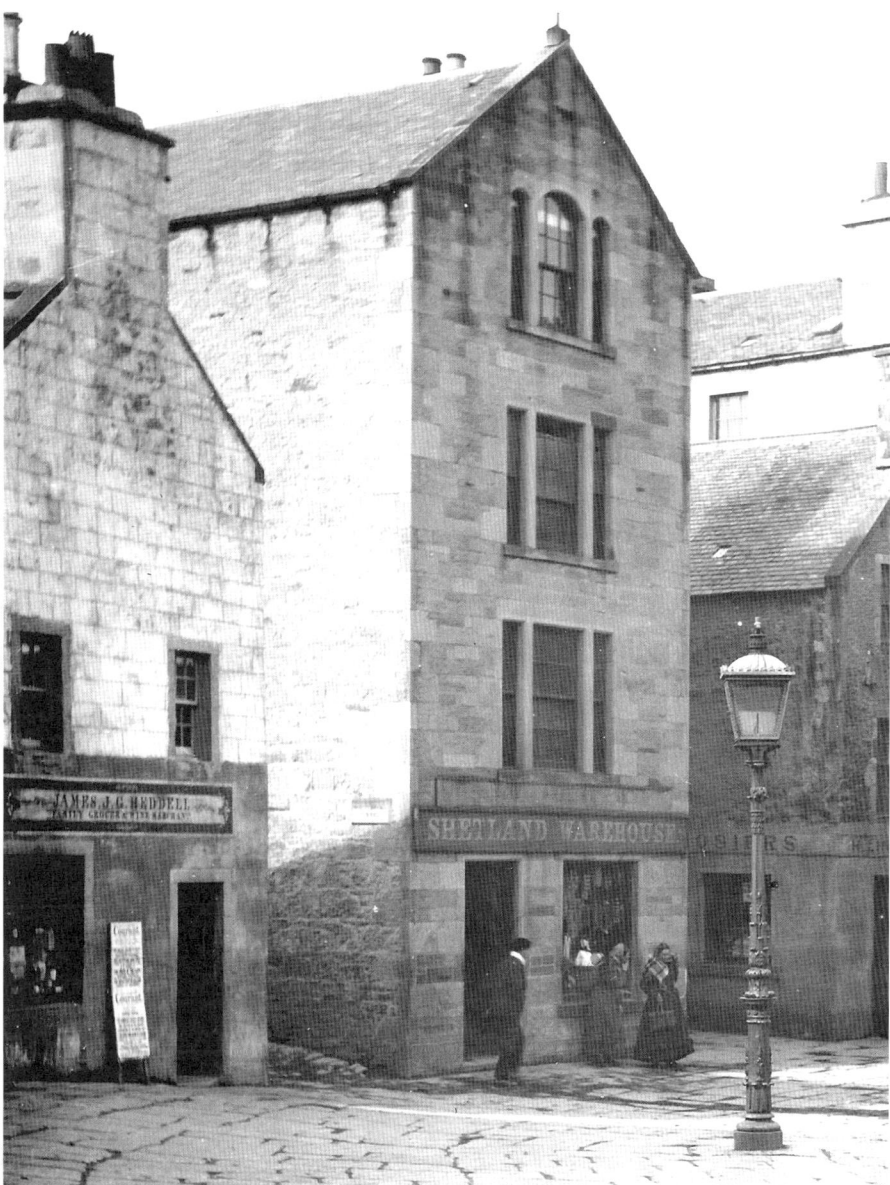

James J.G. Heddell's shop is on the left. Early 1880s

In January the following year Thomas J. Anderson opened his shop there and carried on the business.[4] It became known at "T.J's". He bought the property in July 1893.[5]

In 1899 he reconstructed the building by adding offices at the second level and an upper flat which became a private residence.[6] When Thomas retired in 1935 his business partner, James Gray, became the sole proprietor. Following his death in 1949 his widow, and daughter Mona (now Mrs Tulloch), carried on the business[7] until 1968 when the premises was let to J. & P. Lyons, who continued to operate as a licensed grocer.[8]

T.J Anderson's shop in his restructured building. The entrance to Heddell's Court is to the left of the shop. 1952

In 1976 a Norwegian businessman, Arne P. Moltzau, purchased the premises and renamed it Centron of Shetland. He firstly opened T.J's Coffee Shop for a short time before he went on to sell electrical goods, and advertised A.E.G. Telefunken colour television sets in preparation for the first signal for colour TV expected on 15th November, 1976.[9] The firm ceased trading the following year.

The Highlands and Islands Development Board was the next proprietor and in April 1979 it was granted planning permission to open a tourist office.[10]

The Shetland Tourism Organisation then moved in to the prime site at the Market Cross in 1981.

In October 2005 an extensive refurbishment was undertaken resulting in an open ground floor design, with an impressive reception desk made by Cecil Tait of Paparwark Furniture. The original V-lined shop walls and ceiling were exposed and restored. The staff were decanted to Harbour House while the work was carried out. The public were able to view the newly refurbished premises on 11th April, 2006,[11] and the Centre was opened by Visit Scotland chairman Peter Lederer on 4th May.[12]

It currently functions as Visit Scotland – Tourist Centre.

A reminder of a previous owner of the building remains as the entrance doorstep bears T.J. Anderson, Grocer and Wine Merchant in mosaic.

The mosaic at the entrance to the Tourist Centre.

Heddell's Park

Work has commenced on the Heddell's Park housing scheme. 1956 (Courtesy of Elizabeth Angus)

In 1955 tenders were sought for the building of 54 local authority houses and flats in Heddell's Park, between Queens Lane and Mounthooly Street.[1] These were completed in 1958 and were given the addresses Gardie Lane, Haldane Place, Mounthooly Place, Chapel Place and Queens Place (a continuation of the existing Queens Place). The Heddell's Park housing scheme was awarded a Saltire Society Housing Design Award in 1959 and a plaque is situated on the east wall of the Mounthooly Place block of flats.

In August 1960 Her Majesty Queen Elizabeth II was in Heddell's Park and visited some of the houses.[2]

When the old buildings at Bain's Court were demolished in 1958 the stones were used to build garden walls at the scheme. Also utilised were dressed stones from 22 and 26 Burns Lane which had been demolished the previous year.[3]

Until recent years the residents of Mounthooly Place dreaded the approach of 5th November as some youngsters delighted in setting off fireworks in the

Mounthooly Place flats. 2021

Mounthooly Place walls with reutilised stones. 2021

open area under the flats. The resulting explosions echoed throughout the scheme, frightening both people and pets.[4]

Although still referred to as Heddell's Park the scheme is not signposted. The younger generation call it Mushy Park due to the bollards near the play area resembling mushrooms.[5]

The bollards and play area. 2021

THE MARKET CROSS

The Market Cross is first mentioned in 1838 when the open space of ground near the centre of the Burgh of Lerwick was approved as the site of a "market cross" where public notices could be displayed. This was in response to a petition by James Maconachie, advocate sheriff of Orkney and Zetland, Charles Ogilvy and Gilbert Duncan, magistrates of Lerwick.

Despite the fact that in 1747 the sheriff court had relocated to Lerwick from Scalloway, the capital of Shetland, all public notices had continued to be announced at Scalloway Banks or at Scalloway Castle gate. This state of affairs had caused a great deal of trouble and expense which was resolved when the order for the formation of the Market Cross was finalised on 11th March, 1839, and a stone pillar was duly erected.[1]

In the mid-18th century the area that became the Market Cross was a beach referred to as Heddell's Beach, where boats were hauled up. A burn, later to be known as Miss Heddell's Burn, flowed down Baker's Closs (now Mounthooly Street) under the flagstones then over the beach into the sea. The Heddell family had property in the closs[2] as well as nearby in Heddell's Court.[3]

On the street opposite Gardie Court stood the building known as the "stone block". This projected out so far into the street that the passage between it and the building opposite was only six feet wide and carts sometimes stuck trying to get through. Gavin Goudy carried on business there as a general merchant for some time until about 1840.[4]

An illustration depicting how the Market Cross looked in 1850

Next door was John Foubister's butcher shop. Also in this vicinity was Innes's Lodberry. All these buildings were replaced in 1874-75 by the building that is now Anderson & Company, 60-62 Commercial Street.[5] Peter Innes, merchant, lived opposite his lodberry at what is now 99 Commercial Street. He died in 1793.[6]

A pump well had existed to the south of the beach since the middle of the 18th century and perhaps earlier. It is described as being a rectangular structure of stone with panels on each side with two steps at the base, a plinth and pointed top. Lions' heads were on the north and south panels, from where water poured when a chain was pulled. Although it was called the Market Cross Well it was there long before the Market Cross was erected and is shown in William Aberdeen's 1766 map.[7] The old pump was removed in 1871.[8]

In 1854 a group of local businessmen formed the Lerwick Gas Light Company and erected a gasworks on the site of what is now Charlotte House in Commercial Road. By 1858 the Market Cross was lit by gas thanks to a lamp post presented to the town by Frederick Dundas, who was MP for Orkney and Shetland from 1837 until his death in 1872, apart from five years when he lost his seat to Arthur Anderson.[9] The lamp post was subsequently moved to Victoria Pier.[10] In 1933 the old gas lights along the sea front were replaced by electric lamps. It was claimed that this scheme made Lerwick one of the best-lit ports in the north of Scotland.[11]

The Market Cross with shops. James J.G. Heddell, the Shetland Warehouse, H. Linklater, the Victoria Warehouse with C. Sandison on the right. 1880s

The new electric light fitting that replaced the old gas one on top of the Market Cross was designed by local art

The Gas Pier is on the lower left with what is now Healthcraft and Shetland Community Bike Project at 12-18 Commercial Road. Opposite, on the upper side of the road, is the gasworks. Aerofilms, late 1962

teacher John R. Sutherland. He had been born in Lerwick in 1871 but spent most of his working life in Edinburgh as an art master and heraldic artist before returning in 1931 to teach at the Anderson Educational Institute.[12]

By the way, the gasworks closed in 1963 and in 1976 the site was cleared for the construction of Charlotte House.

In 1875 the barometer that had been presented by the Board of Trade to the fishermen using the port of Lerwick was removed from an inconvenient building near the pier. After having been repaired by the Commissioners of Police it was then attached to the side of the Market Cross facing the sea.[13] The barometer had originally been lent by the Met Office in 1858. In December 1996 it was taken down when the Christmas lights were being wired up but was reinstated the following March when it was discovered that Lerwick Harbour Trust had breached planning regulations by removing it from a C listed structure.[14] [15] It remains in that position.

Permission was granted for the Market Cross to be moved slightly to fit in with the proposed layout of slabs during the reflagging of Commercial Street in 1999.[16]

The Market Cross still carries out the function for which it was created in 1839, namely to display notices and advertise events.

The location of the barometer. 2021

Notices. 2016

Mounthooly Street

The old row of houses in the upper part of Mounthooly Street where Peter Sievwright had the first bakeshop in Lerwick. Navy Lane is on the right. Early 1950s (Courtesy of Elizabeth Angus)

Baker's Closs was renamed Mounthooly Street in 1845. The origin of the name Mounthooly is obscure but was thought to have been in connection with the artillery battery, reputed to have been situated near the present Braeside House, Law Lane. The officer in charge was believed to have lived nearby.[1]

However, the original name of the closs is self explanatory as it contained Lerwick's first bakeshop.

In the late 1700s Peter Sievwright, an Aberdonian, had his bakeshop in a house on the south side of the junction with Navy Lane.[2] These houses were demolished in 1956[3] to be replaced by Lerwick Town Council houses, which were completed in 1963.[4]

Following Mr Sievwright's death in 1830 he was succeeded by a Mr Dingwall,[5] then the business was carried on the following year by John Bannatyne[6] who had relocated to Lerwick from Rothesay. In 1838 Bannatyne bought the house and garden further down the closs, belonging to his brother Robert who was a fishery officer, and John subsequently built a new house and bakeshop in the bottom part of the garden.[7] This is the building we see today at 12 and 10 Mounthooly Street (now "The Bakers" and Jon Stone Hair respectively).

This row of houses replaced Skipper's Court in the early 1960s. On the right is "The Captain's" in Navy Lane. 2021

Originally the bakeshop, now Jon Stone Hair. 2016

On the left is 10 and 12 Mounthooly Street. 2021

The next occupants of the bakeshop were James Sinclair and George Irvine,[8] then Mr Irvine's son who was trading as Irvine & Co in 1892.[9] The next baker was Arthur Russell in 1894.[10] William Hall followed in 1898[11] and when he moved to premises on Commercial Street in 1902 it ended over a century of bakers operating in the closs.

In 1909 the trustees of the late John Bannatyne sold the property to Mrs Margaret Morrison.[12] She let the house and garden to a Laurence Robertson and the cellar as a store to James Goudie, ironmonger, whose shop at 113 Commercial Street is now The Wine Shop.

Mrs Morrison then sold the building to Christina S. Christie in 1924[13] who relocated her bookseller and stationers shop from 67 Commercial Street (now the Antique & Collectable Shop).

In 1930 Frank Williamson, the next tenant, opened his house painter, decorator and signwriter shop[14] and remained there until he retired in 1971. His brother William took over the business, retained the name, but moved to premises at 11 Mounthooly Street (now Aurora Ink), until February 1991 when the firm Frank Williamson moved to the former Co-op Supersave at Grantfield.

In 1940 Mr and Mrs T. Stewart purchased the whole property at 10-12 Mounthooly Street[15] and it remained in the family until bought by Leslie Irvine in 1996.[16]

However, after Frank Williamson retired, the ground floor ceased to be a shop when Peter Black, hairdresser, became the next tenant in January 1972 and moved his business

The mural in Peter Black's hairdressing salon painted by twins Barbara and Wilma Cluness and Lilian Tait. 1972. (Photo by Dennis Coutts, courtesy of Peter Black)

from 1 Gardie Lane.[17] Peter was there until 1997. After renovation Leslie Irvine opened Lerwick Building Centre's "in owre shop" for the summer of 1999. The following year the shop premises was let to Jon Stone Hair – the current tenant.

When the building was renovated in 2011 the original old ovens were found to be still in place but were removed.[18]

Baker's Well

The well – one of the largest and best known of the wells in Lerwick – was in the closs up from bakeshop. In 1835 a public pump was placed over it. The crews of whaling ships and foreign vessels frequently used it which added to a shortage of water during the summer. This resulted in a restrictive order whereby the well was locked up at certain hours to conserve the supply and a fine of seven shillings (35p) for illegally using it was imposed.

In 1856 Simon Laurenson, a blacksmith who had a smithy which stood just below what is now Chapel House, was paid a fee by the Commissioners of Police for looking after the well.[19]

The bakers' ovens. (Courtesy of Leslie Irvine)

The pump was situated over the well. Chapel House is on the left. Early 1950s. (Courtesy of Elizabeth Angus)

The well and pump was at the lower end of these houses.

The row of houses on the left was demolished in 1958. The corner of Chapel House is on the right. (Courtesy of Elizabeth Angus)

There could be a large number of women in the closs patiently waiting their turn to get water, with the queue stretching down to the door of Miss Merrylee's school (now Stems). Multi-tasking was evident. To pass the time they knitted, heard the latest news, gossiped, and obtained enough water for that day.[20]

On one occasion a man who lived nearby came home for his meal to find that it had not been cooked because his wife had been unable to obtain any water due to the length of the queue. "I'll shune get dee some," he said, and, stripping off all his clothes he grabbed the pails and proceeded down the closs. Needless to say the waiting women scattered when he appeared and the resourceful man filled his pails and returned home to enjoy his long awaited meal.[21] Could he have been Lerwick's first streaker?

This is how the area looks today. The well and pump would have been situated approximately in front of the car in the centre of the image

In 1862 a wall was straightened in the lane which had the effect of removing the two corners which formed receptacles for filth. It was reported that the amount of ammonia in a volatile state mixing in the atmosphere with decomposing matter was a health hazard.[22] This was the state of affairs throughout the town prior to the introduction of piped water and improved sanitary conditions.

Following an outbreak of typhoid in 1885 the Baker's Well water was analysed and was certified to be highly dangerous for drinking or cooking purposes. Despite a petition to Lerwick Town Council to reopen the well, the decision was made that it should remain closed and it was covered over.[23]

Looking into the Baker's Well on 4th May 1964. (Courtesy of Elizabeth Angus)

It was not until 1958 that the Baker's Well pump was removed when the nearby row of houses were demolished.[24]

When the well was considered liable to collapse the flagstones were lifted and the well was filled up by Lerwick Town Council workmen between 1st and 5th May, 1964.[25]

Navy Lane, Baker's Court and Wren Court

Navy Lane was officially named in 1845. It is the short, steep lane leading from Mounthooly Street to the Hillhead.

Former names were Battery Closs, which took its origin from the gun battery reputed to have been situated in the vicinity of Braeside House in nearby Law Lane and, secondly, Back Baker's Closs.[1] This originated from the bakeshop at the foot of the lane on the south side, belonging to the first baker in Lerwick, Peter Sievwright.[2]

It is not known for certain but Navy Lane was probably named after Captain William H. Brand, RN. He lived in what is now Navy Cottage, at the top of the lane on the north side. He served as midshipman on HMS *Revenge* at the battle of Trafalgar[3] but had come to Shetland in connection with the making of the "meal roads".[4] As a result of bad harvests in the mid and late 1830s, roads were constructed in the islands using local labour. In an attempt to reduce pauperism the workers were paid in meal, hence the name given to the roads.

The first opening up Navy Lane, on the left, was named Baker's Court in 1845. It was known as "Skipper's Court"[5] and that name remained in use right up until the mid-1950s when the houses were demolished. Gilbert Duncan was said to have given it that name in 1824[6] as it proved to be a popular abode for seafarers. In 1848 Captain John William

Willie Leask, better known as Whalsa Willie, walking up Navy Lane on his way to his home in Skipper's Court. Early 1950s

Navy Lane sign

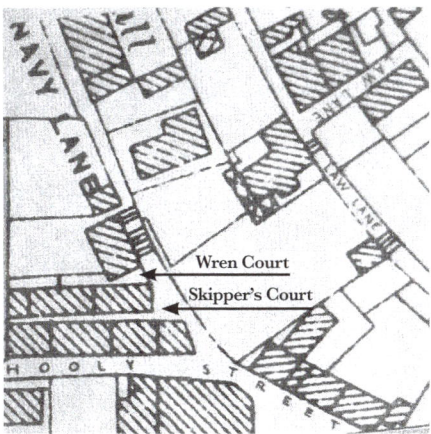

Map showing Mounthooly Street, Navy Lane, Skipper's Court and Wren Court.

Looking down Navy Lane with the entrance to Skipper's Court on the right. c.1920

This photograph taken from the top of Mounthooly Street shows a parallel row of houses. The lower row is Skipper's Court while the upper is Wren Court. Early 1950s

Navy Lane. "The Captains", Hjempåfjaelet, the Ebenezer Hall and Braeview. 2021

Petrie bought property there, bordering Mounthooly Street.[7] He was leading shipmaster in Hay & Company's fleet and was also master of the clipper *Matchless* up until 1865.[8][9] James Jamieson, otherwise known as "Muckle Jeemie Jeemson", was master of the smack *Sprightly* and he lived in the court.[10]

The second opening led to Wren Court, also named in 1845.

Further up Navy Lane, next to Wren Court, on the left was Erland Cottage which Captain James Hughson, a pilot, bought in 1847.[11] It was recently purchased and refurbished by Leslie Irvine to provide luxury self-catering accommodation and renamed "The Captain's". During the early part of 1996 new ornamental streetlights were introduced in the lanes, including Mounthooly Street and Navy Lane. They were custom made, of a high quality and based on the traditional design seen earlier in the area.[12]

The census for 1851 reveals that there were 14 families consisting of 48 people living in Navy Lane and, as can well be imagined, the sanitary conditions were somewhat primitive. In 1862 Robert Coyne, a civil engineer from Edinburgh,

Willie Leask and his dog Fanny outside his front door. (Courtesy Elizabeth Angus)

was requested to examine the state of Lerwick lanes, streets and courts and his report on Navy Lane made depressing reading. Coyne reported: "There are three nooks, angles or corners each of which are used as depositing places for filth and for committing nuisances of the foulest description."[13]

Originally, the lower part of the lane was very uneven with cobblestones two-thirds of the way up. It was extremely difficult to negotiate in frosty weather, resulting in a resident installing a handrail at his own expense. In about 1907 two sets of steps were constructed and at the same time the drystone wall bordering the north side was knocked down to allow the lane to be widened. It was subsequently rebuilt and by 1918 the cobbles had been replaced by granite setts.[14] These remained until 1985 when flagstones were laid.

This row of houses replaced Skipper's Court in the early 1960s. 2021

Memories of one of the latter-day residents remain – namely Willie Leask, better known as Whalsa Willie, and his dog Fanny. He was a docker who was frequently seen around the waterfront and lived in Skipper's Court for some time.

The two parallel rows of old houses forming Skipper's Court and Wren Court were demolished in 1956[15] to provide a site for a Lerwick Town Council housing scheme in Mounthooly Street, which was completed in 1963. One house has a Navy Lane address.[16]

Today there are seven houses in Navy Lane. In addition to the three previously mentioned, Braeview was built in the garden of Braeside House in 1905 for Gifford Gray who was superintendent of County Police and it subsequently had the distinction of having the telephone number Lerwick 1. It is now the home of the author and his wife. In 1978 George and May Anderson's house, Hjempåfjaelet, was constructed opposite Braeview on land attached to Erland Cottage. In 2004 Alan Manson built two houses across from the Ebenezer Hall in the grounds of Alderlodge.

Charles Spence, a later occupant of Navy Cottage, was Lerwick's first professional photographer. He built the Christian Brethren Ebenezer Hall in his garden and it was officially opened on the 1st July, 1885.[17]

Between Ebenezer Hall and Navy Cottage was a little old dwelling house that was only demolished in the late 1980s. During the First World War its occupant gained a degree of notoriety when she and another woman were accused of, and were charged with, using the house as a brothel. There had been complaints by neighbours of large numbers of men frequently visiting the house and of the women being drunk. Although admitting that men did regularly visit the house the women were adamant that no immoral or improper behaviour ever took place as all they had been doing was washing the men's clothes. As the court was reluctant to convict on a mere suspicion the charge was found not proven.[18]

One marked difference between the early days in Navy Lane and now is that at the present time sycamore trees outnumber residents!

11 and 13 Navy Lane on the left. 2021

The alleged house of ill repute. 1965

Sycamore trees. 2021

Law Lane

Law Lane was officially named in 1845.

Until then it was called Sheriff's Closs, after Sheriff Andrew Duncan who built Prospect House at the top of the closs in 1819.[1] Initially there was reluctance by Lerwegians to adopt the new name despite its appropriateness due to the number of lawyers who lived in the lane.

Prospect House remained in private ownership until it was acquired by Lerwick Town Council in 1963[2] and converted into flats for tenants.

In 1992 this was another old house that councillors planned to demolish.[3][4] However, sense prevailed following a public outcry, distressed tenants, a petition, objections from Lerwick Community Council, Shetland Civic Society and the Architectural Heritage Society of Scotland, and the building was saved.[5] Subsequently the interior was redesigned to provide six flats.[6][7]

Sheriff Duncan's son, also Andrew, who was a lawyer, lived opposite in the more modest house at the top of the closs on the south side, now 4 Hillhead.[8] This

Prospect House. 2021

Ortolan House, formerly Windhouse. 2021

8 Law Lane. 2021

house was later the Free Kirk Manse but in recent years became the home of the Goodlad family associated with the firm Anderson & Goodlad, solicitors.

Another Law Lane resident was Robert Niven Spence, solicitor, who had been born in Windhouse, Mid Yell in 1802. He was the grandson of Robert A. Spence of Windhouse.[9] He resided in the house he named Windhouse, at 14 Law Lane, but it has recently been renamed Ortolan House. Mr Spence practised his profession at home until his death in 1863, when he was succeeded by his son John William Spence, also a lawyer, who worked and lived in the house until his death in 1873.[10]

The house on the left, opposite number 8, no longer exists. Braeside House is in the background. c.1910

The title deeds for 8 Law Lane date back to 1689 and, after several owners, it was bought by James Greig, procurator fiscal, in 1813.[11] It was heightened and modernised in the 1850s during Dr John Cowie's ownership. His wife was Mr Greig's daughter, Margaret. The house remained in family ownership until 1952 when bought by Henry R. Gilbertson.[12] The next and current owners are Leslie and Raewyn Irvine who bought the property in 1985.

William Sievwright Snr, born in 1792 and died 1870, was the son of Peter Sievwright, the first baker in Lerwick.[13] He started his business as a solicitor in 1823 and worked from an office in his residence in a house at the foot of the lane, in the building later known as Albert Court House.[14] After qualifying, his son William entered the firm as W. and W. Sievwright, solicitors and public notaries. He moved to New Zealand about 1877, a few years after his father's death.[15]

Access to the bottom of the lane is from Mounthooly Street via an opening at the rear of The Lounge bar.

A very picturesque lane

Albert Court

The entrance to Albert Court with the extension to The Lounge in the centre. 2021

Looking down through the court towards Commercial Street. 2021

Albert Court was named in 1845 and was at one time referred to as Birrell's Court,[1] possibly after Ralph Birrell who was supervisor of excise in Lerwick during the early 1800s.

The entry to the court is situated between Miller Opticians and the Shetland Soap Company at 109 and 111 Commercial Street, with steps at the far end leading to a space between the rear of The Lounge bar at Law Lane and Pirate Lane.

In the 1880s John Byrne, an Irishman, occupied a house that had previously been Mr P.E. Petrie's private hotel, which was in premises at 1 Charlotte Place (above what is now Puffin Republic, previously Save the Children shop until early in 2020). Mr Byrne called his establishment Byrne's Temperance Hotel. However, he left in 1888[2] to become manager of the Royal Hotel at 173 Commercial Street (now Boots UK Ltd). He then went on to open the Albert Hotel in the former Albert Court House in late 1889. The following year he opened the Albert Café in the Coffee House which was at the top of Garthspool Road.[3]

Looking towards the rear of "The Lounge", with the top of the passage leading to the lower part of court on the left. 2021

The site of Albert Court House, looking towards houses in Pirate Lane and Hangcliff Lane. 2021

In 1898 the Albert Hotel was advertised as a first class temperance hotel.[4]

However, in 1903 the seven-room hotel was offered for let.[5] The following year Mr Byrne moved to 69 Commercial Street[6] and he died in the Temperance Hotel there in January 1907, aged 77.[7] John Byrne is the great-grandfather of Ian Byrne, Lerwick, retired painter and decorator.

When the hotel in Albert Court ceased to operate, the building reverted back to Albert Court House. It was a very old building with a courtyard at the back and a pump well.[8]

This house no longer exists.

In 1964 a section of ground in the lower part of Albert Court was sold to Stanley Swanson to enable The Lounge to be extended.[9]

Thirsty customers in The Lounge being served by Stanley Swanson, in the centre, with Jim Goudie and Chrissie Leys. c.1964 (Courtesy of Raymond Swanson)

Pirate Lane

The entrance to Pirate Lane from Commercial Street. 2021

The commonly known Tarry Wumple's Closs was named Pirate Lane in 1845.

The foot of the very narrow lane is situated between the Shetland Soap Company and The Wine Shop at 111 and 113 Commercial Street respectively.

Of all the unusually-named lanes and closses in Old Lerwick Tarry Wumple's Closs must top the list. William Mouat, an Orcadian, his wife and sons – William, Thomas, Richard and Robert – lived in the upper part of the trance house at the foot of the closs. He was employed as a "tide waiter", i.e. a customs officer who checked the goods being carried when a ship landed in order to secure payment of customs duty. It was said that William Snr had bought a boat which the builder had heavily tarred on one side. As to the stability of the boat Mouat announced: "She'll be steady enough by-and-by, it's the tar that makes her wumple," and thereafter he acquired the nickname "Tarry Wumple". He died in 1825.

William Jnr, a lawyer's clerk, inherited the Tarry Wumple nickname on the death of his father. He and Thomas also had a problem with a boat. They subsequently moved to Park Lane where Thomas laid the keel in an upstairs room where they lived. Just before Christmas they invited some important people to see the half-built boat and a youth casually asked if they were sure that it could get out the door. The eccentric brothers looked aghast, then took measurements and discovered

The lane is narrow at the bottom. 2021

Like in many other lanes a tap was situated here in the days before houses had an indoor water supply. 2021

that the beam was too wide to be either taken out through the door or the window. On Christmas Eve they received a bottle of whisky and a large ready-to-be-cooked stuffed goose from a merchant who had nearly choked with laughter when he had heard about the boat. Unfortunately the brothers got extremely drunk and, on Christmas morning, Thomas found the smashed remains of the whisky bottle and the charred and blackened goose in among the ashes.[1] William died there in 1862, followed later by Thomas.

How did Tarry Wumple's Closs became the somewhat exciting and mysterious Pirate Lane and who was the pirate who lived there? Most likely he did not exist except in the imagination of the well-known Scottish author Sir Walter Scott. His novel *The Pirate*, first published in 1821, included the shipwrecked pirate Captain Clement Cleveland. The character was apparently based on the escapades of John Gow the notorious real life "Orkney pirate".

Another character in the novel is Ulla Troil, also known as "Norna of Fitful Head". The Commissioners of Police were obviously so impressed by the novel that in addition to changing Nicol's Court to Norna's Court, Tarry Wumple's Closs was named Pirate Lane in honour of pirate Captain Cleveland.

Pirate Lane widens at the top before turning to join with Law Lane. 2021

Hangcliff Lane

The bottom of the lane. 2021

The top of the lane leading to the Hillhead. The rear of Prospect House is on the left. 2021

Steep Close was given the name Hangcliff Lane in 1845.

The bottom of the lane is situated between The Wine Shop at 113 Commercial Street and the Bank of Scotland and, like the majority of others, the exit is at the Hillhead.

Hang-cliff is said to be derived from the name given by Dutch cartographers to the Noup of Noss – "Hangcliff" or high cliff. It may have been chosen because it was said that the Noup at one time could be seen from the top of the lane, but more likely it was because of its steepness.

Many people lived and died in the closs over the years, including the young daughter of James Laing, a sailmaker. She was the first person to be buried in what is now Lerwick Old Cemetery in Knab Road, which was created in 1834 and opened the following year.[1]

In the early days the lane was difficult to negotiate due to its steep gradient, the loose stones underfoot and an open sewer that ran down one side of the lane.

Despite these conditions the 1851 census reveals that 146 people lived in Hangcliff Lane.

The open sewer remained until 1905, the only lane in Lerwick to have one at that time. During that summer the foot of the lane was widened when it was set back to align with the new bank building which was under construction, now Bank of Scotland Buildings. It replaced the Union Bank which burned down in May 1903. An additional set of eight flights were created and the uneven stones were removed and replaced by paving stones from top to bottom. These improvements greatly enhanced the lane.[2]

The "Steep Closs". c.1890

Many characters lived in Hangcliff Lane. One such eccentric individual was Robert Laurenson, commonly known as "Robbie Snuddie", who was born in Lerwick in 1819 and boasted that he was "ages with the Queen". When young he was expert at swindling Dutchmen with polished buttons passing as coins in exchange for schnapps, tobacco or china-bowled pipes. He was a very good pilot (at least when sober), a smuggler, slaughterman and Arctic sailor. He died in 1881.[3]

The original steps at the bottom. c.1900

Eight flights of steps in Hangcliff Lane. 2021

Robbie Snuddie. c.1870s

Mary Norie. c.1870s

Another individual was Mary Norrie, who lived near the foot of the lane. On a Sunday evening in 1867 a fire broke out there in Mr James Dalziel's grocer shop. In the cellar was stored a barrel of gunpowder, several barrels of paraffin, linseed oil and other flammable material. Mary, in sheer terror and in the scantiest of clothing, rushed out and up the lane crying at the top of her voice: "Da last day is come, da last day is come, fly ta da mountains, fly ta da mountains, da last day is come". However, most people fled to see the fire and assisted to put it out with buckets of water from the sea, wells and pumps. News of the fire soon spread and kirks even emptied leaving ministers in the middle of their sermons. Disaster was averted but one man was severely burned.[4]

Haggis Competition advertisement by "Jim the Butcher" of Smith & Company. January 1991

A more recent "character" who resided for a time in the lane was Jim Grunberg, also known as Jim the Butcher, who worked at Smith & Co, 65 Commercial Street. His parties in the late 1970s were legendary and on one occasion fancy dress was mandatory. Anyone not in costume was handed out appropriate apparel and the well-known musician Ronnie Cooper was given a crash helmet on arrival. With Ronnie's limited eyesight it is doubtful how much he enjoyed the experience. The evening ended with a fireworks display much to the displeasure of neighbours.[5]

Swallow Lane later Bank Lane

James Tait's Closs was renamed Swallow Lane by the Commissioners in 1845. It is suggested that the closs was named after James Tait, merchant, who had his shop at the south side of Park Lane.[1]

Numerous swallows frequented the area in the early 1840s[2] and built their nests in the chimneys of the old houses at the foot of the lane,[3] and in Mariners' Court before those buildings were demolished in 1888.

Swallow Lane has the distinction that the last blazing tar barrel was taken down to Commercial Street from the Hillhead via the (at that time very narrow) lane, despite the fact that the tradition had been prohibited in 1874.[4] Although police and special constables were watching for trouble at the north and south ends of Commercial Street, the boys outwitted

The lane before the handrail was erected in 1945

them by bringing the barrel down the lane at speed. It was then hauled towards the Market Cross where, after three cheers, they quickly dispersed and the barrel was left to burn.[5] This may have taken place in 1877 as there were no tar barrels the following year.[6]

In addition to James Tait's Closs this lane had a further three names. After the Union Bank of Scotland was erected in 1873[7] an unofficial sign was put up at the top of the lane changing the name to Union Bank Lane. Mr Mitchell, the bank agent, was unaware that regulations had been broken but asked if the sign could remain.[8] However, the 1881 Lerwick Census reveals that the lane was still called Swallow Lane, but by 1891 it had been changed to Union Bank Lane. After the Union Bank building was destroyed by fire in 1903, work commenced the following year on building the present Bank of Scotland Buildings, which opened in 1906. The lane then became Bank Lane.

The Myrtle Hall, the meeting place of the Church of God in Lerwick, was built in the lane in 1925 and opened in July of that year.[9] The handrail in the centre of the

Bank Lane with handrail. The St Clair is at Victoria Pier. c.1950

The Myrtle Hall is next to the trees. 2021

lane, with handgrips on each side, was erected in October 1945.[10] The work was initially held up as the trustees of the Myrtle Hall objected on the grounds that the railing would prevent funerals from taking place. The matter was resolved by leaving a gap in the railing opposite the hall's entrance which allows coffins to be taken in and out.

Looking down Bank Lane. 2021

Mariners' Court

Mariners' Court was named in 1845 and was situated between Bank Lane and Reform Lane behind the buildings at Da Roost (not to be confused with another Roost at the south end of Commercial Street). The court ceased to exist when these buildings were demolished in 1888.

Why was this narrow, almost 3m wide, part of the street called Da Roost? It derives from the Icelandic word *raust* – a rapid current; described as "a strong and boisterous current, occasioned by the meeting of rapid tides".[1]

This is the common name attributed to the turbulent tide stream around Sumburgh Head.[2]

This definition would appear to accurately describe the activities that took place on the street during the tar-barrelling days in the mid-1800s, when it was the custom for groups of young men to celebrate Christmas and New Year by dragging blazing tar barrels from opposite ends of Commercial Street, usually at 3am and 4am, with the object of trying to force their way past each other through Da Roost[3] – the meeting of rapid tides being human rather than water. From the north came the "Northerners", a group made up of men who lived at Freefield, Garthspool and Skibbadock, and worked at the docks as carpenters, sailmakers, coopers, cod-splitters and fishermen. The opposing group, the "Southerners", was composed of young men living around Commercial Street.[4]

The replacement building constructed in 1888 between Bank Lane and Reform Lane. 2021

The old buildings at Da Roost

The frontage of the two shops on the right was set back in 1936 and is now part of Conochies

A vivid account states that:
"Yells, shouts and curses rend the air. The police are swept aside as they try to delay the progress of one side or the other to allow the tar barrels to pass… The tar barrels crash together, and boiling blazing tar is scattered in all directions: the tug of war commences, and now between the combatants there is a veritable inferno of fire and scorching heat. Neither side relaxes for an instant: the curses, shouts and yells grow louder… … Tempers break loose and fists come into play. Masked figures hit out indiscriminately at other masked figures, but still the struggle for supremacy goes on."[5]

Shopkeepers and people living nearby would have been relieved when tar barrelling was banned in 1874.

However, in 1886 the burgh surveyor reported that the buildings at the foot of Union Bank Lane, Reform Lane, Mariners' Court and the lower house used as a baker's shop, were in a dangerous state and unfit for habitation.[6] Subsequently a letter was submitted to the Commissioners of Police by Arthur H. Harrison, merchant, along with plans for a new building to replace his buildings at Da Roost.[7]

These old buildings were occupied by Hugh McKay, butcher, who had been a farmer born near Tongue, Sutherland, but now lived at Sound,[8] and Charles Gifford, pilot and shoemaker, who lived with his family in the adjacent building. They must have been

Hector Morrison's shop on the right, also James Bain's shop. Early 1880s

Commercial Street 2021

terrified many times when the tar barrels stuck before their door. The next shop had been occupied by various bakers over the years, the last being John Black.[9]

However, by 1888 the foundation of the new building was laid, five feet (1.5m) further back at the Bank Lane corner and 11 feet (3.3m) further back at the Reform Lane corner.[10] The new block, with a façade of Hildasay granite, consisted of three large shops with offices above and Mr McKay returned to occupy the middle shop.[11] These shops are now Juice Culture Lerwick (from May 2021) and the British Red Cross Society, 125-127 Commercial Street.

Opposite the new building was the premises of the Harrison family who gave their name to Harrison Square. Gilbert lived at 76 Commercial Street while the firm's drapery shop at 74 was in line with the present day Camera Shop. The house along with their licensed premises at 78 Commercial Street protruded into the street and later became Hector Morrison's and Andrew Nicolson's shops. The frontage of these was set back in 1936.[12] Today the three shops comprise Conochies.

Another shop that protruded into the street was that of James Bain, tailor.[13] This shop has often been mistaken for 84 Commercial Street (currently R.A.M. Knitwear). Messrs. George Harrison & Co, who was Arthur Harrison's father, had earlier occupied Mr Bain's premises. Next was a ruinous building at the north end where there had been a fire in 1824. It was thereafter called the "Brunt Hoose". In 1905 these buildings were purchased by E.S. Reid Tait & Co, and razed to the ground.[14]

The replacement building now houses Ninian and Aurora at 80 and 82 Commercial Street respectively, while at the rear in Harrison Square are Coffee Culture and Lerwick DIY, with residential accommodation above.

Following the demolitions on both sides of the street, and the construction of the new buildings, Commercial Street was widened from nine feet (just under 3m) to 19 feet (almost 6 metres).[15]

It is ironic that in 1887, following a petition, magistrates agreed that due to increasing traffic every effort should be made to widen Commercial Street in the best interest and prosperity of the town. However, today emphasis is on discouraging traffic and promoting pedestrianisation.

Reform Lane

The cold water tap can be seen at the side of the woman who is standing below the steps. The outdoor toilet is the little building on the right. c.1935

Reform Lane was named in 1845. This was probably a reference to the 1832 Scottish Reform Act, which introduced wide-ranging changes to the election laws of Scotland. However, the old name of Gilbert Tait's Closs remained in use for many years afterwards.

Gilbert Tait was born in Fetlar in 1789. He was an ironmonger, general merchant and herring curer who had his shop and business at the bottom of the lane, on the north side.[1] In 1841 he was living, along with his family, at Tait's Pier, then ten years later in Mariners' Court.

Gilbert Tait's lodberry and pier were near the site of the present day Ninian and Aurora at 80 and 82 Commercial Street.[2]

Gilbert died in 1860.

He was succeeded by his son Richard, an ironmonger and hardware merchant who also had a saddlery department.

The 1911 census reveals that a total of 92 people, in 10 houses, were living in the lane.

By the 1960s many of the houses were derelict but these were later renovated and the lane is now a desirable place to live.

Park Lane

The entrance to Park Lane from Reform Lane. 2021

The closs was commonly known as Robert Cheyne's Closs before becoming Park Lane in 1845.

Robert Cheyne had a small school there, many years before the building of the Anderson Educational Institute in 1862.[1] John Jamieson, his daughter's husband, was a tailor and they lived in a small house in the lane.

Park Lane is accessed from Commercial Street by steps next to the Nordsterna Shetland Crystal Boutique.

The lane sweeps to the left with further flights of steps bordered by drystone walls and trees.

The entrance from Commercial Street. 2021   *Park Lane sign. 2021*

Another flight of steps. 2021   *Several more leading to the cross lane. 2021*

The top part of Park Lane is a cross lane with Reform Lane at one end and Pitt Lane at the other.

A green field, or park, in the distant past gave its name to Park Lane and it is appropriate that the Park Lane Community Garden can now be found at the top of

The cross lane part of Park Lane. 2021

the lane. It stretches to Pitt Lane then beyond towards the car park. The garden was built on the site of three blocks of social housing containing eight flats which were demolished in 2010 due to the use of inferior concrete blocks in their construction. There were no plans to replace the housing so neighbours Frank Johnston and Andrew Sandison, whose properties bordered the waste ground, decided to create a garden on part of the site in 2014. Over the years it has expanded and now covers a much wider area. Recently the "Food for the Way" or FFTW Community Garden Club took over responsibility for maintaining the garden. The club was created in March 2021 and is based in the Methodist Church.

Part of the Park Lane Community Garden. 2021

Pitt Lane

The entrance to Pitt Lane. 2021

Pitt Lane was named in 1845 in recognition of William Pitt the Younger. He was a prominent Tory statesman who became the youngest prime minister at age 24 and served on two occasions, from 1783-1801 and from 1804 until his death in 1806. He is known as "the Younger" to distinguish him for his father, who was also a former prime minister.

This lane was known by three different names. The first was Mowbray's Closs, after John Mowbray, merchant, who was living in the closs in 1716. His name appears several times in local legal documents in the period 1699-1721.[1] He was at one time a kirk elder and held the post of treasurer.

In October 1819 Captain Thomas Leask purchased a house, shop and tenement block called Mowbray's Houses from Magnus Jamieson, merchant.[2] The property was situated at the foot of the lane on the north side.

The Leask family had moved to Lerwick from Whalsay in 1806. In 1822, when the eldest son Joseph was about 25 years old, he set up his business[3] – Joseph Leask & Co – in what is now R.W. Bayes, 143 Commercial Street. It consisted of a drapery and clothing establishment and office. The entrance was from the lane at the top of the first flight of the original steps. He was also a ship and boat owner and one of the principal shipping agents in Lerwick at that time. The shop and office were the scene of great activity in the days of the Greenland whaling and seal trade when, at the end of March each year, local men queued to sign on as crew on the whale ships. It was said that on occasion there were so many people in the shop, and in the lane trying to get in, that men resorted to being hoisted up from Commercial Street to gain entry by the window. His popular and successful licensed premises was at ground level.[4]

Mr Leask bought property at Garthspool in 1852 that became known as Leask's Dock, and added fish curing, ship chandlery, sail making and carpentry to his business. He was also the owner of several smacks[5] and carried on extensive business there until his death.

In public life Joseph was chief magistrate and a member of most public bodies. He acquired a considerable amount of landed property included the estate of Sand, also premises at Seafield Court and at 52 Commercial Street, which is now Anderson & Goodlad, solicitors, where he lived for several years. Joseph Leask of Sand died at Seafield, Lower Sound in 1882, when he was 85.[6]

Mowbray's Closs gradually became referred to as Leask's Closs and eventually to Pitt Lane, but Lerwegians were slow to adopt the official new name. Perhaps not surprisingly, as William Pitt had died so much earlier.

Pitt Lane, the entrance to Park Lane and part of the Community Garden. 2021

The houses that were built towards the top of the lane in the late 1970s have been demolished and the Park Lane Community Garden has been created in their place.

BBC Radio Shetland broadcasts from its base at the top of the lane. The station began life with just two members of staff – local journalist Jonathan Wills and BBC television producer Suzanne Gibbs, back in May 1977. Mary Blance joined the team as the first full-time secretary in 1978 and rose to be head of the station before leaving in 2000. She still contributes freelance work to the station. In 1998 the station moved from an overcrowded office in Brentham House to the purpose-built new premises near the top of the lane.[7]

Radio Shetland. 2021

Kelday's Court

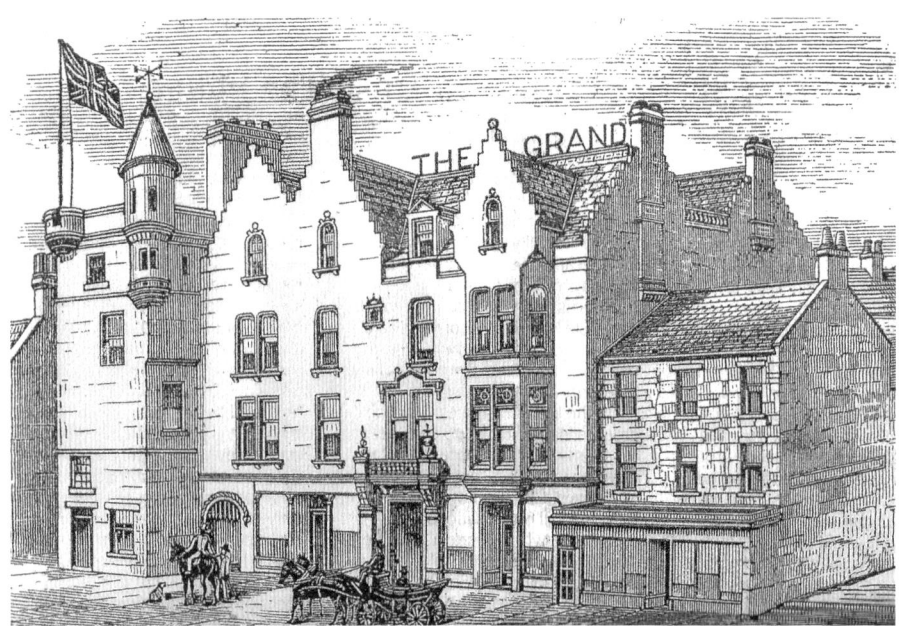

An illustration indicating that the Grand Hotel was now open. August 1887

Kelday's Court was the largest of all of Lerwick's courts and became the site of the Grand Hotel.

The court was enclosed by a substantial, high stone wall and it was said that the gateway, with its stone vases on the side posts, was more like the approach to a country mansion that an entry to a town house. About the middle of the 18th century it belonged to John Kelday, merchant. The house stood with its front to the south, with a large garden to the west and in the gable facing Commercial Street there was a shop. His daughter Elizabeth married Andrew J. Grierson and the house passed down through the Grierson family for nearly one hundred years.

The large house later became the property of Thomas Stout, merchant, and was then known as "Stoot's Hoose", which he let to tenants as he lived at Stout's Court. The old house ultimately deteriorated and was deemed to be dangerous but, despite several offers by the directors of the Commercial Bank who wished to buy the site in order to build a new bank, he repeatedly refused to sell. Eventually the house was demolished and the rubble remained during his lifetime. Following his death in 1879, his representatives sold the ground to Joseph Leask's nephews, Thomas and Charles, and they built the Grand Hotel. The foundation stone was laid on 23rd June, 1886, and the hotel opened for business in August 1887.[1]

In 1888 the Leask brothers were suffering financial difficulties due to the intemperate behaviour of Charles, and an accountant took charge. David and George Goudie Kay, whose father and Joseph Leask were cousins, then took over the business of Joseph Leask & Co. In 1900, along with their brother Theodore, they bought the whole complex but, as their forte was retail, they did not wish to become involved in running a hotel. Consequently, over the next 50 years a series of managers were appointed, and bookings for accommodation could be made by telephoning Lerwick 18.

The Grand Hotel. The sign on the wall states "Grand Hotel Bar Pitt Lane Now Open". c.1888

Mrs Jemima Henry bought The Grand from the Kay family in 1950.[2] The next owner was her daughter Irene Cheyney, and then James Bewick, Irene's second husband.

In 1980 local businessman Charlie Fordyce became the proprietor[3] but his plans did not materialise.

The hotel changed hands again in 1984 when it was bought by Mr and Mrs Neil Wilkins. The following year Posers Nightclub was opened.

The Grand Hotel was sold early in 1994 to local wholesalers JWG plc, with managing director George Hepburn.[4] Renovations were carried out in 1999.

In April 2019 the Grand was again offered for sale and was bought in January 2021 by Cornwall businessman, Harvey Richmond.

Quendale Lane

Quendale Lane sign. 2021

The lane looking up. 2021

Quendale Lane, named in 1845, was previously commonly known as Grierson's Closs.

It is situated to the north of what was Andrew J. Grierson of Quendale's town house (now 155 Commercial Street). The Grierson family's principal estate was Quendale, Dunrossness.

The house was built by Andrew in about 1810 and was entered by a door which stood in the middle of the building and was on the first floor. A stone staircase gave access to the courtyard in front and this courtyard now forms part of the shop, facing Commercial Street. What was the Grierson's drawing room and parlour upstairs was converted to be part of the shop.[1] There was a well in the floor of the house's kitchen.[2]

The house and grounds were purchased from Andrew J. Grierson by Charles D. Jamieson, bookseller, in 1875.[3] He made the extensive alterations to the front and had the steps removed to create a shop for his business.[4] He died in 1891.

His nephew Charles J. Duncan, who had returned from America, carried on business here as a stationer, bookseller, newsagent, dealer in fancy goods and Goss china, agent for The Gramophone Co Ltd, Zenophone Co, and as a pianoforte tuner.[5] He lived in the house above, at 153 Commercial Street, until he died very suddenly in 1915.[6]

Robert Ollason, bookseller and stationer, newsagent and fancy goods merchant, then took over the business and extended into 153 Commercial Street. The shop at 155 Commercial Street continued under the Ollason name until the 1970s when it was owned and occupied by John R. Robertson and L.A. Sinclair. They called the shop Telenews.

Soon after television was transmitted to Shetland for the first time, on 15th April 1964, Tom Stove began selling television sets from his home. In 1966 he obtained premises at 73 Commercial Street, selling television sets and other electrical goods, trading as Televiradio. In 1980 the firm moved to 155 Commercial Street. After Tom retired in 1996 his partners, Tom Smith and James Sinclair, carried on the business until 2003.[7]

The premises then became The Stage Door and recently Shetland Clinical Services Ltd.

Looking down the short lane. 2021

155 Commercial Street in the centre. 2018

Fox Lane

Fox Lane 2021

Why the lane was commonly referred to as either Sutherland's or Manson's Closs is not known, but it was officially named Fox Lane in 1845, presumably after Charles James Fox, the Tory statesman. He was an arch-rival of prime minister William Pitt the Younger and, by coincidence, they both died in 1806.

Half Closs was a cul-de-sac entering from the Hillhead and was situated between Quendale Lane and Fox Lane. It was previously called Braeside Court.[1] The closs disappeared in the 1960s when the whole area was cleared to provide a site for a swimming pool. In 1969 permission was given for the building of the £120,000 pool, which opened in 1973[2] but was demolished before the new pool at the Clickimin Leisure Centre opened in July 1995. The site became an addition to the car park.

Fox Lane gained notoriety as the result of a gruesome event that took place on 25th March, 1858.[3] At the foot of the lane, in the house above the premises at 159

The lanes as viewed from the Town Hall. c.1895

The swimming pool under construction. c.1971

Commercial Street, Peter Williamson (general merchant, draper, grocer and agent for the Peterhead whalers), in a fit of insanity brutally attacked his sleeping wife with a hammer and razor and she died soon afterwards. He also murdered their young daughter and two sons, then attacked his 15-year-old son who had tried to stop him. Although badly injured this son escaped and sought refuge with the servant. He survived, along with a sibling who was not at home at the time. Mr Williamson then committed suicide.[4]

Not surprisingly, afterwards it was said that nobody wanted to live there and the premises became a customs house for a time before relocating to Fort Charlotte.[5]

On a lighter note, on the opposite side of the lane was Malcolmson & Co, bakers, at 157 Commercial Street. William Malcolmson bought the property in 1858[6] but had established his business in 1855, possibly in his house at the top of Church Lane where he was living in 1851. The bakery was inconveniently situated some distance up Fox Lane and a mass concrete section was built about 1880 (now part of Peerie Foxes nursery). Prior to 1946 when the buildings were connected up, a familiar sight was the bakers delivering baked bread down the lane to the shop by the means of boards on their heads.[7]

Malcolmson's was the longest established firm in Lerwick when the doors closed for the last time on Saturday, 12th January, 2013.[8]

The following year Aa' Fired Up moved in and currently occupy the premises at number 157.

Malcolmson's bakers outside the bakery in Fox Lane. c.1957. Left to right George McMaster, Andrew Johnson, George Anderson, Leslie Sinclair, Harry Blance. (Courtesy of George Anderson)

Pilot Place now Pilot Lane

Pilot Place was the name given in 1845 to the narrow closs to the north of Fox Lane. It is now Pilot Lane.

It reflected the occupation of seamen who lived there, including Magnus Thomson, pilot,[1] but it was named after John Gifford, another pilot. The Dutchmen called him "oude Jan Gifford, opp die klein straat" (old John Gifford, up the small street).[2] His three sons – John, Charles and William – were born during the early years of the 19th century and followed in his footsteps. They owned a large sixern, referred to as the "pilot boat", and were said to be the foremost pilots in the town at that time.[3]

The entrance to Pilot Lane is easily missed as it very narrow. 2021

Looking down the short lane. 2021

Burns Lane

The entrance to Burns Lane is through the trance. 2021

Burns Closs was renamed Burns Lane in 1845. The lane is very narrow at the foot, with access from Commercial Street through a trance.

The name is attributed to the Burns family who had been resident in the area for many years.

Magnus Burns was born in Unst about 1758. He was pressed into the Royal Navy in 1793, was a quartermaster and lost an arm on active service in Lord Howe's victory of 1st June, 1794.[1]

Mr Burns became a merchant and built and owned considerable property at the bottom part of the lane, in Pilot Lane and also between the two, on Commercial Street.[2] His house and business was on the site of the present M&Co, 102 Commercial Street. A flight of steps out into the street led to the kitchen.

Burns Walk was the area in front of his house over to the present Virgin Money. (For many years this was the Clydesdale Bank and earlier was Laurenson & Co.) Between the two buildings there was a parapet with an

The lane with the original trance building at the foot. 1950s (Courtesy of Elizabeth Angus)

The present day Burns Walk. 2021

The inscription in the trance. 2021

Houses at the top of Burns Lane. Late 1950s

iron railing to prevent people falling to the beach below.[3] However, the current Burns Walk is the area between M&Co, the bank and Esplanade.

Burns Lodberry was at the back of the shop and Burns Pier was on the south side of the lodberry.

Magnus Burns died in 1846. His son David died two years later, but his daughter Janet, referred to as Miss Burns, lived in the property until her death in 1878.[4]

In 1977 Roy Greenwald, who was the owner of the property at 161 and 163 Commercial Street, had it demolished and rebuilt an almost replica building, complete with trance, on the site. A stone with the initials M.B. and the date 1846 (the year that Magnus Burns died), with an inscription stating "Rebuilt 1977 Roy Greenwald" can be found on a wall in the trance.

Burns Lane was densely populated, with houses extending upwards from Commercial Street and at the Hillhead. Those there met the fate of many others in Old Lerwick when they were demolished in the late 1950s.

Others were demolished during the following years and the site forms part of the car park at the Hillhead which is still referred to as "the swimming pool car park".

Houses in Burns Lane. Late 1950s (Courtesy of Elizabeth Angus)

On the right is Tait's Lodberry, now part of the Thule Bar. To its left is what was Burns's house and lodberry. The long building on the far left was Greig's Lodberry (now the Peerie Shop and Peerie Shop Café). c.1880

From Grierson's Lodberry on the left to Laurenson & Co on the right. The restructured building is now Virgin Money. c.1890

The North of Scotland & Orkney & Shetland Steam Navigation Co headquarters replaced Grierson's Lodberry in 1900, (now LHD shop). Greig's Lodberry is now the Peerie Shop and Peerie Shop Café. M&Co now covers Magnus Burns's house and lodberry. 2021.

Hill Lane

The foot of the lane with what was called Hill House on the right, now Intersport. 2021

Hill Lane was appropriately named in 1845. In the early days it led up to what was known as "da green yairds".

The building at the foot of the lane on the north side, now 167 Commercial Street, was called Hill House and for some years was the home of Laurence Laurenson, draper and hosier. He was born in 1799 and in 1818 founded the firm Laurenson & Co at 106 Commercial Street, where Virgin Money is now. He died in 1867 but family members retained the business and reconstructed the building in 1886, then enlarged it in 1893. The firm expanded to include

Laurence Laurenson's firm, Laurenson & Co. c.1895

Looking down Hill Lane. 2021

dressmaking, millinery, gentlemen's tailoring and outfitting, but primarily became a wholesale warehouse for Shetland hosiery. It specialised in lace shawls and scarves and induced knitters to produce superfine articles in new designs. The firm existed at 106 for over 100 years, until 1925, when it transferred across to the other property belonging to the firm at 167 Commercial Street.[1]

Laurenson & Co at 167 Commercial Street. Late 1940s

In 1947 Laurenson & Company was under the ownership of Mr H.C. Adam and he retained the name until 1950. From then on he traded only in hosiery as H.C. Adam.[2]

The shop is currently Intersport.

Laurence Laurenson also owned property at the top of the lane which his son Arthur inherited.

Jerome J. Anderson was born in Fetlar but, after a period at sea and in the Californian goldfields, he moved to Sacramento and worked in the salmon industry. He returned to Lerwick in 1870 and the following year bought the premises from Arthur for his father and brother before returning to Sacramento, where he died in 1888. Jerome's nephews, Messrs A.T. & D. Anderson, later established a business in the house as watchmakers and jewellers.[3]

Messrs A.T. & D. Anderson were in business in the house adjacent to the Town Hall. This building still exists, as does Gladstone Terrace on the far right, but the others were demolished in about 1957. The site is now a car parking area. Early 1930s

Back Charlotte Lane

Thatch House Lane was officially named in 1845 due to the two "tekkit" roofed houses in the vicinity. One, occupied by Baabie Ratter, was situated where Willowbrae now stands in Charlotte Street and the other, with its south gable on the lane, was occupied by Jeannie Gordon.[1] It would seem that the name was not popular as in 1851 it was recorded as Thatch Lane, in 1861 as Charlotte Lane, and by 1881 it had become Back Charlotte Lane. It was paved in 1873.[2]

Back Charlotte Lane. 2021

Looking down the lane. 2021

Towards the bottom of the lane. 2021

Charlotte Street

Charlotte Street. 2021

Fort Charlotte and Charlotte Street. Late 1960s

The most northerly closs was commonly referred to as Garrison Closs, due to its proximity to Fort Charlotte, but in 1845 it was named Charlotte Lane.[1] By the 1880s it was referred to as Charlotte Street.

At this time at the north end of Commercial Street there was a walled-in space of ground. The front wall facing the street was old and weather stained, and a torn down ragged formation of ground sloped with degrees of irregularity from the boundary of the roadway to the formation of the wall.[2] On this site in 1884 Thomas Ogilvy built a block containing three modern shops, with houses above, which was ready for tenancy during 1886-87. The block became known as Ogilvy's Buildings.[3]

The shop at 177 Commercial Street was occupied by Mr Ogilvy, flesher, then for many years by James S. Smith, butcher. It is currently occupied by Love from Shetland. The middle shop has been occupied by Smith & Robertson since 1894 and the end shop has been occupied by C'est la Vie, the French café, since March 2018.

Ogilvy's Buildings. 2021

CHAPTER 3

FROM TOLBOOTH QUAY TO THE ESPLANADE

Tolbooth Quay, Hay's Corner and the Towbooth Walk

The Old Tolbooth is on the right with Hay's Pier and Lodberry to the left. On the far left is "The Lodberrie". c.1880

Hay's Pier was named the Tolbooth Quay in 1845.

In 1804 James Hay, along with his sons, took the first step towards establishing a retail trade. They acquired a site on the foreshore to the southeast of the Old Tolbooth and built a small house with warehouse and stone jetty with steps where goods could be transported ashore from vessels anchored in the harbour. These became known as Hay's Lodberry and Hay's Pier.[1]

In 1914 Lerwick Harbour Trust began work on extending the pier to form the breakwater and create the small boat harbour. By doing so the backwash from the breakwater began to cause damage to the lodberry and Queens Hotel.[2] Miss Margaret E. Hay, the owner, entered into a legal dispute with Lerwick Harbour Trust that lasted from 1915 until 1917 when the Trust resolved the matter by building a protective sea wall alongside the lodberry.

Hay's Corner was the space between the Queens Hotel, Hay & Company's shop, which was opposite the hotel at 59 Commercial Street, and the Old Tolbooth.

The Towbooth Walk was the part of Commercial Street in front of the Old Tolbooth.[3]

The sea continues to cause damage to the foundations. 1930s

The word tolbooth, or tow böd, simply means a townhouse where tolls (taxes) were collected. The foundation stone of the Tolbooth was laid in 1767 on the site of a previous tolbooth that was over 100 years old and had been in a ruinous condition.

Over the years the iconic building has been used for a multitude of functions such as a court room and prison, a sheriff clerk's office and the office for weights and measures. When the ballroom was not in use the room became a customs house. The Masonic Lodge met there until 1859.

When the prison relocated to Fort Charlotte this allowed the Post Office to return to the building, having previously been there in the 1850s. The Shetland Literary and Scientific Society used rooms as a library and museum until 1897. Another room was an office for an auctioneer and commission agent. Eventually the Post Office occupied the whole building, until 1910.

In 1912 the building was completely renovated and the Royal Mission for Deep Sea Fishermen moved in and occupied the building until 1962.

In 1962 the Old Tolbooth passed to council ownership and it became the headquarters of the Civil Defence. It was even a hall for Up-Helly-Aa for five years from

The Old Tolbooth when it was a Post Office. 1890s

Hay's Corner. Hay & Company's licensed grocer shop is extending into Commercial Street. It was demolished in 1892 and replaced with the building that is there today. c.1885

1964. In 1968 it was sublet to the British Red Cross, the WRVS, and Shetland Tourist Association.

The Hoversta Dairy initially operated from the basement, and then from the early-20th-century extension which ran the whole length of the rear of the building. The dairy ceased in 1963 and the premises became the Red Cross Shop in 1976. At the other end of the extension was the Lerwick Old People's Welfare Committee rest room, previously occupied by Mr R. Paton, barber.

Due to its deteriorating condition the main building was condemned in 1999. The Red Cross Society was forced to leave and relocated to 125-127 Commercial Street.

In 2001 the Old Tolbooth became the property of Shetland Amenity Trust and it was leased to the RNLI. However, the pensioners' rest room was allowed to remain open until July 2003. In August that year the renovation contract was awarded to building contractors DITT and work commenced in September to renovate the building and return it to its original appearance.

By 2005 the building became the fully functional RNLI Lerwick Lifeboat Station at 24 Commercial Street.

Mouat's Lodberry

James Mouat's former residence. At the time this photograph was taken the shop was occupied by E.H. (Hancie) Smith, general merchant, who also lived with his family above the shop. Late 1960s

Mouat's Lodberry was next to the Old Tolbooth.

In 1798 Walter Scott of Scottshall sold a house, byre and garden in South Kirk Closs (now part of Church Road), and also an old lodberry to James Mouat,[1] which thereafter became known as Mouat's Lodberry.

In 1805 James used the site of the property in the closs to build his residence. Part of it is the shop we see today at 67 Commercial Street, which currently contains the Antique & Collectable Shop.

That same year he also built a shop and office opposite, on the lower side of the street, with a house above and cellar below. It became known as Da Cockstool shop.[2] James was a shipping agent for the Leith traders *Dolphin*, *Magnus Troil* and *The Sisters*.[3]

His son later sold Da Cockstool premises to Capt. William James, who then sold to Daniel R. Williamson who bought the lodberry along with the house, shop and cellar in 1885[4] (the shop was later named Seaview Stores).

Jamieson's Knitwear. c.1960   *Seaview House just before demolition in 1968*

Seaview House is to the right of the Old Tolbooth. Early 1900s

Seaview House being built. c.1896

Daniel built a dwelling house on the site of Mouat's Lodberry in 1896 called Seaview House.[5]

This house had several occupants over the years. The upper floor was the Simmer Dim Restaurant for a short time until 1964 when the building was sold to Shetland Islands Council.

The shop underneath, accessible from the Esplanade, was occupied by Jamieson's Knitwear from 1952 until the early 1960s and then by Jim Burgess, who sold agricultural and motor spares until 1967. He then moved to newly built premises at 20 Commercial Road.[6]

Seaview Stores and Seaview House were demolished in 1968 to allow the completion of Church Road.

Clark's Court

Faerdie-maet. 2018

Clark's Court was named in 1845. The court entered from Commercial Street and was behind William A. Clark's dwelling house which is now Faerdie-Maet (previously P. Solotti & Son) at 42-44 Commercial Street. It was also referred to as Clark's Place.

In 1796 Nicol Sinclair had bought what was referred to as "William Farquhar's lower house" from the Rev. John Mill.[1] This was most likely a small house with a very small pier.[2] In 1808 William Hay, merchant, bought what was then a new house and offices, together with shop, cellars and a lodberry behind, from the trustee of the sequestrated estate of Nicol Sinclair.[3]

The next owner was William A. Clark who was born in Unst in 1782. He was a merchant and in 1834 he bought this property from William Hay along with warehouses that been built on the lodberry yard.[4] This now became known as Clark's Lodberry. The main property became his house and shop at 42-44 Commercial Street.

William Clark passed the various buildings to his wife Elizabeth in 1852,[5] two years before his death. Their daughter Catherine, who had married Robert Grant, was the next owner. Their son, William A. Grant, had been born in Lerwick in 1828.

Towards the end of September 1860 Stephen de Djunkowsky, who had been appointed Prefect Apostolic of the Arctic Regions, visited Lerwick. Although said by some to be Polish, he was actually a Russian who had grown up in St Petersburg and was the son of a Russian nobleman and a Dutch mother.[6]

During his two-week stay he lodged at the Zetland Hotel, 77-79 Commercial Street (now the building containing The Shetland Times Bookshop), run by an Irish couple, Mr and Mrs O'Brien. He wasted no time before celebrating what was probably the first mass since the Reformation and converted some local people to Catholicism, including William A. Grant.[7] William allowed the lodberry building to be used as a chapel, which was dedicated to St Anne. It was said to be gothic in appearance and could hold 100 people,[8] although this number is highly unlikely.

In 1864 the property was listed for sale as consisting of a commodious dwelling house and two shops at 40, 42 and 44 Commercial Street, with cellarage underneath and with a lodberry, cellar and lofts behind. There was also a four-roomed house in Clark's Place that was adjoined and connected to the above house.[9] It transpired that the property was not sold on that occasion.

William died in Glasgow in June 1865, 20 years before his mother. He had written poetry and had begun to compile a Shetland dictionary. Surviving extracts are to be found in an archive in Bilbao, Spain. Thomas Edmondston acknowledges in the preface to his *An Etymological Glossary of the Shetland and Orkney Dialect*, published in 1866, that he included many words from Grant's papers in the book.[10]

William's mother, Catherine, sold the property to John Walker of Bressay in 1870.[11] Nicknamed "the director general of Shetland", Walker was the notorious factor for the Garth and Annsbrae estate and was responsible for the eviction of many families from crofts who were then replaced by sheep. He began to convert the lodberry buildings to create his proposed "co-operative store" but the scheme did not materialise.[12]

In 1873 all the buildings were sold to The Shetland Fishing Company Ltd.[13]

A committee had been set up to collect funds for the provision of suitable accommodation for the large number of Royal Naval Reserve (RNR) men who travelled to Lerwick to drill during the winter months. The warehouse buildings were renovated, remodelled and additions were made by building between and over the two lodberry buildings with their gables in the sea. The Seaman's Home was thereby created, with an entrance from the court. This venture was not a success as the reservists preferred the lodging houses in the town which were cheaper. The "home" closed in 1879,[14] but the buildings continued to be called the Seaman's Home.

The Shetland Fishing Company Ltd sold the buildings to Arthur Laurenson and Arthur J. Hay, merchants, in 1879.[15] Part of the Seaman's Home was used as a drill hall by the Zetland Volunteer Corp until 1884, when it was disbanded.[16]

Several families then occupied the building on Commercial Street. In 1896 Arthur J. Hay sold the property to the trustees for the Seaman's Home and Institute in Shetland.[17]

In 1897, due to lack of space, The Shetland Literary and Scientific Society relocated the library and news room from the Old Tolbooth to the vacant Seaman's Home. To give some background to the history of the society, it had been formed in 1861

The Old Tolbooth is on the left. The large building next to it is the Seaman's Home and adjoining it is the Clark's former house, which is now Faerdie-maet. Sinclair's Beach is to the right. c.1880

to promote the formation of a museum of natural history and antiquities and the establishment of a public library. The following year two rooms were made available in the Tolbooth. Initially book donations were received and that same year books were transferred from the General Zetland Library which had been founded in 1828. The Public Library formally opened in 1863 and held 1,100 volumes.

A suggestion was made in 1865 that another library, namely the Lerwick Subscription Library, founded before 1823, should amalgamate with The Shetland Literary and Scientific Society's library.[18] However, it is not known why the Subscription Library was discontinued and the complete collection of its books was sold by public auction in 1877.[19]

The society's library and museum relocated to a room in the Auld Kirk, now the Masonic Hall, from 1878 until 1881 when a move was made back to the Tolbooth. In 1882 the museum items were sold to the Society of Antiquaries of Scotland but the extensive collection of books was retained by the local society and moved to the Seaman's Home in 1897, as previously mentioned. That same year Alexander R.S. Ratter, who was a tenant in part of the Seaman's Home buildings, was appointed curator. He also undertook the duties of librarian and caretaker of the public library, reading room and news room.[20]

In 1904, due to the fact that the library was situated in a comparatively dark corner of the reading room, the society procured additional accommodation for the library in rooms above what is now Faerdie-maet that had been vacated by the Order of Oddfellows. The reading room and news room remained in the hall of the Seaman's Home.[21]

At the outbreak of the First World War special subscriptions were taken up for the service of war telegrams. The service proved so popular that sometimes it was difficult to get near the notice board on which the telegrams were displayed on the wall of

Delivering books to country schools. Mr Ratter, librarian, is in the doorway. 1920s

the Seaman's Home accessible from Commercial Street.

In 1915 the Carnegie United Kingdom Trust, based in Dunfermline, introduced a pilot scheme whereby library books were provided to people in Orkney, Shetland and Lewis. By the end of 1916 a total of 47 rural libraries had been established. In Lerwick it became necessary to rent a further room from the trustees of the Seaman's Home to house the ever increasing number of books supplied by the Carnegie Trust. However, in 1924 the education authority accepted responsibility for administrating the rural library scheme, hereby creating a County Library, with the Carnegie Trust donating all the books and reimbursing the local authority for the cost of obtaining and equipping extra accommodation.

In the same year Mr Ratter, librarian and curator of the Literary and Scientific Society, became the first county librarian[22] but soon found that due to the large number of people borrowing books he was unable to carry out all his duties without the help of his daughter, Lizzie. Consequently, she was appointed assistant librarian at a salary of £5 per year and became curator of the reading room and news room.

Both libraries then operated as close but separate entities with the County Library offering a free service and a better choice of books.

Conditions in the library were often chaotic during the Second World War due to the large numbers of service personnel requiring assistance. A grant of £100 from the feuars and heritors enabled the society to provide free-of-charge facilities in the reading room and a daily service of telegrams. Both were greatly appreciated by locals, members of H.M. Services and visitors to Lerwick.

At the end of 1943 the posts of county librarian and the curator of the reading and news rooms were amalgamated following the death of Mr Ratter, and the subsequent resignation of Miss Ratter. Mr Andrew W. Jamieson was appointed to fill the posts.[23]

In January 1947 the education committee bought from the Church of Scotland the redundant forces canteen in St Olaf Street, now the site of King Erik House.

In July 1948 the library closed for issue of books and a week later books were transferred to the new headquarters with Mr George Longmuir appointed as county librarian. In August 1948 Mr E.S. Reid Tait, last president of the Shetland Literary and Scientific Society, opened the new premises in St Olaf Street.[24] It remained there until February 1966 when the move was made to the purpose-built museum and library on the Lower Hillhead.[25]

In March 2002 the library relocated to the nearby, refurbished, former St Ringan's Church. However, in October 2021 the library and learning centre moved back across Union Street to the original building, which had been completely renovated. It reopened on Monday, 15th November. The former church and the building containing the learning centre were retained by Shetland Islands Council.

Constructing the Shetland Museum and Shetland Library. 1965 (Courtesy of Dennis Coutts)

Following the removal of the library in 1948, the Seaman's Home was used by other organisations. The cellar was used by Lerwick Boating Club to store sails.[26] Access was by large doors from the Esplanade.

The rooms above were occupied by Lizzie Ratter and the National Insurance Office. Mr John P. Shewan, clerk, had his office upstairs, overlooking the small boat harbour. This was later occupied by James Daniels, accountant.

When the National Insurance Office moved to Alexandra Buildings in 1960[27] the Lerwick Club was granted occupancy of the vacant rooms. It had been in existence since 1885 and had occupied the top floor in the Town Hall for 63 years, but the lease had not been renewed. Members played snooker, billiards and bridge. The club remained there until 1965 when it moved to its new clubroom in Annsbrae House, and then to Islesburgh Community Centre in 1981. Members still meet there but the Lerwick Club now exists solely as a bridge club.[28]

The Seaman's Home unfortunately met the same fate as others in the vicinity when it was demolished in 1968 to facilitate the completion of Church Road. In doing so Clark's Court no longer existed.

However, William Clark's former house was unaffected.

From the left are the Queens Hotel, the Old Tolbooth, Seaview House and the former Seaman's Home (both demolished in 1968). The Post Office building is on the right. Early 1960s

After the library moved out, the rooms above were utilised by the Zetland Executive Council. It had been established following the introduction of the National Health Service on the 4th July 1948, with the responsibility for pharmaceutical, dental, ophthalmic and medical services. There were two rooms, separated by a small corridor and a toilet with its window overlooking Commercial Street. Upstairs was an attic used for storage. Following the NHS reorganisation in 1974 the staff transferred to the new purpose-built Shetland Health Board Headquarters at 28 Burgh Road in January 1977.[29]

In 1985 the Alcohol Resource Centre moved from Stout's Court to the rooms vacated by the Zetland Executive Council. Also included was the basement which was unused.[30]

In 1991 the centre was replaced by the Community Alcohol and Drugs Service Shetland (CADSS) but, due to chronic underfunding, it closed its doors on 30th March 2016.[31] These rooms and the basement were then converted into private flats.

It is believed that Alex Solotti, who was of Italian descent and a confectioner and ice cream manufacturer, first opened for business in a shop made out of fish boxes at Baltasound, Unst. In 1904 he moved to Lerwick and resided at the foot of Church Lane (now Church Road). Trading under the name P. Solotti & Son, he commenced selling ices at 40-42 Commercial Street in the shop that is still often referred to as Solotti's but is now Faerdie-maet.

However, he was not the first Italian to sell ice cream locally. Emanuelle Valle arrived in 1895 and opened his shop at 67 Commercial Street (now the Antique & Collectable Shop). In 1904 Mary & Harry Corothie also opened a shop in part of what is now Westside Pine, and seven years later another at 175 Commercial Street (currently Sleeping Beauty). Their business was sold to Alexander & Bruschi in 1913. Andrew

Walter Robertson and Alex Solotti selling ice cream from a stall in the Gilbertson Public Park shortly after the Second World War

George Batty with Solotti's ice cream cart. Mid 1960s (Courtesy of Jenny Murray)

Cabrelli, confectioner, had a shop in what is now the Thule Bar in 1927 until 1931 and was followed by Alfred Vettese until 1935.[32]

By the early 1950s there were no longer any Italian families in Lerwick. The only surviving shop was Solotti's, now run by long-time employee Walter Robertson, ably assisted by his wife Molly, who carried on trading under the name P. Solotti & Son.

A popular figure around the town in the 1960s was George Batty, pushing his three-wheeled cart, selling Solotti's popular ice cream. This was made in the small factory in Church Lane (now Church Road).

In 1985 Walter sold the shop to Brenda Westmoreland.[33] She continued to trade under the Solotti name until the end of an era came in 1998 when she replaced the sign with "Faerdie-maet" and all reference to Italian ice cream manufacturers disappeared.

Sinclair's Steps and Greig's Pier

Sinclair's Beach was in front of what is now The Shetland Times Bookshop but at this time was a piece of waste ground. Sinclair's Steps are shown as a continuation of Queens Lane and are between the beach and William Sinclair's former property. Late 1890s

Sinclair's Steps were not officially named in 1845. These were in line with North Kirk Closs (now Queens Lane)[1] and led down to what was referred to as Sinclair's Beach, Sinclair's Pier and Lodberry, which were situated on the north side of the beach.

Brothers Robert and William Sinclair, merchants and ship agents, came to Lerwick from Dunrossness in 1806. They built a small house on the beach, which they also used as an office. John, another brother, was also a partner.[2]

In 1811 Robert, the senior partner, bought a new dwelling house nearby, with wharf and lodberry, shop cellars and other adjoining buildings.[3] The house was at 48 Commercial Street, which was opposite the present day Royal Bank of Scotland. Unfortunately he was drowned in 1813 when the *Doris*, a two-masted vessel trading between Lerwick and Leith, foundered in a storm.[4]

William initially prospered. He heightened the Commercial Street premises in 1815 and also dug down to solid rock in front of the premises, laying foundations of cellars (or smuggling caves) with elaborately constructed subterranean arches. By doing so this built up and levelled the street.[5][6]

However, James Greig, lawyer and later procurator fiscal, purchased the property along with the lodberry and pier from Sinclair's sequestrated estate in 1824.[7] Thereafter Sinclair's Lodberry became known as Greig's Lodberry.[8]

Sinclair's Pier was officially named Greig's Pier in 1845, but the pier was later referred to as Ollason's Pier, after Charles Ollason, bootmaker, who lived in the small house on the beach with his family of three sons and a daughter.[9] He died in 1873.

The top of Sinclair's Steps was between the two walls on the right and the area to the further wall was Greig's Walk. 1880s

There were high walls projecting out into Commercial Street from each gable of the house and the space between them was referred to as Greig's Walk.[10]

The house was later occupied by the somewhat unusually named Mr Hay Hay, who was a grocer in the 1880s, and then by E.S. Reid Tait & Coy, draper, until 1903. The property was subsequently passed through the Greig family to Miss Mary C.E. Umphrey of Reawick,[11] until it was sold to the Postmaster General in 1907, along with the beach which by now was the property of Andrew Smith.[12] The new post office was erected on the site and it opened on Monday, 9th May, 1910.[13] The counter closed for the last time on Wednesday, 26th February, 2020, before moving to Conochies at 74-78 Commercial Street.[14]

The original steps were removed when the site was cleared for the construction of the Post Office. The present day Sinclair's Steps are between Faerdie-mact and the post office building.

Sinclair's Steps sign. 2021

Sinclair's Steps. 2021

Leask's Lodberry

On the left are the Clark's properties then Sinclair's Beach and Lodberry. Leask's Lodberry is next, then the large house at Taylor's Pier, now Phusiam Restaurant and Takeaway. c.1880

Leask's Lodberry still exists, but the building is now residential accommodation. It is between the Esplanade part of the Post Office building and Phusiam Restaurant & Takeaway.

Joseph Leask lived at 52 Commercial Street from the 1850s until 1881 in the house built by Charles Ogilvy Snr in 1811.[1] (This is now Anderson & Goodlad, Solicitors.) The lodberry was at the back of his house.

Joseph was a prominent businessman, ship owner, landowner and property holder, including premises in Pitt Lane.

Leask's former lodberry is on the left. 2021

Taylor's Steps and Taylor's Pier

Taylor's Steps are between the Tangled Salon at 56 Commercial Street and ICare Shetland at 58 Commercial Street. They led down to what the Commissioners named Taylor's Pier in 1845.

Ship agent William Taylor, born in 1748, and his sister Remmy lived in the premises,[1] now occupied by Phusiam Restaurant & Takeaway. It is not certain when this house on what is now the Esplanade was built but it was certainly before 1792.[2]

The house was bordered on the east and south by the lodberry and house later owned by Joseph Leask, but to the north by the sea and on the west partly by the sea

The entrance to Taylor's Steps. 2021

From underneath the trance with the steps leading to Commercial Street and across to Crooked Lane. 2021

The Phusiam Restaurant & Takeaway. The entrance to Taylor's Steps is hidden behind the front extension to the building. 2021

and partly by Taylor's Pier. The 1871 census was still listing Taylor's Pier as the address of numerous families.

Incidentally, the building was acquired by Goodlad & Coutts, boot and shoemakers, in 1902[3] and the iconic K boot mural was painted[4] on the sea-facing gable soon after as an advertisement for the K-brand boots and shoes which the firm stocked. However, in another capacity the landmark serves as a guide for vessels making a direct approach when berthing at the south side of Victoria Pier,[5] and also as an aid when adjusting compasses.[6]

Goodlad & Coutts with the K boot advertisement. Early 1900s

Victoria Wharf

Victoria Wharf. 1870s

Morrison's Pier was renamed Victoria Wharf in 1845, but the former name remained in use for the next 20 years. It would seem that John Morrison, mason, along with Robert Deans, came to Lerwick in 1781 to work on the extensive repair to Fort Charlotte.[1] [2]

Morrison settled in the town and in 1785 he bought a piece of waste ground[3] on which he erected a house[4] and entered into business. This was on the site of the present

Victoria Wharf. c.1880

The opening of Victoria Pier on 23rd June, 1886. The Earl of Zetland was the first vessel to berth alongside. (Courtesy of Elizabeth Angus)

High Level Music Centre. He also built a substantial pier that projected from the east gable and was then involved in a legal dispute with nearby merchants over building below the high water mark. He lost his case and the costly legal expenses caused his bankruptcy. It was said that he died of a broken heart in 1820.[5]

Morrison's Pier or Victoria Wharf had a slip on the north side but in 1866 it was extended by public subscription, therefore becoming a public pier. A slip was added to the south side and it was the main pier in Lerwick at that time.[6]

In 1876 it was proposed that the pier should be extended and work commenced in March 1883. On 31st July the foundation stone of Victoria Pier was laid with full Masonic honours near the northeast corner of the old pier by Brother G.H. Thoms, vice-admiral and sheriff of the county.[7]

Crowds gathered on Victoria Pier to greet the "new" Earl of Zetland. The "old" Earl is on the left and the St Sunniva is in the harbour. 19th August, 1939. (Courtesy of Elizabeth Angus)

The 23rd June, 1886, was an important day in Lerwick, for in the morning the foundation stones of the Grand Hotel and the Lerwick Combination Poorhouse (later Brevik Hospital then Brevik House) were also laid with full Masonic honours by Sheriff Thoms. In the afternoon a large crowd watched as the sheriff and a group of dignitaries representing the various bodies boarded the S.S. *Earl of Zetland* at Albert Wharf and were taken for an hour-long cruise before returning to Victoria Pier where the *Earl* had the honour of being the first of the "north boats" to berth alongside. Sheriff Thoms then stepped ashore and formally opened the pier.[8]

The provision of the pier was a godsend for passengers who could now step ashore instead of being ferried in an open boat between the steamer and dry land.

The *Earl* was built in 1877 and had a long career providing the service between Lerwick and the north isles. In 1939 she was renamed *Earl of Zetland II* when the launching of her successor was imminent and she continued to serve the north isles under that name throughout the Second World War. In 1946 she was sold and renamed *Anal*. The intention was to run illegal immigrants into Palestine, however, she was arrested by the British Navy in 1947 and beached at Haifa. In 1950 the ship was broken up.[9]

The "new" *Earl of Zetland* arrived in Lerwick on Saturday, 19th August, 1939. The "old" *Earl* and *St Sunniva* sailed out as far as Mousa to meet her. However, due to the outbreak of war the following month she was on active service in the Pentland Firth until returning in 1946. The *Earl* then served the north isles until February 1975. With the introduction of roll-on roll-off vessels she was no longer required and finally sailed from Lerwick to Aberdeen on 3rd March of that year.

After a short time the *Earl* was sold to Middlesbrough Ocean Surveys, was converted to a diving support vessel and renamed *Celtic Surveyor*. She even took part in a BBC soap opera about North Sea oil. Around 1981 she was sold and two years later, after another conversion, became a restaurant and entertainment centre at the South Quay, Great Yarmouth until late spring 1986. The *Celtic Surveyor* then found herself in the India Dock at the Isle of Dogs as a floating restaurant and also the canteen for *Daily Telegraph* staff. Three years later, and now reverted back to her original name, the *Earl of Zetland* had moved to Eastbourne and was a venue for functions, meetings, dinners, lunches, bar meals etc. At this time it was alleged she had participated in the Dunkirk evacuation but this is unfounded. In 1997 the *Earl* was sold again and towed to the Albert Edward Dock within the Royal Quays Marina in North Shields where she became a popular floating restaurant.[10] Many Shetlanders visited her over the years at the various locations, including members of the Shetland Family History Society who paid a visit in May 2006 and the author had the honour of being asked to give a talk on the history and family link with the vessel.

Unfortunately the *Earl* became expensive to operate and the economic pressures of the Covid-19 pandemic in 2020 marked the end of this vessel's 81 year existence. The decision was

Extending the pier. 18th December, 1957. (Courtesy of Elizabeth Angus)

The newly constructed arm. (Courtesy of Dennis Coutts)

reluctantly made to have her dismantled and this took place between October and December 2020.

Plans were drawn up for the widening of both Victoria Pier and the North Esplanade in 1937. Work was about to commence when war broke out in September 1939 and all work on improvements was suspended.[11] The North of Scotland & Orkney & Shetland Steam Navigation Company Ltd was renamed the North of Scotland, Orkney & Shetland Shipping Company Ltd in 1953.[12] It was not until early in 1955 that work commenced on widening and extending the pier. Activities normally carried out on Victoria Pier moved to Alexandra Wharf where the company was given the use of a store in the new Alexandra Building. Unfortunately, berthing at Alexandra Wharf proved difficult due to exposure and, after a few months, the steamers returned to Victoria Pier after specially constructed fenders were introduced to protect the concrete from damage.

Victoria Pier with the pump station control building on the left. 2021

Cruise ship visitors waiting to board tenders to continue their cruise on the MSC Orchestra. 2018

The arm at the point of the pier was constructed in 1959[13] and on 10th August, 1960, her Majesty Queen Elizabeth II formally opened the new harbour works.[14]

By 1970 it became apparent that Victoria Pier was unable to cope with the increased volume of cargo being handled by the "North of Scotland" – as the company was commonly known – and it was finding it difficult to operate by using conventional cargo vessels. Roll-on/roll-off vessels were required.[15]

On 1st October, 1975, the North of Scotland, Orkney & Shetland Shipping Company Ltd became known as P&O Ferries, Orkney and Shetland Services.[16]

The new Holmsgarth Road was constructed during 1976, along with a pier, link-span and terminal.

On Saturday, 2nd April, 1977, the M.V. *St Clair* sailed from Victoria Pier for the last time. The following Tuesday the new roll-on/roll-off ferry *St Clair* arrived at Holmsgarth. The terminal was officially opened by Mr Bruce Millan, Secretary of State for Scotland, on Friday 15th April.[17]

After the steamers' store – or transit shed to give it the proper name – was removed early in 1987, the pier was converted into a car park and taxi rank by its owner, Lerwick Harbour Trust. The trust changed its name to Lerwick Port Authority in 1999.

Richard Gibson Architects designed the pump-station control building at the head of the pier, with work beginning on its construction in 1998 and it opening the following year. The mosaic by Paul Grime, entitled *Pattern and Place*, was unveiled by Tavish Scott MSP on 10th September, 1999.

The popular clock at the head of the pier was removed as a result, and the Diana Fountain was repositioned yet again, this time to the left of the car park entrance.

Numerous events have been held on the pier including Johnsmas Foys and RNLI open days.

Victoria Pier was regularly used by oil related and fishing vessels, yachts of all sizes, pleasure craft, tall ships and cruise ships, until the arrival of the Covid-19 pandemic in 2020. It is hoped that in the near future the pier will return to be once again an important and vibrant part of Lerwick's waterfront.

Trance Closs

Trance Closs. 2018

Trance Closs is between Santander and High Level Music Centre at 66 and 62-64 Commercial Street respectively.

The closs refers to Yorston's Trance, known as the South Trance,[1] and also as the Dark Trance.[2] The trance was an opening at street level in the middle of a tenement of houses that stretched across the street where Santander and the Wine Shop now stand. The trance allowed access along the street to pedestrians and very narrow carts. *(See page xiii)*

James Yorston was a merchant who bought the tenement of houses called the South Trance, along with buildings down to the beach and another tenement of houses joined on the upper side of the trance, from Andrew Heddell in April 1793.[3] He sold the upper tenement to William Mouat that same year, in November.[4] William was known as Tarry Wumple. His son, William Jnr, sold this property to Robert Goudie in 1836.[5] In that year, or in 1837, the trance house was removed,[6] Mr Goudie renovated his property and the street was widened. His firm, R. Goudie & Son, ironmonger and general dealer, had been established in 1821.

The firm existed at 113 Commercial Street until September 1973 when Alistair Robertson, the last proprietor of "Goudie's", announced that after a clearance sale the business would close a month later, on Saturday 20th October.[7]

The Clerical, Medical & General Life Assurance Society then reconstructed the property and owned it until 1982.

Mr I.C. & Mrs G.P. Caldwell bought the building and retained the shop until 1985 but sold the office to Smith & Rutherford in 1983.

Keith Brothers Environmental Service Ltd rented the shop from 1978 until 1985 when it became The Wine Shop.

The Trance House

James Yorston's nephew, also James, inherited the South Trance tenement and sold it to Alexander C. Irvine in 1820. Following Alexander's death in 1830 his brother John T. Irvine inherited and sold the buildings to Robert Robertson in 1833.[8]

This is the location of the South Trance. "Goudie's" is on the right (now The Wine Shop) and the building opposite is now Santander. c.1900

After the trance house was removed Robert built a new house and shop. He is listed in a directory for 1854 as a fishcurer, grocer and clothier at 66 Commercial Street and 4 Victoria Wharf.[9] He tragically contracted cholera and died in 1855.

His son John, or John o da Trance as he was known, inherited the property. He was born in Lerwick in 1826 and became a merchant, was a Commissioner of Police, a Lerwick Town Councillor and a member of several boards. When he was young he lived in the trance house and in 1898 he gave a vivid description of how he remembered it to be. He described that the roof of the trance was part of the floor of the kitchen; the width of Commercial Street under the trance was about 2 metres, the depth about 3.7 metres and the height just over 2 metres. In his opinion a small Shetland pony and cart could pass through it. He also remembered that at Christmas time the guizers passed through the trance with a large crate, set on wheels, with fiddlers and a drummer seated at each end. The crate had flags which required to be lowered to allow access through the trance.[10]

The Esplanade had been built at a higher level, leaving a drop protected by a fence between it and the old row of houses that were purchased by George Leslie. These were demolished and Ellesmere Buildings were constructed on the site. The building on the right was Lerwick Co-operative Society Ltd and then Aitken & Wright for many years. 1905

John Robertson was unmarried and, following his death in February 1905, his trustees sold his whole property to George

Ellesmere Buildings are under construction. 1906

Leslie of Laxfirth House. This consisted of the houses, shop and cellar that Robert had built prior to 1847, along with the various buildings at Victoria Wharf.

The old buildings there were demolished in 1906 and Mr Leslie had Ellesmere Buildings constructed on an extended site.

Mr Leslie retained the building at 66 Commercial Street but the front was set back to align with the neighbouring building and the street was widened.[11]

After John Robertson's death the shop was occupied by John Russell Anderson, trading as J. Russell Anderson, licenced grocer. He died in 1922 but the firm remained until about 1943, when George Leslie's son John Robert opened an agricultural shop selling "everything for the fisherman, farmer and crofter." This included piltock or sillock flies, trout and spinning rods and remedies for sheep, cattle poultry, dogs and cats. Following George's death in 1950, John inherited the property which he sold to the Aberdeen Savings Bank, later amalgamated into TSB. In 1978 the Alliance & Leicester Building Society moved in and in 2010 it transferred to Santander.

Irvine Closs

Irvine Place is to the left of Arthur Simpson and Irvine Closs is on the right. 2021

Irvine Closs, from Commercial Street to the Esplanade. 2021

Irvine Closs, originally Irvine's Closs, is between what is currently Arthur Simpson Estate and Letting Agents at 68 Commercial Street and Santander at number 66.

Irvine Place is between Arthur Simpson and The Camera Centre (with Richard Gibson Architects above). It stretches down to between the TSB and Harbour House and also towards the back of the public toilets to join Harrison Square.

Andrew Irvine, merchant, was born in 1760 and in 1798 he obtained the land on which he built the property at 68 Commercial Street.[1] It was his sons Alexander, then John, who owned the lower part of the adjacent trance house from 1820 until 1833.

Irvine Place. 2021

The large building to the right of the ship's mast is Anderson & Company. The double row of houses with gables facing the sea were demolished to provide sites for Ellesmere Buildings and Victoria Buildings. The large building on the right is 68 Commercial Street. c.1880

Another view of these buildings behind the Diana Fountain. 1890s

The Lerwick Co-operative Society Ltd at Victoria Buildings with Dutch fishermen on the Esplanade. c.1910

From left are D.G. Leslie at Ellesmere Buildings, the entrance to Irvine Closs, the TSB, Harbour House and the public toilets. 2021

Irvine's Pier, officially named in 1845, was sometimes called Irvine's Lodberry. It was described as a platform built on to the end of his property, with steps on the south side.[2] Andrew Irvine died in 1850.

Victoria Buildings were constructed in 1905 by rebuilding on a row of houses owned by James. H. Allan.[3] It was firstly occupied by Lerwick Co-operative Society Ltd – the first Co-op in Shetland – at ground level with W. Leslie & Company, ship brokers and fish merchants, on the floor above. In 1912 John & James Tod & Sons Ltd, wholesaler merchants, opened a small depot in Victoria Buildings for about three years. Aitken & Wright, wholesalers, were the next occupants, until March 1972 when the firm ceased trading in Lerwick and "Tod's" took over the Lerwick stock.[4]

The Aberdeen Savings Bank moved to the ground floor from 66 Commercial Street and the Shetland Islands Council planning department and motor taxation department was on the first floor.[5]

Victoria Buildings was demolished in February 1994 to be replaced by the current, glass TSB building.[6]

Harrison Square

●

The "Brunt Hoose" is on the left and the space in front is the site of the present day Harrison Square. The building to the right is now the Cancer Research UK Shop and on the far right is part of what is now Da Harbour Chippy. Mullay's Steps is between the two buildings. c.1890

What is now Harrison Square was originally a beach behind what is now the Camera Centre, towards the Cancer Research UK Shop. It developed into a square when the waterfront was filled in to create the Esplanade.

Gilbert Harrison was born in Unst in 1798. The firm Messrs Harrison & Son carried on an extensive business as ship owners, fish curers and fish traders. In addition they were general merchants, wine and spirit merchants and had an export trade with Spain.[1]

Mr Harrison had his drapery shop at 74 Commercial Street, his grocer shop at number 78,[2] and his house was number 76. He resided there until his death in 1882

The street was widened when the frontage of the two shops on the right was set back in 1936, now part of Conochies. The building in the centre was demolished in 1905.

when he was 84 years old.[3] Conochies is now at these addresses.

William B.M. Harrison, Gilbert's son, lived for a short time in a house at the foot of Reform Lane, with the address Harrison Place,[4] before moving with his family to Prospect House. He died in 1880, aged 36.

In 1904 what was described as a "smuggler's hole" was discovered when the front of the north part of the building, presently occupied by Conochies, was set back to widen the street. The hole extended a good distance along the street and legend has it that at one time it was possible to reach the Hillhead through this subterranean passage, but this has never been verified.[5]

However, in the 1950s a Pitt Lane resident unexpectedly landed in a well-constructed stone passage while digging a hole to set potatoes. It ran under the lane towards what is now the car park. Then, in the early 1970s when the site was being prepared for the swimming pool, a JCB sank into a similar passage.[6]

Harrison Square, with the public toilets on the left and then the building constructed by E.S. Reid Tait in 1905. The Cancer Research UK Shop and Da Harbour Chippy buildings are unchanged. 2018

Conochies. Early 2018

Lower Tait's Closs, now Reform Lane

Gilbert Tait, born 1789, was listed as an ironmonger, general merchant and herring curer in 1854. He had his shop and business at Gilbert Tait's Closs. It was renamed Reform Lane in 1845.

Lower Tait's Closs, on the lower side of Commercial Street, is now signposted as a continuation of Reform Lane. It is between Conochies at 74-78 Commercial Street and Ninian at number 80.

Tait's Place was officially named in 1845 and was described as the area from where the houses along the beach there reached up towards Reform Lane. It was in his home here that Gilbert died in 1860. He had previously lived at Mariners' Court.

Tait's Pier was also named in 1845. A bulwark extended from the pier in a northerly direction. Fish were cured here.[1]

Tait's Lodberry was on the north side of the pier and had been built in 1775 by James Malcolmson, sheriff substitute of Shetland, who at that time owned two properties nearby. (These are shown on the *Perspective View of Lerwick* 1766 to the south of the Middle Trance.)

James Ogilvy, merchant, bought the lodberry building in 1821 but it burned down in 1824. It was thereafter known as the "Brunt Hoose" and stood roofless until bought by Gilbert Tait in 1830. He replaced the floor to form a roof and this cellar was used as a cooperage.[2]

Lower Tait's Closs, now a continuation of Reform Lane. 2021

This building was constructed by E. S. Reid Tait & Co in 1905. 2021

In 1875 Mr G. Harrison Jnr opened a public bar in his new building at the top of Tait's Pier. It was described as having an open counter but there were no "boxes" where customers could sit down in the hope that seamen would be more temperate in their drinking habits.[3]

These buildings had several owners and occupiers until bought by E.S. Reid Tait & Co in 1904 (Mr Tait was the grand-nephew of Gilbert Tait). These were demolished in 1905. The building we see today was constructed on the site[4] and now houses Ninian and Aurora Jewellery at 80 and 82 Commercial Street, Coffee Culture and Lerwick DIY at Harrison Square, with residential accommodation above.

The public toilets, Harrison Square with Coffee Culture and Lerwick DIY, Cancer Research UK. 2021

Angus Pier and Angus Closs

Angus Closs. 2021

Angus Pier was officially named in 1845.

Angus Closs, previously Lower Park Lane, is between R.A.M. Knitwear and Aurora Jewellery on Commercial Street and the Cancer Research UK Shop and Lerwick DIY at Harrison Square.

Gilbert Angus, merchant, was born in Toft in 1777. He was in business at 84 Commercial Street until 1813, when he was unfortunately a passenger on the ill-fated

An illustration by Fred Irvine from his book Believe it or Not, published in 1952.

Doris when she was wrecked at Cruden Bay, on route from Leith to Lerwick. However, his son John carried on the business at the same address.[1]

Gilbert Bain, in whose memory the local hospital is named, was Gilbert's nephew.

In 1905 a passage, possibly for storing smuggled goods, was discovered under Angus Closs. This was when a site was being prepared for the construction of Mr E.S. Reid Tait's building.

The tunnel was said to extend from the steps at Angus Closs round to the front of Mr Angus's former shop at 84 Commercial Street.[2]

Angus Pier was in the vicinity of the present Cancer Research UK Shop.

The steps in Angus Closs. 2021

Mullay's Steps

Mullay's Steps is between R.A.M. Knitwear and what was for many years Da Noost, at 84 and 86 Commercial Street respectively.

Robert Mullay started his own business in 1830.[1] He was a licenced grocer and general merchant, fish curer and owner of the home fishing sloop *Mariner*. It would seem that he was originally in business at 86 Commercial Street where he succeeded Gilbert Peterson who was a merchant there.

Mr Mullay later concentrated on his shop business which was opposite the top of the steps, at 141 Commercial Street, and was there until his death in 1884.[2] (For many years number 141 was S. & R. Swanson and is now, since summer 2020, Nordsterna Shetland Crystal Boutique.)

Mullay's Pier was a continuation of Peterson's Pier and could be accessed via the steps.[3]

In 1998, when Commercial Street was being repaved and old sewer/water pipes were replaced, a tunnel measuring about 1.5m in height, with a curved stone roof, was rediscovered in front of number 86. Jim Henry had been aware of this blocked up tunnel extending from the cellar when he bought the property but had never been in it. It ran under the street in the direction of R.W. Bayes at number 143 and contained some empty bottles, presumably left by a previous merchant. It was filled in at that time.

Mullay's Steps sign. 2021

Mullay's Steps. 2021

Peterson's Closs

Peterson's Closs was named after Gilbert Peterson (also Paterson), merchant, who had a shop at 86 Commercial Street (until recent years Da Noost) prior to his death in 1828.[1] The closs is between what was his shop and the adjacent premises, currently No. 88 Kitchen & Bar and led down to Peterson's Pier and Peterson's Place.

Peterson's Place was named in 1845, but was later changed to Albert Place.[2] This is now part of Harrison Square.

Peterson's Pier extended in an easterly direction from the gable of Gilbert Peterson's property. This is now Da Harbour Chippy. Mullay's Pier was a continuation of this pier.[3]

The closs looking down towards Victoria Pier. 2021

Gilbert Peterson's property is shown centre left. Grierson's Lodberry and Greig's Lodberry are to the right. The long building is Tait's Lodberry and on the far right is the North Lodberry. 1870s

Grierson's Lodberry

The building that is now Da Harbour Chippy is on the left, then Grierson's Lodberry. On the right is Greig's Lodberry (now the Peerie Shop). c.1890

The "North of Scotland's" building was erected on the site of Grierson's Lodberry and opened in 1900.

Andrew Grierson of Quendale's town house was situated on the south side of Quendale Lane, at 155 Commercial Street (now Shetland Clinical Services Ltd).

Grierson's Lodberry, along with cellars and warehouses, neighbouring property and ground, covered an area from the Esplanade up towards the back of 90 Commercial Street (now part of J.G. Rae Ltd).

The North of Scotland & Orkney & Shetland Steam Navigation Company moved from their lodberry and office at 16 Commercial Street to number 90 in 1875[1] and bought Grierson's property in 1897.[2] In 1899 the buildings were demolished to provide a site for the building of their new premises on the Esplanade, which opened the following year.[3] It consisted of office space at ground level, the shipping agent's/manager's office on the first floor and residential accommodation for the manager on the second floor. The stable on the north side housed the agent's horse and gig and the store to the rear contained coal for bunkering the first *Earl of Zetland*.

There was a painted plaque over the entrance to the building. The inscription N of S & O & S S N Co reflected the name of the company in 1900, but "1836" indicated when its predecessor, the Aberdeen, Leith, Clyde and Tay Shipping Company's steamship the *Sovereign* began a regular fortnightly service. Unfortunately the plaque deteriorated over the years and in 2021 was replaced by an unpainted replica.

In the late 1960s a decision had been made to reorganise the shipping service to Shetland and the facilities at Victoria Pier were found to be unsuitable for roll-on/roll-off ferries. Following the construction of the new Holmsgarth Road and ferry terminal during 1976, the *St Clair* sailed from Victoria Pier for the last time on 2nd April 1977 and the "North of Scotland" staff moved to Holmsgarth.[4]

The building was vacant until early 1978 and on 8th May Ian Byrne and Martin Garrick opened a cash and carry shop called Unification. They undertook a major renovation and the former stable was incorporated into the building.[5] The stock included paints, wallpapers, tiles, bathroom fittings, doors and a large selection of kit furniture. The firm closed in November 1979.[6]

The plaque

The floors above are now privately owned flats.

John Leask & Son, travel agent, bus operator and coach hirer, bought the premises and opened in January 1980 after relocating from 56 Commercial Street (now Tangled hairdresser). The travel agency division closed in December 2011 but Peter Leask and a small number of staff remained in the premises to manage bus operations before moving, in February 2014, to premises at Gremista. On the evening of Sunday, 16th August, 2020, John Leask & Son's bus service left Viking bus station for the very last time. This was due to the retirement of the two partners, brothers Peter and Andrew Leask, whose grandfather John had established the firm 101 years earlier in 1919.[7] [8]

LHD Marine Supplies Ltd opened in the vacated premises on Saturday, 12th April, 2014, after moving from Albert Building and is the current occupier.[9]

The painted-over plaque above the door. 2021

Greig's Closs

Greig's Closs was named after James Greig of Leog, merchant and ship agent, whose property was built in 1798. The house is the part, nearest to Loose Ends, of the present J.G. Rae Ltd at 92 Commercial Street, but previously also had the number 94. As a matter of interest, the house plan was the same as the premises of Anderson & Goodlad, solicitors, at 52 Commercial Street.

The original closs to the south of Greig's building indirectly ran right through from Commercial Street to the Esplanade. The original house entrance was from the closs but Mr Charles Stout Snr blocked off the top of the closs by creating a large entrance hall accessible from Commercial Street.[1] Only the lower end of the closs still exists.

The house had an interesting feature common with others in Lerwick at that time. This was a carved mantelpiece, said to have been brought from France, with an emblem of the thistle and rose intertwined. This confirms that the house was built before the union with Ireland in 1801, as afterwards a shamrock would have been included.[2]

John Deans Campbell obtained the property in 1843 from his sister, Ann Deans, who was married to James Greig.[3]

The top of Greig's closs, now part of J.G. Rae Ltd., was previously the house entrance. 2021

Greig's Closs from the Esplanade. 2021

The Peerie Shop and Peerie Shop Café. 2021

The property was let to Mrs Bouwmeister, the widow of a Dutch physician, who managed a private hotel. In 1849 Lady Franklin, accompanied by her niece, resided here while in Lerwick to meet the whale ships returning from the Arctic. She was hoping to hear news of her missing husband, Sir John Franklin, who had set out in 1845 on an expedition to discover the middle part of the north-west passage. Lady Franklin was unaware that he had died in 1847. Both women kept diaries and the niece wrote that fleas in her bed kept her awake on the first night.[4]

In 1859 Mr Hicks, chemist, relocated here from 169 Commercial Street and opened the first Medical Hall. On his death in 1863 it was sold to Dr Petrus Loeterbagh, who

The Esplanade entrance to Greig's Closs. The sign carved into the stone to the right of the entrance identifies the original location of Greig's Pier. 2021

Towards the left are Grierson's and Greig's Lodberries. c.1880

had been a surgeon accompanying Dutch fishing vessels to Shetland. He married Miss Ann S. Heddell in 1859. Charles B. Stout Snr was an apprentice to Dr Loeterbagh who died in 1871. John Spence was the next owner followed by James Linklater. Mr Stout purchased the house and Medical Hall business in 1878 or 1879. Following his death in 1928 his son, also Charles, carried on the business. It remained there until 1948 when the new Medical Hall opened next door in 96 Commercial Street.

The next occupant was The Gift Shop which moved from 143 Commercial Street in 1950. The proprietor, Mrs. J.A. McWhirter (known as Queenie), was Charles Stout's sister. The shop stocked jewellery, watches, brush sets, etc.

Shetland Silvercraft, established in 1953, took over The Gift Shop in 1965 and has traded as J.G. Rae Ltd since then.[5]

An underground passage was discovered in 1932 during roadworks in Commercial Street for the installation of electricity cables. The broad passage extended along the front of what is now the north part of J.G. Rae Ltd and towards 155 Commercial Street, where two deep vaults were found. It was evident that the passage had at one time connected with the top part of Greig's Closs.[6] However, it was not until 1955 when the stone flags were removed to resolve a water leakage that workmen rediscovered the passage and it was filled in.[7]

Greig's Lodberry was restored by Richard Gibson in 1987 and the Peerie Shop opened the following year.[8] The Peerie Shop Café was opened in 1999.[9]

Greig's Pier was on the south side of the lodberry.

Greig's Hol was a small dock between the pier and Grierson's Lodberry to the south.[10] It was said that it was an ideal secluded spot for the consumption of alcohol or, on a dark night, for the smuggling of Dutch tobacco.[11]

Campbell's Lane, now Campbell's Closs

The top of Campbell's Closs. 2021

The Peerie Shop Café is at the bottom right of the closs with Bressay in the distance. 2021

Campbell's Lane, now signposted as Campbell's Closs, is between J.G. Rae Ltd and Loose Ends. It was named after John Deans Campbell who obtained the property between the lane and Greig's Closs from his sister, Ann Deans, in 1843. She was married to James Greig.[1]

Campbell's Pier, officially named in 1845, was at the foot of the lane. Not so long ago a large iron ring was still attached to the wall of the current Loose Ends shop on the north side of Campbell's Closs. It was fixed there in the distant past by a fisherman named James Tait who used it to fasten his boat.[2]

In earlier times Maikie Moad's Beach stretched from Greig's Lodberry – now the Peerie Shop and Peerie Shop Café – north to Magnus Burns's lodberry and pier, now the site of M&Co. Maikie lived in a house at the foot of Campbell's Lane.[3]

Campbell's Closs, leading up to Commercial Street and Quendale Lane. 2021

Nicolson's Closs

Nicolson's Closs is between Loose Ends at 96 Commercial Street and The Dowry at number 98.

Andrew Nicolson was born about 1771. He was a shipping agent and spirit merchant during the early part of the 1800s and his business is listed at 98 Commercial Street in a 1854 directory.[1] The building he occupied was very old. His pier was a built-up bulwark, the width of the building, with steps down to the sea.[2]

Following Andrew's death in 1856 in Swallow Lane, now Bank Lane, the family left Shetland. Laurence J. Nicolson, one of his sons, was eleven years old at the time. In 1894 his verse was collected and published as *Songs of Thule*, which proved to be his only book. He became known as "The Bard of Thule" and resided in Edinburgh until his own death in 1901.[3]

The building at 98 was renovated in 1868 by Laurence G. Stove who, on returning to Shetland after having spent some time south, opened an ironmongery and ship chandlery shop with a large window. He was described as "the pioneer of the 'big shop window movement' in Lerwick" as, before then, the shop windows along Commercial Street were old fashioned with small panes. It wasn't long before other shop keepers had followed his initiative and soon all the shops had large windows.

The pier and sheds were cleared when the Esplanade was created and the shop was then extended.

The incredibly narrow Nicolson's Closs with the manhole cover over the cellar. 2021

Following Laurence's death in 1889 the business passed to his son, also Laurence. Two years later he sold it to his uncle, Alfred Stove, and John Smith, the shop manager, who had commenced employment as an apprentice in 1874.

In 1897 Alfred disposed of his interest in the business to his nephew Thomas Stove and the firm then became Stove & Smith.[4]

Like so many old Lerwick premises, number 98 had a secret. Stove & Smith had a cellar under the street. At the far end there was an opening into a narrow tunnel in the direction of Fox Lane which may well have been used by smugglers. It had been blocked up, leaving only a small gap at the top. It was said that an individual going

Stove & Smith, ironmongers, with the original windows. (Shetland Museum and Archives)

The Dowry. 2021

down Nicolson's Closs unexpectedly fell down a hole which subsequently became the shop's coal cellar.[5] It was subsequently provided with a manhole cover.

Over the years subsequent owners retained the Stove & Smith name and were well-known for supplying hardware, gifts, glass and china, toys, garden supplies, fishing tackle, etc. and continued to do so until 1988.[6]

Gair & Smith was the next occupier, selling DIY equipment, plants, flowers, household goods and toys.

In 1996 the premises became the Scottish Hydro Electric shop until it closed in April 2016.

The building was vacant until it reopened in June 2018 as The Dowry. The popular Scandinavian-style cafe/bar currently serves quality local produce, artisan coffee, beers and spirits.

Merran Moad's Steps

Merran Moad's Steps lead up to Commercial Street. 2021

Merran Moad's Steps are between Virgin Money and Specsavers Opticians, 108 Commercial Street.

Marion Mouat, otherwise known as Merran Moad, was born in Orkney in 1765. It is not known how or when she met her husband, whose name was either John or Andrew[1] Anderson. They lived, along with their two sons Robert and Peter, in a small four-roomed house in Charlotte Lane (now Charlotte Street), opposite the path leading to the Fort's south entrance.[2]

It would seem that Merran was habitually at odds with her neighbours from whom she cadged milk. Local merchants were also not immune from her visits[3] and on one occasion she had a civil action raised against her for alleged violence.[4]

During the Napoleonic War press gangs made numerous visits to Lerwick to seize men to crew Royal Navy warships. On one such trip they encountered Merran, a meeting they no doubt regretted.

Considered to be slightly odd and a "character", she proved to be smarter than people thought when the Press Gang knocked on her door with the intention of impressing her husband. Merran, apparently, neither made a scene nor objected, but invited them in and offered them home brew and bannocks which they readily consumed. When the naval men "fell by" she rushed to her husband who was hiding upstairs and helped him to escape through the skylight. He ran over the field where Lystina House and the Town Hall now are but it is not known if he was successful in evading capture.[5]

In the 1830s she moved to a small house, the site of which is now part of Virgin Money. It bordered a beach, which became known as Merran Moad's Beach possibly because of a ducking she received there. She was a spinner and had a special wheel for the purpose of spinning hemp twine which was used for making fishing nets. A local worthy coming down the steps from what became Commercial Street to the beach either trampled on her hemp or knocked over her wheel and she gave him his character in front of others. He was so angry that in retaliation he carried her out into the sea where she received the immersion. He was soon to regret his action because she never let him forget it.[6]

In 1841 she was living with her son Peter and his wife and family in a house on the north side of Irvine's Closs (this would be approximately where the TSB is now).

Merran died in 1843 when she was 78 years old.

Although Merran Moad's Beach disappeared with the formation of the Esplanade, the steps ensure she is not forgotten.

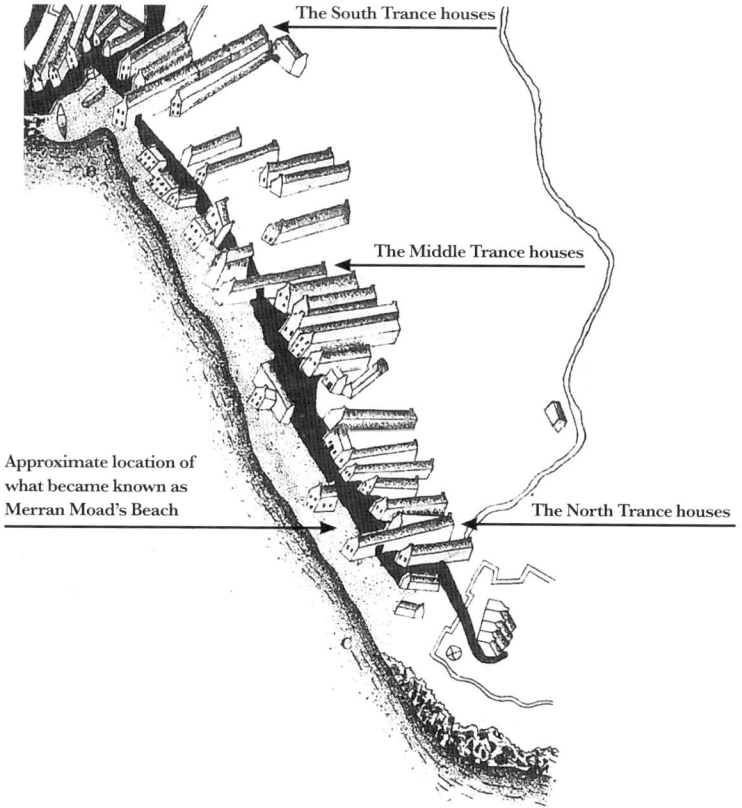

A section of William Aberdeen's 1766 map showing the beach along The Shore from the Market Cross area towards Fort Charlotte

Tait's Lodberry

●

Most people are unaware that the present Thule Bar was originally Tait's Lodberry before the Esplanade was constructed.

George Reid Tait, draper and shipping agent, bought a tenement block at 108 Commercial Street in 1860, consisting of shops and dwelling house with cellars below and a lodberry at the back.[1] He reconstructed the block in 1874 by adding a shop at the north side and extended the whole shop premises towards the sea. These shops now are Specsavers at number 108 and Envi hairdressers at 110 Commercial Street.[2]

The lodberry became known as Tait's Lodberry. It was a large, open lodberry in which boats had been built and, after roofing it over, Mr Tait used it as stores and rigging lofts for his vessels engaged in the Faroe fishing. He then converted these buildings into workshops for joiners and contractors.[3]

In 1879 the lower stores were occupied by William Macfadyen, general merchant and second-hand dealer.[4] In 1885 Robert Thomson opened Cocoa and Coffee Rooms

Tait's Lodberry on the left and the North Lodberry. c.1880

here in addition to his grocery business.[5] The following year he was granted a licence for his new public house – The Sea View Vaults at Tait's Place.[6]

Following the death of Mr G.R. Tait in 1889, Messrs D. & G. Kay, merchants, purchased all the buildings.[7]

Tenant Robert V. Kean operated "The Vaults", as it became popularly known, from 1893 until 1896 when his brother Thomas succeeded him and changed the name to The Thule Refreshment Bar.[8]

David G.K. Hunter, licensed grocer, became the licensee in 1905.

However, a momentous event occurred in Lerwick's history in 1920 when, under the Temperance (Scotland) Act, prohibition came into effect. No-licence elections were held in every Shetland district and only three parishes – namely Yell, Northmavine and Delting – decided to remain "wet". The Thule Refreshment Bar's licence was revoked, along with other establishments throughout Shetland, and Lerwick was "dry" for the next 27 years.

Reid Tait & Co and the Seaview Vaults. c.1890

From 1921 until 1925 the premises was classed as a restaurant and then in 1926 it became a shop. The following year an Italian, Andrew Cabrelli, confectioner, took over

The Thule Refreshment Bar.

from Mr Hunter. Fellow countryman Alfred Vetesse, confectioner, followed him from 1931-32, operating during the summer months selling ice-cream, tobacco and confectionary. William C. Bain, agent, replaced John White, shoemaker, in the neighbouring shop (now New Harbour Cafe). Around the same time Robert Burgoyne, hairdresser, opened in a section that had been partitioned off to the north of Mr Vettese's premises.

In 1935 Alfred Vettese left and the premises were utilised by D. &. G. Kay, and at one time housed a weaving loom. During the early 1940s Mr William C. Bain used the building as an egg grading station, before relocating to premises at Freefield in 1947. In 1954 the firm moved to Garthspool to the "kippering kiln and bothy" they had purchased from Williamson & Co (now Bulter & Mulhern). Hay & Company bought the Freefield premises to be used as a store.

Notice at the Market Cross regarding the no-licence elections. 1920 (Courtesy of Aileen Robertson)

During the dry period alcohol could only be sold wholesale, in amounts of two gallons of whisky or beer (just over 9 litres). In order to legally obtain a dram, groups of men clubbed together and bought a case of whisky or the equivalent amount of beer from the wholesaler which was then distributed. Many wholesalers employed boys whose job it was to deliver the alcohol purchased, by barrow, to the "thirsty" customers. The other option was for the favourite tipple to be obtained illegally by "under the counter" transactions.

The NAAFI at Da Lang Bar

"Da Lang Bar"

However, during the Second World War service personnel could have a drink at "Da Lang Bar" at the Hillhead which was run by the NAAFI (*Navy, Army and Air Force Institutes*).[9] After the war the occupants were C. & J. Byrne, confectioners and fruiterers, then in 1949 their son-in-law Mr Nick P. Carter traded as the Hillhead Stores. In 1962 Sylvester Marnoch sold sweeties, groceries, small ornaments and gifts, until it was sold to the Ma family in 1979. The building will be remembered as The Golden Coach Chinese Restaurant, the first in Shetland, which was there from 18th October, 1979, until early in 2009. The building was then converted and is now private accommodation.

Thule Bar

Prohibition lasted until after the war ended. On Friday, 29th May, 1947, following the result of a poll, Lerwick was "wet" again and the Thule Bar was the first public house to open its doors in Lerwick since 1920.[10] James W. Gray was appointed manager and the bar fittings from the old Grand Hotel Bar[11] (now R.W. Bayes) were fitted in the newly furbished premises. The opening of the Thule Bar was a long awaited occasion for many Lerwegians. As 11.00am approached many intending customers and curious sightseers gathered on the Esplanade. A large number of photographers also assembled, eager to snap the many camera-shy patrons. The first customer was Mr John Mouat, a veteran of two world wars and commissioner of the North Star picture house.

While George T. Kay retained ownership of the Thule Bar, the rest of the property was sold to Tulloch of Shetland in 1955. Mr Gray bought the bar the following year from Mr Kay[12] then carried out refurbishment and renovated the upper storey to become another bar, now the private function bar.

After several owners the Thule Bar was taken over by JWG plc in early 1994.[13]

Although Mr Tait died in 1889, Tait's Place was, and still is, situated from the bottom of Merran Moad's Steps and along the south side and front of the Thule Bar, and is the bar's address.

The Thule at Tait's Place. 2018

Muir's Steps and Osy Anderson's Pier

Muir's Steps are between Universal Stores at 114 Commercial Street and Puffin Republic (previously the Save the Children Shop, until March 2020). The steps were named after Thomas Muir of Messrs Muir & Son, watchmakers and jewellers, who was in business at 1 Charlotte Place from the 1920s until the mid-1940s.[1] The address changed to 116 Commercial Street.

Osy Anderson's Pier was on the south side of the opening between the above shops. The pier extended into the sea beyond the line of Tait's Lodberry which was to its south.[2] Hosea, or Osy, Anderson was a general merchant, draper and spirit dealer who had his business earlier at 1 Charlotte Place and tenanted the house

Muir's Steps and Back Charlotte Lane. 2021

The Puffin Republic with the top of Muir's steps on the right. 2021

Muir & Son, Watchmakers & Jewellers. (Courtesy of Aileen Robertson)

above from the 1840s until 1863. He then emigrated to New Zealand.

Osy Anderson's Pier was also called Linklater's Pier or the North Pier.[3]

Robert Linklater is listed as a merchant, hosier and Shetland veil manufacturer in 1854, at 173 Commercial Street.[4] Upper floors were added in 1868[5] and this is now Boots UK Ltd. He lived opposite, at 112 Commercial Street, and some years later moved his business into part of the house.[6] This is now Universal Stores, 114 Commercial Street.

Universal Stores. 2018

Charlotte Place

Drawing of Charlotte Place with Tait's Lodberry and the North Lodberry in front. (From Lerwick During the last Half Century published 1923)

Charlotte Place was officially named in 1845. The name was due to the proximity of the building to Fort Charlotte.

Between 1827 and 1829 James Sinclair, mason, erected a building for William Hay but, in 1835, it was rebuilt by the firm Hay & Ogilvy, of which William was a partner.[1] This impressive block at 116-126 Commercial Street is situated between Muir's Steps and Tod's Steps.

It was an unusual building for Lerwick at that time with the style of architecture more commonly found in both the old and new town of Edinburgh. The residential accommodation was on the top floor, with shops underneath, at street level. The basements were reached both through doors from the back, which faced the sea, and from the street by sunken areas accessible by steps, protected by iron railings. These were at each side of the doors leading to the five business premises, later six,

Charlotte Place is on the left with Ogilvy's Buildings opposite. c.1900

at street level. One feature that distinguished the building from its neighbours was the size and height of the rooms, which were modern in style and appearance and each property was completely self-contained. Over the years there was a frequent change of occupancy of both the houses and shops.[2]

In 1906 the railings were removed and the space was covered over to create a wider pavement,[3] with glass panels inserted to light the passage below, as can be seen in the pavement today.

Prior to Charlotte Place being constructed there was a house on the site called Colvin's. It is not known who he was.

Parker's Pier

Parker's Pier resembled a stair head with steps down to the sea and was in close proximity to where Mr Parker lived, possibly in the house known as Colvin's. Mr Parker was a retired soldier from Fort Charlotte who settled in the town after 1815[4] and was said to be a road surveyor who understood road-making and all kinds of paving to perfection, despite being unable to read or write. He was able to draw in a fashion that was understandable to others and consequently he was employed by the Commissioners of Police.[5]

The passage under Commercial Street, originally the sunken area protected by railings. This was included as part of a walking tour by Elma Johnson and the author. 2008

The North Lodberry

The North Lodberry with Charlotte Place on the right. The workmen are marking out the position of a wooden fence to be erected for safety reasons. c.1880

The North Lodberry was one of the largest and busiest in Lerwick with a sizeable yard between two stores.

It is not known when the lodberry was constructed but, in 1851, when James Mouat bought the property from the sequestrated estate of William Hay, it consisted of the Bulwark Wharf and enclosed lodberry with cellars, also a dwelling house and pier on the south side of the lodberry.[1] James died very soon after, as did his son and heir, also called James. A brother, William, inherited the property and he sold it to Peter, another brother, in 1853.[2] Peter unfortunately died in 1855 and his remaining brother, Alexander H. Mouat, inherited the property.

In the early days there were a number of tenants who rented the lodberry stores and yard for keeping fish and salt, as premises for joiner shops and also sail lofts.[3]

Alexander H. Mouat, who was resident in Canada,

Tait's Lodberry and the North Lodberry. 1870s

E. S. Reid Tait and the Seaview vaults are on the left with the North Lodberry on the right. c.1890

sold the property to brothers Thomas and Charles E. Leask, nephews of Joseph Leask, in 1884.[4] They later used the north part as a coal store.[5] In the block on the south side they opened a ship and boat supply store and a licenced shop under the firm name of Joseph Leask & Co.[6] (This is now the greetings card section of Harry's Department Store.)

In 1890 the whole property was sold to sisters Catherine Schoor and Barbara Muir (née Colvin), the partners of Schoor & Company, Shetland hosiers.[7] Two years later they sold the north part of the North Lodberry to brothers Robert D. and Thomas Ganson.[8] At that time they had property which they had built in 1882 in Whisky Lane (now Market Street). The brothers initially built a store at the North Lodberry and then, during 1895,[9] a large four-storey building, the one we see today. Included was a large room that was used for house furniture auction sales etc. In 1909 the American Bazaar Company advertised a great sale to be held for a short time in Ganson's Hall.[10]

Shoor & Company's premises on the left, David and George G. Kay's building in the middle and Robert D. and Thomas Ganson's building on the right. The Kays' building burned down in 1916. c.1910

In 1900 the partners of Schoor & Company sold the piece of ground between their property and that of Ganson Bros to David and George G. Kay, merchants.[11] By 1906 they had built a significant property on the site.[12]

However, during a violent storm on 13th January, 1916, a fire broke out in the early hours in Messrs D. & G. Kay's property occupied by Mr Eric Charleson, who had a restaurant on the ground floor with a billiard room upstairs. The next floor was where Mr Fred Salmon, fish merchant, kept fishing nets, oilskins and other material used in the fishing industry, while on the top floor there were nets and wool. The fire soon spread to the adjacent Ganson Brothers' property to the north where Mr H.G. Hall also had a restaurant. Ganson's auction sale rooms were on the first floor, and above were the offices of Mr G.W. Hoggan, solicitor. On the top storey were two houses and the stores of Messrs Smith & Robertson, drapers.[13] Residents and tenants of the offices rescued what they could before the flames forced them to leave. It was not until the roofs of both properties fell in and the buildings were practically gutted that the fire was brought under control. By evening the fire had been extinguished and the front wall of Mr Charleson's shop was demolished as it was in a dangerous condition. The cause of the fire was not established. Fortunately, the fire did not spread to the neighbouring Charlotte Place as there was a passage between the two buildings.[14]

The Schoor & Company buildings had been sold to George Leslie Jnr the previous year[15] and were relatively undamaged in the fire. However, the firm Schoor & Company continued to trade under different management.

In 1917 what remained of the Ganson Brothers' building was bought by John & James Tod & Sons Ltd, Leith wholesaler merchants.[16] It was extensively altered and reconstructed.[17] Five years later they bought the adjacent building from Messrs D. & G. Kay.[18] In 1920 the house and shop on the north end of Charlotte Place on Commercial Street had also been purchased[19] and the buildings were joined up. A further purchase

Tod's renovated and restructured all three buildings. The Esplanade was extended during the mid-1950s. (Courtesy of Elizabeth Angus)

The Thule, Harry's, Westside Pine and Albert Building in 2021

was the Schoor & Company buildings in 1932,[20] although the firm was in business until about 1935. The property of J. & J. Tod & Sons Ltd then comprised the whole row of buildings on the Esplanade and extended from there to the north end of Commercial Street.

"Tod's" continued in business until the firm moved to Gremista in 1978.[21]

The vacant premises were acquired by Mr Arne Moltzau, a Norwegian who had until then been in business as Centron of Lerwick at the Market Cross. He had ambitious plans to turn the former warehouse buildings into a shopping centre with various units available to be open by Christmas of that year. A proposed nightclub did not materialise, nor did Mr Moltzau's scheme.[22] He later sold the various sections. However, he did have a footwear shop at 124 Commercial Street for a very short time.

In 1980 Patricia Watts opened a shop which she advertised as "The Complete Dress Shop" in the street-level part of the building at 126 Commercial Street, and was there until 1984. The shop was then occupied by Micro Management to be followed by Sixty North Ltd then the Sandwick Baking Company and The Street Café. The upper floors were bought by Harry Jamieson in 1990. The shop premises were purchased from the Sandwick Baking Company in 2003.

Also in 1980 the Sandwick Baking Company moved into 124 Commercial Street, to be followed by Telenews in 1988. The premises were bought by Harry Jamieson in 1996 and is now the street entrance to Harry's Department Store.

The south part of the former North Lodberry, consisting of two ground floors, hairdressing department and store above, was sold to Harry in May 1978. The upper store was bought the following year and is now the toy department. The first, second and third floors above the card department were built in 2010.[23]

The Esplanade part of the building became a furniture store during April 1981 when R.L. Arthur relocated his shop from Charlotte Street. He was followed by Westside Pine in 1996, the present owner.[24] Harry Jamieson bought the floor above Westside Pine from the proprietors in March 2007 and this is now the linens section of the household department.

Tod's Steps

Tod's Steps. 2021

Tod's Steps were only officially named and signposted in 2005,[1] in recognition of the firm Messrs J. & J. Tod & Sons Ltd Leith, whose wholesale business had been based there from 1917 until 1978. The steps are situated adjacent to the Westside Pine shop.

Ross Smith had a photographic studio with cellar next to his property at the north side of Charlotte Place in the 1870s. After this burned down he was given permission by Lerwick Town Council to erect a baker's oven on the condition that he built a flight of steps there. He did so but these steps that led from a walkway, or platform, were badly constructed.[2]

In 1895, when Ganson Brothers built their large premises on the site of the north part of the North Lodberry, they were given permission to rebuild the adjacent steps and extend the platform to gain an access to the upper floor of their premises. These were constructed alongside the building together with a store under the steps.[3]

The firm commonly referred to as Tod's was established in 1841. There had been a local connection since the 1850s but it was not until 1907 that Henry Mouat was appointed the first local manager. In 1912 the firm opened a small depot in Victoria

Lerwick's south end and the North Lodberry in the early 1870s. This date arises from the fact that the building that is now Anderson & Company, built during 1874-75, does not appear in the illustration

Buildings on the Esplanade, in part of the building later occupied by Aitken & Wright.[4] (Victoria Buildings was demolished in February 1994 and the TSB was built on the site.[5])

As a result of business expansion, Tod's moved into larger premises in 1915[6] at what is now Vaila Fine Art, at 61 Commercial Street, but soon this was also inadequate.

Following the fire in 1916, in premises owned by Ganson Brothers at the former North Lodberry, the building was bought the following year by Messrs John & James Tod & Sons Ltd Leith, wholesale merchants.[7] Ganson Brothers transferred their right and interest in the steps and store to Tod's in 1919.[8]

In 1922 the firm bought the adjacent building from Messrs D & G. Kay.[9] After the buildings at the south part of the

Vehicles next to Aitken & Wright. The Bank of Scotland is on the right

lodberry and the house and shop at the north end of Commercial Street were also purchased, the buildings were extensively altered and reconstructed. The warehouse premises then extended from the Esplanade to Commercial Street. (This is now Harry's Department Store and Westside Pine.)

Tod's trading address was Commercial Buildings.

When Henry Mouat retired in 1939 he was succeeded by his nephew, Harry J. Mouat, who had worked for the firm since 1917.

Tod's premises on the Esplanade. J.W. Robertson (Albert Building) is on the right with the top of the fish market immediately behind. Albert Building underwent major refurbishment during 1989-90

In 1946 Sir Gilbert Arthur, who had joined Tod's in 1896, accepted an offer from Beecham Group Ltd for the business and his son John remained on as managing director in Leith. However six years later, in 1952, John announced that he had acquired the firm back from the Beecham Group.[10]

Following the retirement of Harry Mouat the next manager, Mr Furnival, was transferred from Edinburgh for a short time. Local man Tammy Balfour, who had joined the firm in 1956, was then appointed manager assisted by his son Hamish.

The Esplanade

Major pier expansion took place during the mid-1950s enabling the Esplanade to be widened. Tod's is on the right. (Courtesy of Elizabeth Angus)

The north part of the building was the flour store. A large door allowed a truck to drive inside and be loaded by means of a chute. Soap was stored towards the back and further back at a lower level there was a boiler, which was under Commercial Street in the direction of what is now C'est la Vie. Above the flour store cigarettes were kept and the floor above held the toilet rolls. Animal feed was stored in the middle section of the building on the Esplanade, while lemonade and water was kept in the south part. Access to the upstairs offices was from Commercial Street.[11]

In March 1972 Aitken & Wright, wholesale grocers, ceased trading after over 50 years in business in Lerwick and Tod's took over the Lerwick stock.[12]

The firm moved to Gremista in 1978.

Tod's of Lerwick is now incorporated into J.W. Gray & Co, wholesalers.[13]

Messrs J. & J. Tod & Sons Ltd extended their building to join with the north part of Charlotte Place. The top of Tod's Steps is at the door on the side of the building. 2021

THE ESPLANADE

The waterfront below Fort Charlotte. c.1883

In the early 1880s Lerwick Harbour Trust began to develop the shoreline and, by doing so, many small piers were demolished or built over and some lodberries no longer stood in the sea. Many continued to be used as stores, while others were converted. One example is Greig's Lodberry which was converted to become the Peerie Shop in 1988[1] with the Peerie Shop Café opening in 1999.[2]

The proposal to construct a proper pier had been under discussion by Lerwick's business community for some time prior to *The Shetland Times* being founded in 1872. The newspaper then contained numerous references to the question. In 1876 a conference was held between Lerwick Town Council and a committee appointed by the Commissioners of Supply and it was agreed that a proper pier could be constructed by extending Victoria Wharf.[3] The existing roads and streets leading to the area were obviously too narrow to facilitate access. Therefore, harbour improvements were proposed stretching from near the Gas Pier (which was behind what is now Healthcraft) to Victoria Wharf and then to Hay's Pier behind the Old Tolbooth. Included in the scheme was a proposal to construct a wide esplanade and improve the very narrow road below Fort Charlotte by extending it from the north end of Commercial Street to join with the new road.

A Bill was duly drafted and presented to parliament and, despite opposition from the North of Scotland & Orkney & Shetland Steam Navigation Shipping Company and Mr George H.B. Hay, representing the residents of the south end, the Bill passed through parliament. In August 1877 the Lerwick Harbour Improvement Act received Royal Assent and consequently Lerwick Harbour Trust was formed. The scheme,

Constructing the South Esplanade and extending Victoria Wharf

however, was unable to proceed due to lack of funding and the fact that the bank did not consider the project to be viable. It was not until 1882 that funding was secured and work could commence in creating the Esplanade and extending the pier.[4] The foundation stone was laid in 1883 and Victoria Pier was formally opened by Sheriff Thoms in June 1886.

When the harbour works were completed the wooden railing directly below Fort Charlotte was extended. A second railing was erected along the seaward side of the newly constructed lower road at the north Esplanade. It stretched to the building that is now Healthcraft.[5] Unfortunately, by 1896 over 100 of the posts were affected with dry rot and required to be replaced.[6]

The Esplanade. c.1910

At Victoria Wharf the Esplanade stood higher than the foundations of the old row of houses where the boatmen had lived who made their living by ferrying passengers and goods to and from the steamers anchored in Lerwick Harbour.[7] A sunken passage was retained along the east end of the houses with a safety railing to protect the public from falling in. In 1905 George Leslie purchased this property and the following year replaced the houses with Ellesmere Buildings (presently D.G. Leslie at street level). The ground to the east side was built up to the level of the Esplanade and in the process the sunken passage and old railings were replaced with a wide pavement. In fact, the Esplanade was, and is, at a higher level than most of the buildings it borders.[8]

The police and sanitary department's office is the small highlighted hut. 1905 (It was moved and later became Lizzie's Lodestar Café)

In 1905 two landmark structures were to be found near the top of Victoria Pier. One was a drinking fountain while the other was a little hut that was later to be known as Lizzie's Lodestar café.

The Diana Fountain

During the 19th century whaling ships from numerous ports throughout the UK called along Lerwick each spring to sign on crew for voyages to the Arctic. Locally the best known is the *Diana* of Hull. In 1867 she drifted into Ronas Voe after having been away for fourteen months, with food and provisions long exhausted. During six of these months she had been locked in the Arctic ice. Somehow she

The Diana Fountain. 1929

escaped the fate of being crushed by the ice and when she eventually arrived in the voe 13 of her crew lay dead, included nine of the 26 Shetlanders on board.⁹ Few of those remaining alive were able to stand.

Dr Charles Edward Smith, who had been surgeon on board the *Diana*, died in 1879. Ten years later his brother, Alderman Frederic Smith, then Mayor of West Ham, erected a commemorative marble drinking fountain on the pier close to where the crews of the whaling ships used to land.¹⁰ It was formally inaugurated on Monday, 24th May, 1890.¹¹

Incidentally, a great-granddaughter of Magnus Gray Jnr, one of the survivors of the ill-fated voyage, was christened Diana with water from the memorial fountain.¹²

Although the fountain has been moved at least twice from its original location, and no longer dispenses water, it still dominates Victoria Pier and stands there as a lasting memorial to the return of the *Diana*.

Lizzie's Lodestar Café

In 1905 Lerwick Town Council erected a hut with a corrugated iron roof as an office for the police and sanitary departments on a spot overlooking Victoria Pier. The work was carried out by Andrew Coutts, joiner, at a total cost of £73 10s, and the rent to Lerwick Harbour Trust was £1 per annum. The area had previously been occupied by building contractor John G. Anderson, who relocated to a yard at Sinclair's Beach (the site of the present Post Office sorting office) in 1904.¹³

The hut was not to remain very long in that location because it occupied part of the site designated for the proposed new Harbour House offices. Lerwick Harbour Trust wrote to the Town Council stating that it was necessary for the police hut to be removed and that the harbour trustees were willing to pay the purchase price and take immediate possession of the building. They also offered to move it to another site and agreed to provide accommodation in Harbour House for the "police, sanitary and water office".

In 1906, when work commenced on constructing Harbour House, the hut was duly raised from its foundations and transported north along the Esplanade to a site opposite the present Bressay ferry terminal. Here it assumed a new role when it was let, the same year, to Messrs Malcolmson & Co as refreshment rooms. The following year it was let to Mrs Ann Jamieson as a restaurant, but in 1910 it was discovered that she was using part of it as a butcher shop – a practice the trust suppressed immediately. The refreshment rooms carried on and were widely used by fishermen and crofters. A watering trough situated to the north of the refreshment rooms was provided for horses and other livestock prior to shipment.¹⁴ In 1947 a weighbridge was built on the site of the trough.¹⁵

Mrs Jamieson carried on business until 1938 when the building was taken over by Miss Annie Manson.

The hut was moved to this site in 1906. It was The Computer Clinic in 2008

Land being reclaimed from the sea to create the Esplanade

In 1944 Miss Jessie Bolt became the new tenant and she continued to provide a valuable service to customers, including the large number of naval personnel stationed in Lerwick during the war. On one occasion two Norwegian sailors arrived exhausted in Lerwick Harbour having had nothing to eat for over 36 hours but, immediately after mooring their vessel, they headed straight across the road for a much appreciated meal.

The café became known by its appropriate nautical name, "Lizzie's Lodestar",[16] soon after Mrs Elizabeth Wilson became the next occupier in 1953. The café had continued to be a popular venue sought out by seafarers who visited Lerwick and also regularly used by the large numbers of men working around the harbour area. This included the author who remembers as a student enjoying a well-earned "smoko" at Lizzie's while working as a docker during summer holidays. An acquaintance recalls "da fried eggs sweemin in fat".

Lizzie's Lodestar changed hands in 1975 with the arrival of Mrs Mary Leask who carried on until 1983 when Mrs Barbara Smith took over as the Harbour Café.

It was the end of an era when the café closed in 1994 as the premises,

The public toilets nicknamed "Da Crystal Palace", demolished 1958. Early 1950s (Courtesy of Elizabeth Angus)

with minimal alterations, had operated for over 88 years as a refreshment rooms/café providing a valuable service to the general public.[17]

However, its useful role to the community continued when Mr Brian Priest opened Last Ditchology. After working from a nearby shed he moved into the former café and continued to turn his hand to repairing electrical appliances. He became an expert at making things work and remained there for ten years until he relocated to Cope's premises at Gremista in 2005.[18]

The next tenant, Mr Bill MacGregor, opened The Computer Clinic, repairing computers in addition to providing a facility for TV repairs.

Early in June 2010 the former Lizzie's Lodestar was no more, but not without controversy. The badly corroded structure was in very poor condition and, although a building warrant had been granted to Lerwick Port Authority for its demolition, conservation consent should also have been sought. Many people were shocked that the building had been demolished as it had been in that location for 104 years. It was a landmark building and had become a tourist attraction.[19]

The site is now a car parking area.

The destruction of an iconic small building. June 2010

Improvements

Several improvements took place in time for the visit of the Tall Ships to Lerwick in July 2011 and continued over the following years.

In a joint venture between Lerwick Port Authority and Shetland Islands Council, Harbour House was renovated in 2008 by Richard Gibson Architects. The new offices are now leased to private businesses. In addition, public toilets were built on the adjacent site and opened in June 2009.

However, this was not the first public convenience to have occupied this site as, in 1908, a much-needed facility was funded jointly by Lerwick Harbour Trust and Lerwick Town Council. It soon acquired the tongue-in-cheek nickname "Da Crystal

Boats in the small boat harbour. 1950s

Palace". The ladies' section was tactfully called the "waiting room". It was a typical building of that time, with tiles and blue stained-glass windows. The sanitary provision was very basic, particularly in the gentlemen's area, and privacy was virtually non-existent. The facilities consisted of a row of porcelain urinals, while "the throne" was a long wooden bar, placed over running water, on which to sit. A favourite prank was to launch a rolled up piece of burning newspaper and wait with anticipation as it sailed towards the unsuspecting user sitting above.

The redeveloped small boat harbour. 2021

The convenience served the public for 51 years until, in 1958, after the Esplanade had been widened as part of the pier expansion and harbour developments, a new toilet block was built opposite Burn's Walk. "Da Crystal Palace" was then demolished. The new facility also served the public for 51 years, before being demolished following the opening of the new toilets in 2009.

Hay's Pier was extended in 1914 to create the "smaa boat harbour". During 2010-2011 the wall at the small boat harbour was redeveloped and replaced by modern railings and the wooden deck was also replaced and enlarged. The pavement was widened which allowed seating to be safely installed.

Two sculptures have since been erected near the seating.

Shetland South Atlantic Whaler Memorial

In May 2011 a memorial to honour the Shetland seamen who worked in the South Georgia whaling industry was unveiled by Willie Tait, the former chairman of the Shetland ex-whalers Association. The memorial was designed by Davy Cooper and

The Shetland South Atlantic Whaler Memorial. 2021

the plinth was built by Shetland Amenity Trust using Enviroglass panels. The plaque is made of black Indian granite with an engraving of South Georgia and inscriptions:

Erected by the Shetland ex-whalers Association in tribute to all the Shetlanders who, from 1905 to 1963, worked in the Antarctic with the whaling fleets of Chr. Salvesen & Co Leith.

Through the 1930s depression and post war austerity, money earned at the Antarctic Whaling sustained many families and helped stem the flow of emigration from the islands till the fishing industry improved in the 1960s and the oil industry arrived in the 1970s.

"They did business in great waters and saw the wonders of the deep"

Da Lightsom Buoy

This cast bronze sculpture is situated a short distance from the whaling memorial and celebrates the role the pelagic fishing industry plays in Shetland life, economy and culture. The sculpture, created by artist Jo Chapman, depicts a large fishing buoy and includes images and text in dialect. It was commissioned by fish agents LHD, Lerwick Port Authority, Shetland Catch and Shetland Fish Producers' Organisation. It was unveiled in October 2016 by Rosabelle Halcrow, an ex-gutter, and Callum Irvine who was Shetland's youngest pelagic fisherman at the time. It was designed to have a light shining through an opening in the sculpture but visitors thought it was an elaborate litter bin and the decision was made to forego the original plan and block it up.

The Lightsom Buoy sculpture. 2021

The seating, cycle stand and water tap at Burns Walk. 2021

Further developments

In 2013 three bollards were erected between M&Co and the Clydesdale Bank, now Virgin Money, to prevent vehicles using the pedestrian precinct to access the car parking area below Fort Charlotte. Vehicular access was and is allowed from the foot of Harbour Street.

Harrison Square was pedestrianised that same year.

In 2017 there were changes to road markings, along with traffic-calming measures and the introduction of a new crossing with traffic lights. This new layout and crossing initially caused confusion among motorists, pedestrians and cruise ship passengers. Also a seating area was created at Burns Walk together with a modern, steel letter, cycle stand outlining the word "SHETLAND".

In September 2019 Scottish Water installed "Scotland's most northerly top-up water tap", also at Burns Walk. The tap digitally tracks water usage and records cost savings. It was part of a national initiative to get more people to carry a reusable bottle to reduce plastic waste.

CHAPTER 4

OTHER NAMES AGREED IN 1845
GULLET'S BRAE
WHISKY LANE

Other Names Agreed in 1845

In 1845 it was decided that Bullet Loan should be renamed London Road, but it would seem that the name was never used. It was renamed Knab Road in 1924.

The short stretch of road bordering the old cemetery, between what is now Knab Road and Lovers Loan, was designated as Cross Lane but it is now part of Breiwick Road.

From west of St Magnus Scottish Episcopal Church towards the top of what is today Church Road was named Greenfield Place and from there to the top of Mounthooly Street received the name Annsbrae Place. Annsbrae was named after Annsbrae House, which was and is situated at the foot of Knab Road.

The road between the top of Mounthooly Street and Reform Lane was called South Hill Place. From Reform Lane to the top of Charlotte Lane was North Hill Place (now the Upper Hillhead).

The road leading from near the top of Charlotte Street and around the corner down to Fort Charlotte was named Anderson's Place (now Anderson Place). It was named after Joseph Anderson, a builder and contractor whose property was opposite the entrance to the Garrison Theatre.

The road from South Hill Place westwards to the Burgh Road was named Waterloo Road in 1845 but was officially named Scalloway Road in 1884. The upper part continues to be referred to as Gullet's Brae.

Whisky Lane was named Freefield Lane, but the former name was used until 1884 when it was renamed Market Street.

The road from the north end of Charlotte Place northwards to Burgh Road was named Commercial Road in 1845 and the North Ness was officially named.

Freefield Docks was named and the road forming the west boundary of the Burgh of Lerwick, from the Freefield Docks to Breiwick, was officially named Burgh Road.

Gullet's Brae

Scalloway Road is between the two walls on the left leading up to Alder Lodge and Clairmont Place on the top right. The house where Johnnie Goodlad or Gullet lived is highlighted and is next to the brae that bears his name. Recognisable on the Hillhead are the Adam Clark Methodist Church and Manse, Grindislea, Rosegarth, Navy Cottage, Gordon Cottage, Alder Lodge and Clairmont Place. c.1878

Although the road between South Hill Place and down to the Burgh Road was named Waterloo Road in 1845, it would seem it was never popular as it was renamed Scalloway Road in 1884. However, the upper part continues to be referred to as Gullet's Brae after John Goodlad, known as Johnnie Gullet, who lived nearby.

Not so long ago Denis Jamieson kept sheep and ducks in the park surrounding his property at Brae Cottage on South Road, adjacent to the Lerwick Hotel. It is now the site of the Brae Court semi-retirement housing scheme built in 2010.

However, Denis was not the only person to have kept ducks in the vicinity as, in 1858, seamen from the Peterhead vessel *Kate* were petitioned for theft of ducks from John Goodlad,[1] or Gullet, after whom Gullet's Brae is named. There is uncertainty as to his place of birth as one record shows him to be born on 20th August 1785 in Gulberwick, while another suggests the small farm of Holmsgarth, Lerwick.[2] Nevertheless, it would seem that he spent the most of his life in Lerwick.

John, or Johnnie, was married twice – first to Robina Anderson and they had seven children, the eldest of whom was born in 1806. In 1839 he married Jane Sinclair, but they had no family.

When he was a young man, like so many Shetlanders Johnnie went to the Greenland whaling. On one occasion French vessels attacked the whalers and burned four of the ships, but fortunately he managed to escape injury. However, the journey home was still fraught with danger as this was the period when Press Gangs were used by the Royal Navy as a crude and violent method of recruiting seamen into naval service, mostly against their will. The recruitment of sailors voluntarily was difficult as the conditions on board ships were poor and serving in the navy, especially at time of war, was dangerous. On returning from whaling voyages there was always the possibility of being seized by the Press Gang, but Johnnie had devised an ingenious method of avoiding the risk of being captured. He was a member of a Voluntary Corp, probably the Shetland Fencibles, a unit of local volunteers commanded by a regular army officer attached to Fort Charlotte. On returning to Shetland he would go into hiding and somehow get a message to his wife detailing his whereabouts. She would rendezvous with him, bringing his voluntary uniform with her. He changed clothes and confidently walked home safe in the knowledge that, as a consequence of wearing the uniform, he would not be impressed.[3]

Afterwards Johnnie was a bank messenger with Mr Yorston, bank agent for the National Bank of Scotland in Braeside House, Law Lane, but the branch did not remain for very long.[4] It was replaced by the Union Bank of Scotland on 3rd October 1838,[5] also there for a short time, before moving to what is now Alder Lodge, 6 Clairmont Place.

In 1841 Johnnie is recorded as a post runner. The volume of mail handled in Lerwick increased after 1840 under the direction of William Rae Duncan, postmaster.[6]

In 1854 Johnnie's fellow post runners were his son Andrew, also Robert Laurenson and Thomas Tullock.[7] The Post Office frequently moved but at this time it is likely that it was at the County Assessor and Collector's Office (now 53 Commercial Street) opposite the Queens Hotel.[8]

Where exactly did Johnnie Goodlad live? The census for 1851 lists his address as Roadside Hut and his dwelling can be clearly seen in the photograph – located on the lower corner of the junction of what is now Scalloway Road with St Olaf Street, on the south side. When the earlier mentioned theft took place it was reported that the seamen had gained access to the ducks by removing a section of the tekkit (thatched) roof from the byre or stable adjoining his house.

His grandson, Mitchell Abernethy, followed in his footsteps by going to the Arctic whaling. He was a harpooner on the ill-fated *Diana* and died there, due to scurvy, on 4th March 1867.[9]

Johnnie Goodlad died on 4th January 1877.[10] He was aged 91 according to records, but his gravestone in the lower section of Lerwick Cemetery states that he was 100 years old.

Regardless of his age his memory lives on. Although the brae between King

Johnnie Gullet. Early 1870s

Harald Street and the Hillhead is signposted as Scalloway Road, this section is most commonly known and referred to as Gullet's Brae.

The following is an old poem penned by "Yacob"[11] who recalls the enjoyment of sledging in Gullit's Brae (his spelling), an activity not possible to undertake safely today.

JOHNNIE GULLIT'S BRAE

Aft haes a poet painted bright
Da beauties o a simmer day,
Bit what aboot a winter's night,
Spent sledgin on John Gullit's brae?

Wi modesty ithin his lap,
Nae winder whin shü says its nice;
He tinks da world's no wirt a rap,
An Gullit's brae is Paradice.

He hads her tightly as dey dash,
Right doon da brae juist laek a train;
An next you see da couple mash,
Ta hae da pleasure ower again.

An sae da sweet night wears awa,
While wingéd Cupid wi his dart,
Lies secretly among da snaw,
An woonds some tochless youngster's heart.

Oh! Let us hope each boy an lass
May aften hae ta bless da day
Dat brought sic happy lives ta pass,
Through sledgin on John Gullit's brae.

Whisky Lane

Market Street. Late 1880s

Although Whisky Lane was given the name Freefield Lane in 1845, the former name was used until 1884 when it was renamed Market Street. A request had been made to have the address changed because of its past dubious history and due to the number of houses being built and the increasing number of residents and businesses in the area.[1]

In the mid-1800s the link between what is now the Hillhead and Freefield was simply a rough and ready track, bordered by grass parks and dry stone dykes. Behind the dyke on the east side were middens and pigsties. These sties were an ingenious place to hide and store tar and materials to make the tar barrels that were set alight to celebrate Christmas and the New Year. The tar was readily available from the nearby gas works[2] (now the site of Charlotte House).

The foot of the track was a favourite place for working men to congregate, mainly on Saturday evenings, to enjoy a dram. It was as a result of this particular activity that Whisky Lane received its name.[3]

In the early days there were no buildings in the lane apart from the small smithy erected by Robert Ridland in 1865 near the roadway at the lower east side (near the present Home Furnishing). Here, he and his brother Abel carried on their trade until 1882 when they moved to new premises which would have been on the site of the present Brentham Place.

Rapid developments took place in the lane with residential accommodation mainly on the west side and commercial/industrial premises on the east. A description and location of some of the buildings follows:

The chimney on the right identifies the location of the gas works. Late 1960s

The County Buildings
The County Buildings, comprising the sheriff court, police station and prison, opened in 1875 at the top of the lane on the west side.

Lerwick Town Hall
In 1880 a group of Lerwick businessmen formed a Limited Liability Company in order to provide the money for the establishment of a purpose-built town hall. One year later the tender by John M. Aitken, architect and contractor, to erect the building was accepted. The following morning the first sod was cut on the site acquired from local merchant George Reid Tait.

In January 1882 Prince Alfred, Duke of Edinburgh, laid the foundation stone of Lerwick Town Hall and in 1884 came the official opening.

The building was designed by architect Alexander Ross in the Scottish baronial style and stained glass windows, designed by James Ballantine & Son, were installed in the building. These include a depiction of the marriage between Margaret of Denmark and James II of Scotland in 1469. There are also windows presented by the Corporation of Amsterdam and the Corporation of Hamburg.

Slaughterhouse and Market Green
In 1877 a public slaughterhouse was built on a piece of waste ground between Whisky Lane and Fort Charlotte.[4] Previously animals were slaughtered in the numerous lodberries which were to be found along the foreshore. One place where such activity was carried out was a cellar under Robertson's Lodberry,[5] later "The Lodberrie",

which in recent years has found fame as the home of the factitious detective Jimmy Perez in the *Shetland* crime series.

Adjacent to the slaughterhouse was the new Market Green, on the corner of Whisky Lane and what became known as Slaughterhouse Road, until it was named Harbour Street in 1884.

The old slaughterhouse. Used for auction sales until 2003

In the early 1980s the redundant slaughterhouse became the venue for Harry Hay's saleroom. After he left it stood empty for a short time until 2003 when it was demolished. The neighbouring Scottish Hydro Electric building, which had been constructed in 1947, was also demolished along with related buildings. In September 1996 the "hydro" shop had moved to 98 Commercial Street[6] (presently The Dowry). The site, including the unused Market Green, became a car park.

Before 1877 the Market Place, or Green, had been situated on the site of St Ringan's Church.[7] The church was built in 1886 and closed in 1997 to reopen in 2002 as Shetland Library and Learning Centre. In October 2021 the library moved back across Union Street to the completely renovated former Shetland Museum and Library. The former church and the building containing the learning centre were retained by Shetland Islands Council.

Residential

From the 1880s onwards more and more buildings were constructed in Whisky Lane, with the tendency for commercial enterprises to be on the east side and dwelling houses on the west. These included the properties of a group of six well known Lerwick seamen – John Gear, James Moffat, John Johnson, Alexander Sandison, John Irvine and Thomas Manson. Later to be called the Market Street Company, they pooled their resources and bought the herring sail-boat *Camperdown*, which was skippered by

John Gear. In her first season she earned more than double her outlay on boat and gear. Encouraged by the success the *Prince of Liberty* was purchased and James Moffat was made skipper. Later the *Pioneer* was added to the fleet, under the command of John Johnson. This venture turned out so well that in addition to obtaining a huge profit the men were each able to erect a substantial house in the lane.[8] For example, in February 1882 Thomas Manson placed an advert in a local newspaper for builders to erect a house for him.

In 1881 John M. Aitken had built his new business premises and offices near the foot of Whisky Lane (now Home Furnishing's upper building). These structures were the first purpose-built workshops in Lerwick. Up to that time any ramshackle shed, letting in wind and rain, was considered good enough to work in.[9] John Aitken started his business in 1873 and was a prolific builder. Of the 140 or so buildings constructed by him the most notable was the Town Hall. He also built his own residence, Summerside House, in King Harald Street.[10]

The Zetland Aerated Water Company

In 1901 Mr Aitken was contracted to specially design and construct a two-storied building near his workshop for the purpose of manufacturing soft drinks. The Zetland Aerated Water Company began production in May of that year but it was soon styled "Da Fizzy Factory". The building at 36 Market Street may be remembered as the Lerwick Laundry before it closed down in 2002.

Mr Alex Simpson from Aberdeen was employed as manager as he had 36 years of experience in the business. Six to eight local people were employed to work in the factory. For those readers who are interested in the technical side of things, the plant consisted of a horizontal steam engine by Bisset & Co, Aberdeen, developing four horsepower. The engine was fitted with Pickering's patent governor, which enabled a steady pressure of steam to be obtained. Steam was obtained from a multi-tubular boiler, which apparently was the first of the kind to be erected in Shetland.

Messrs Bratby & Hinchcliff's aerated water plant was used throughout. This included the gas retort where the gas was made. From this machine it passed into a purifier, then to the gasometer, and finally the aerated water machine. In this machine the gas and water was mixed, and put under pressure, the amount of pressure for the different kinds of waters ranging from 100 to 160 pounds to the square inch. When this process was completed the product was conveyed by pipes to the bottling machines. The first was the Monarch turn-over bottling machine, for bottles in which a glass ball stopper was used. The next was the patent corking machine in which the stopper was an ordinary cork with wire fastening. The third was the siphon filler.

On the same floor was a Hill's patent washing machine which cleaned the bottles before they were re-filled. Connected to the bottling machines was the syrup plant upstairs.

An area for brewing ginger beers, hop ales, etc. was situated at the back of the building. This was fitted with a steam apparatus for thoroughly cleaning the casks. Ground at the back was utilised for stores.

In the upper storey was a laboratory for making the essences used in the production of the various drinks and over 50 different kinds were used for flavouring purposes.

A patent filter ensured that the water was perfectly pure.

The plant was capable of turning out an astounding 9,600 bottles each 10-hour working day.[11] Young boys were eager to acquire the bottles with the glass ball stoppers as they were a cheap source for obtaining "bools" for playing marbles.

However, in 1904 the company went into liquidation and was subsequently purchased by A.L. Laing, chemist, who carried on the business under the existing name.[12]

An advertisement in the *Shetland News* from 1904 lists the variety of table waters manufactured: Ginger Ale; Lemonade; Kola; Ginger Beer (Stone); Champagne Ginger Beer; Hop Ale; Cherry Cider; Claret and Lemonade; Zolakone; Lime Juice and Soda; Tit-bits; Kola Champagne; Ciderette; Football Stout; Soda Water; Polass Water; Seltzer Water; Lithia Water; also a variety on non-alcoholic Fruit Wines.

The drinks were delivered around the town by a high-stepping bay pony pulling a brightly painted float, which was kept in immaculate condition.[13] The driver was Mr Gilbert Ratter who was now the manager of the factory.

The float was later replaced by a Model T Ford lorry. This created some interest as one of the drivers was young Miss Lily Sinclair, Mr Ratter's sister-in-law. She must have been among the earliest female drivers in Shetland.

In 1919 the company was purchased by the wholesale provision merchants Messrs Aitken & Wright, in a venture with the rival company J. & J. Tod's Ltd. It was renamed Zetland Manufactory Co Ltd with T.A. Wright (of Aitken & Wright) and G. Archer (of J. & J. Tods Ltd) as directors, with Henry Mouat and Mitchell H. Williamson as joint managers. In 1924 George H. Burgess replaced Mitchell Williamson as joint manager. Mr Mouat was also manager of J. & J. Tod's Ltd while Mr Burgess was manager of Aitken & Wright.[14]

In January 1932 the business of the aerated water manufactory was advertised for sale as a going concern, along with the premises, stores, machines and plant.[15]

Unfortunately it would appear that there was no interest and consequently much of the machinery plant was sold to Mowat & Co, bakers and grocers of Scalloway, to be used in the operation of an aerated water factory in Scalloway.

Also in 1932 Alexander J. Laurenson (who had received the nickname Al Capone) had returned from America. He was married to one of Henry Mouat's daughters. He opened a plumbing, heating and electrical engineering business at 98 Commercial Street but a short time later he moved to the vacant factory at Market Street and carried on his business there.[16]

In 1962 James M. Mouat (no relation to Henry Mouat) returned from a spell in New Zealand and purchased the premises where he also started a plumbing, heating and electrical engineering business. The premises were sold to R.W. Offshore Services Ltd in 1975, who carried on providing a similar service until 1981, retaining the name James M. Mouat in addition to their own.[17] When alterations were made at the rear of the building around that time hundreds of old Zetland Aerated Water Company bottles were unearthed with many in remarkable condition, including their glass ball stoppers. Consequently an army of local scranners and bottle collectors descended on the site and had a field day.

In 1983 Robert Sinclair, Ertie Fullerton and Willie Hunter purchased the property[18] and relocated their laundry from the building further up Market Street, presently occupied by Shetland Islands Broadcasting Company (SIBC). In 1983 this building was bought by the BBC for the purpose of becoming a team-based transmission centre.

The Home Furnishing shop is on the left then the building that was originally John M. Aitken's workshop. Private accommodation is next then the former Zetland Aerated Water Company building, latterly the Lerwick Laundry. Now also private accommodation. 2021

However, it never happened and instead it was used by transmission engineers as a team-based centre and a new transmission centre was built next door (now Arqiva). Following an unsuccessful attempt to sell the original premises to IBA (the regulating body for ITV and Channel 4), it was sold in 1985 to SIBC. The independent local commercial radio station came on air in November 1987.[19]

The Lerwick Laundry was taken over in about 1989 by Margaret and Dougal Reid, who provided a service until 2002 when the laundry closed. The building was sold in 2004 and subsequently converted into two flats.

However, the Lerwick Laundry was not the first laundry in the street as Bairnson's Steam Laundry had earlier been established further up, at 4 Market Street, in the building that now houses part of The Lerwick Dental Practice.

Dr Skae, medical officer of health for the Burgh of Lerwick and Bressay (1877-1891), had written: "The Sandy Loch water is quite wholesome but contains so much peaty matter that it might be said to be both meat and drink."

This peaty water was a problem for Lerwegians and the main obstacle to be overcome by Robert W. Tait when, early in 1914, he planned to open a laundry in the town. The second problem he encountered was as a consequence of the outbreak of war. However, in partnership with his brother-in-law George L. Bairnson, a Shetlander who resided in Glasgow, both difficulties were successfully addressed.

There had been talk of opening a laundry in Scalloway because of its clear water supply, but this idea had been dropped when Mr Tait announced his plans. This new

Bairnson's Steam Laundry. Early 1930s (Courtesy of Bertie Tait)

business enterprise was to meet a great need in Lerwick as until then laundry had been sent south, with excellent results and no peaty tint.

Without an abundance of pure water there could be no laundry and, at considerable expense, the partners found a solution. Sandy Loch water samples were sent to experts in Glasgow and London and, in fact, Mr Bairnson personally visited London on several occasions. A system whereby the water passed through filters was devised resulting in water as "clear as crystal".

The partners then aimed to acquire the very best machinery but, with the outbreak of war, this was almost impossible to obtain. However, with perseverance and a degree of good fortune they managed to do so.

An experienced architect was hired to design and draw up plans. Tait & Bairnson's Steam Laundry was duly built and opened for business on 16th October, 1915.

This was a new venture for Mr Tait, a cabinetmaker and upholsterer, who had his business and home next door at number 4, in premises built for him in 1902.

The laundry was a large building on three floors and rooms were spacious, well-lit and ventilated. The heavy machinery for washing and starching was on the ground floor, along with the steam-heated bed and roller through which clothes passed to be dried and pressed. The temperature in the hot air room could be raised to 160°F if required. A qualified engineer was in charge of the steam engine which was situated in a lean-to at the rear of the building, along with a large chimney. The receiving office and clerk's office were at the south end of the building.

The work room on the second floor accommodated the finishing machinery, the testing room, cloak room, wash room and toilets. Ironing was carried out using gas-heated irons and a gas compressor ensured that the irons kept a steady temperature. A machine for pressing collars was also installed.

The store room was on the top floor, in addition to the collecting water tank which was capable of holding 15,000 gallons. The filter system resulted in water so pure that it was fit for domestic purposes. Mr Bairnson even suggested that if the same system of purification had been adopted by Lerwick Town Council, the town could have had a supply of perfectly clear water at that time. Instead, the population had to wait until 1931 before a system of filtration was installed.

The up-to-date machinery was capable of dealing with the laundry requirements of the whole of Shetland. At the opening Mr Bairnson visited Lerwick from his base in Glasgow, then recognised as the hub of the laundry industry. He was connected with the Laundry Associations in the city and in a position to introduce newer systems to the local laundry as time went by.

To ensure that first class work was produced a manageress, Miss Doig, was employed. She came from south and was said to be widely experienced in the laundry business. Later on Mrs Tait took over the management of the laundry. Mr Tait concentrated on his other business interests while Mr Bairnson, who was Mrs Tait's brother, became the sole proprietor trading under Bairnson Bros., whose head office was in Glasgow.

This new industry provided employment for many young women and at one time the workforce numbered 20 people.[20]

The laundry provided a valuable service to the community until 1937 when a combination of the cost of replacing equipment, ill health and advancing age forced closure. In August 1937 a letter was sent to all customers informing them of the decision to discontinue trading. The business ceased on 25th September that same year. On 31st August, 1938, the firm of Bairnson Bros. was dissolved.[21]

Mr Tait then used the vacant building as a store and showroom for furniture and as a transport office. In addition to his furniture business Mr Tait had, in 1924, created a transport firm along with his sons Alex and George, and traded as R.W. Tait & Sons. The firm consisted of lorries, taxis, buses and large delivery vans which ran a weekly

Market Street from the Town Hall. Mid 1930s

service west and north. A petrol pump was installed between 4 Market Street and the Garrison Theatre. In 1930 a garage was built in St Sunniva Street (then Parkfield).

During the Second World War part of the ground floor of the former laundry was occupied by the Food Office, from where ration books were issued.

The first floor later became a sale room with Bertie Robertson, and later Harry Hay, being employed as the auctioneers. The top floor was used for storage.

In the 1950s Robert Tait's grandson, Bertie, demolished the old laundry chimney stack.

Both buildings were sold in 1960 to Zetland County Council to become council offices[22] and since 2016 these have been Lerwick Dental Practice.[23]

The Garrison Theatre

It was not built as a theatre but as a drill hall, gymnasium and school of arms by the 7th Volunteer Battalion The Gordon Highlanders, assisted by the Lerwick Gymnasium Trust and by public subscription. The Drill Hall Trust administered the building.[24]

On 22nd July, 1903, the memorial stone was laid with Masonic honours by Captain Commandant Moffatt of the battalion. A selection of coins and copies of the local newspapers were deposited in the cavity of the stone. In addition to providing a drill hall and headquarters for the volunteers, the gymnasium was accessible to local people.[25]

The drill hall was formally inaugurated by Vice Admiral Lord Charles Beresford on 17th September, 1904.[26]

Some years previously a scheme to provide a gymnasium had been suggested and with the formation of the Volunteer Corps this was now possible. A Gymnasium Club was formed in 1904 which was open to Shetland residents of both sexes and all ages. Running costs were met by grants from Zetland County Council, Lerwick Town Council and public donations. The club employed a qualified instructor and within three weeks of opening there were a total of 238 members.[27]

The 7th Volunteer Battalion became Territorials in 1908 and along with the Royal Naval Reserve men they drilled in the hall every winter. "Da dreel haal", as it became referred to, played a valuable role in the whole community, town and country. It was also used for Boy Scouts activities, school PE, boxing, fencing, sales of work, as an Up-Helly-A' hall, a venue for exhibitions and by badminton clubs.

Following the outbreak of war in 1914 Lerwick became an important naval base and the drill hall was required for wartime use.

After the war the TA was not in operation and the hall continued to be used for badminton, with the adjacent rooms let as offices, including estate offices for the Garth Estate.

Following mobilisation of the Territorial Army (TA) in 1939 the hall was requisitioned as headquarters for the Shetland Defence Battalion and later for the 7th Battalion Black Watch. The

The Garrison drill hall and gymnasium. 1904

population of Shetland doubled with the influx of servicemen and initially the building was used as an army meat store and canteen.

In 1940 the Entertainments National Service Association (ENSA) commandeered the hall as a theatre to entertain service personnel. For example, boxing matches were organised in which servicemen participated.[28]

It was soon dubbed the "Garrison Theatre". Following conversion to a proper theatre by the Royal Engineers and Pioneers it was officially named so when it reopened on 7th December, 1942. A new stage had been erected at the Market Street end to replace the temporary stage at the other end.[29] It was constantly filled to capacity as army personnel and locals alike were entertained by servicemen, touring concert parties, film shows and famous celebrities. In February 1943 the well-known stage and film comedian George Formby and his wife paid a flying visit[30] and in August the equally well-known and popular Gracie Fields entertained the troops.[31]

After the Second World War the Zetland Territorial Association leased the building to the education authority. In 1958 the stage was set back and raked seating for nearly 400 people was installed in the auditorium. Ownership passed to the Zetland County Council in 1966.

Responsibility for running the theatre passed from the education committee to the Islesburgh House committee on 1st April, 1974, and to the newly formed SIC Leisure and Recreation Department the following year. Islesburgh management committee provided input to the running of the theatre through the Garrison Theatre sub-committee.[32]

A complete refurbishment of the theatre was carried out in 1989 and the "Garrison" was reopened on 31st October, 1990, by SIC Convener Edward Thomason, OBE.

Islesburgh Trust became owner/operator from 1999 until April 2006 when the management and staff of the Garrison Theatre were transferred from the Islesburgh Trust to Shetland Islands Council, with Shetland Arts Trust (now Shetland Arts) taking over responsibility for its operation.

Despite the opening of Mareel in 2012, the 280-seat Garrison Theatre can facilitate the provision of a varied programme of community and professional shows, including live theatre, concerts, and pantomime.

Ganson Brothers

The name probably most associated with Market Street is Ganson. In 1882 work commenced on constructing the building that is now part of Market House. It consisted of shops, offices, flats, stables, grain and feeding stores.

The driving force was Robert Dowell Ganson who was born in Delting in 1855. He moved to Lerwick and, after working as a clerk for the procurator fiscal, he formed the business of carters and hirers along with his brother Thomas. Another brother, Laurence, joined them for a short time when he moved his ironmongers business from the foot of Reform Lane. Farm implements were then stocked along with horse harness and a saddler was employed. Laurence went south very soon afterwards.

The Ness of Sound farm was purchased, which Thomas managed, and milk was sold from Ganson Brothers dairy in Harbour Street. Additional premises were built in 1895 at the North Lodberry on the Esplanade, which they used until 1917.[33]

Within a few years the carriage hiring business had 20 horses available along with American buggies, dog-carts, pair and single-horse wagonettes, to mention but a few.

The business steadily grew and premises extended around the corner from Market Street into Harbour Street and most of lower Harbour Street when they built Brentham Place in 1903 and Brentham House on the upper end in 1910. It became the permanent residence of the Ganson family.

In 1911 the first motor vehicle became available for hire and the firm were now pioneers in motor transport. They became the agent for Ford cars and held the contract for the Royal Mail services until it was taken over by the General Post Office in 1947. They were also contracted to carry passengers to and from Sumburgh Airport for Fresson's Highland Airways. The business expanded over the years from horse-drawn carriages to a fleet of buses and Gansons became a household name in the process and the largest and most extensive hiring company in Shetland. The passenger carrying business was sold to John Leask & Son in either 1963 or '64.[34]

Brentham Place before Brentham House was built. 1904. Following a disastrous fire the year before, when the Union Bank on Commercial Street was completely destroyed, temporary accommodation for the bank was provided on the ground floor on Commercial Road.

Robert D. Ganson died in 1936 and, as both his brothers had passed away before him, the business passed to his son Robert, better known as Bertie, who had been responsible for the trucking section.

The long connection with the Ganson family ended in June 1973 when the premises was sold to Leask Motor Garage (Lerwick) Ltd who were there until 1995.[35]

Shetland Islands Council was the next owner and, after renovation, the building was used for various departments until 2003 when it became Market House, administered by Voluntary Action Shetland.[36]

From its early beginnings Market Street has developed from being simply a rough and ready track dotted with middens and pigsties to become an important hive of both business and entertainment activity and a desirable residential area of Lerwick.

Market House. 2021

REFERENCES

Perspective View of Lerwick from the North End
1. Donaldson Gordon, *Court Book of Shetland* (Lerwick 1991) p. 126
2. SA6/398/194
3. *The Shetland Times* July 31 2020 'From the Archives', words by Brian Smith and Allan Beattie
4. *The Gunner* Vol. XLI. No.2, February 1959 p. 49
5. SA4/2541/29 Brian Smith 'John Paul Jones and the Mousa Men' *Unkans*, November 29 2011, p. 4
6. *The Gunner* Vol. XLI. No.2, February 1959 p. 49
7. *The Shetland Times* April 14 1995
8. SA1/3/5 1682-92 Register of Sasines
9. It is the 6th building from the left
10. Tait E.S. Reid, *A Lerwick Miscellany* (Lerwick 1955) pp. 9-10
11. *Shetland Advertiser* November 24 1862
12. SA D1/619/8/3 Special edition of *The Shetland News* 'The Lerwick Paving Case' July 15 1898
13. Sandison William, *A Shetland Merchant's Day-Book in 1762* (Lerwick 1934) p. 69
14. SA4/523/1 January 8 1785
15. SA D1/619/8/3 Special edition of *The Shetland News* 'The Lerwick Paving Case' July 15 1898
16. SA SC12/6/1781/5
17. *The Shetland News* June 25 1887 Article 'Shetland During Queen Victoria's Reign'
18. SA4/523/1 February 29 1844
19. Robertson Margaret Stuart, *Sons and Daughters of Shetland 1800-1900* (Lerwick 1991) p. 116
20. *The Shetland News* June 25 1887 Article 'Shetland During Queen Victoria's Reign'
21. *The Shetland News* March 26 1898 Article 'Old Lerwick'
22. SAD6/117/11 March 2 1847
23. SA D1/619/8/3 Special Edition of *The Shetland News* 'The Lerwick Paving Case' July 15 1898
24. *The Shetland News* June 25 1887 Article 'Shetland During Queen Victoria's Reign'
25. Manson Thomas, *Lerwick During the last Half Century* (Lerwick 1923) p. 89

Naming Lerwick's Lanes, Closses and Courts
1. Jakobsen Jakob, *The Place-names of Shetland* (London 1936) p. 24
2. Tait E.S. Reid, *A Lerwick Miscellany* (Lerwick 1955) p. 38

3. Agreement and Disposition between the Heritors of Sound and the Feuars and Heritors of Lerwick (Lerwick 1909) pp. 4-16
4. SA TO/10/163 Great Seal charter erecting Lerwick into Burgh of Barony, February 10 1818
5. SA TO/3/1 Minutes of Commissioners of Police, February 14 1845
6. Bundle of papers in S.R.O. Charlotte Square, Edinburgh CS 235 M31/1
7. Nicolson James R., *Lerwick Harbour* (Lerwick 1977) pp. 28-29
8. *The Shetland Times* May 14 1938

Twageos Road and Lovers Loan
1. SA D1/619/8/3 Special edition of *The Shetland News* 'The Lerwick Paving Case' July 15 1898
2. SA GD150/257A/1 James Isaacson's chamberlain accounts with the Earl of Morton
3. Stewart John, *Shetland Place-names* (Lerwick 1987) p. 119

Leog Place and Leog Lane
1. Jakobsen Jakob, *An Entomological Dictionary of the Norn Language in Shetland Part II* (Lerwick 1985) p. 520
2. *Shetland Advertiser* November 24 1862
3. From notes by Margaret Stuart Robertson
4. SA Sasine dated September 22 1687
5. Information from Brian Smith SA
6. SA Sasine dated June 15 1757
7. SA1/14/3/24/p.8 *The Shetland News* June 11 1887
8. Grant F.J., *Zetland County Families* (Lerwick 1893) pp. 197-199
9. SA4/523/1 February 3 1816
10. Robertson Margaret Stuart, *Sons and Daughters of Shetland 1800-1900* (Lerwick 1991) p. 35
11. SA SC12/53/10/folio 231v dated October 23 1829
12. Knight G. Roger, *Empire in Early Nineteenth-Century South East Asia* (Suffolk 2015) p. 114
13. SA CO.8/1/10/10 Valuation Roll 1864-65
14. SA CO.8/1/13/1 Valuation roll 1867-68
15. *The New Shetlander* Summer Number No. 85 1968 pp. 17-18
16. SA4/523/5/December 10 1897
17. SA4/523/11 October 26 1953
18. *The New Shetlander* Summer Number No. 85 1968 p. 18
19. Author's personal knowledge
20. SA SIC1/8/4 Monthly report by Director of Social Work December 4 1978
21. SA SIC1/8/4 Minute of Social Work Committee December 4 1978

Copland's Pier
1. Manson Thomas, *Lerwick During the last Half Century* (Lerwick 1923) pp. 140-141
2. SA4/523/1 March 24 1815
3. Manson Thomas, *Lerwick During the last Half Century* (Lerwick 1923) pp. 140-141.
4. Robertson Margaret Stuart, *Sons and Daughters of Shetland 1800-1900* (Lerwick 1991) p. 55

5. *ibid.*, p.8
6. Graham John J. and Robertson T.A., *Nordern Lichts* (Lerwick 1964) p. 20
7. Tait E.S. Reid, *A Lerwick Miscellany* (Lerwick 1955) p. 2
8. Charter by the Commissioner of Thomas Earl of Zetland in favour of Dr James Copland dated May 27 1840
9. SA4/523/1 October 29 1857
10. SA12/6/1947/1
11. SA4/523/11 July 27 1951
12. SA TO11/64 August 13 1964
13. *The Shetland Times* November 20 2020
14. SA4/523/13 February 12 1961
15. *ibid.*, January 25 1964
16. SA4/523/14 July 5 1966
17. Lerwick Boating Club, *The First Hundred Years* (Lerwick 1980)
18. SA Valuation Rolls Lerwick, covering the years 1983-2000

Miss Chalmers Stair and Murray's Lodberry
1. Tait E.S. Reid, *A Lerwick Miscellany* (Lerwick 1955) p. 3
2. *The Shetland Times* September 13 1902
3. Smith Mark Ryan, *The Literature of Shetland* (Lerwick 2014)
4. Chalmers Margaret, Lerwick, Zetland *Poems* (Newcastle 1813)
5. Sandison William, *A Shetland Merchant's Day-Book in 1762* (Lerwick 1934) p. 14
6. SA Sasine July 8 1724 Robert Scollay from Dick of Wormadail (sic)
7. SA Sasine March 7 1758 Arthur Scollay for Patrick Torrie
8. Sutherland Paul J., *Morton Lodge No. 89, 250 years of a Lerwick Institution 1782-2012* (Lerwick 2012) pp. 5-7
9. SA Sasine September 9 1765 Patrick Torrie for Samuel Scollay
10. Robertson Margaret Stuart, *Sons and Daughters of Shetland 1899-1900* (Lerwick 1991) p. 176
11. *ibid.*, p. 196
12. SA D1/619/8/3 Special edition of *Shetland News* 'The Lerwick Paving Case' July 15 1898
13. *The Shetland News* March 26 1898 Article 'Old Lerwick'
14. SA D1/619/8/3 Special edition of *Shetland News* 'The Lerwick Paving Case' July 15 1898
15. SA Minute of Meeting of Lerwick Town Council October 12 1954
16. Robertson Margaret Stuart, *Sons and Daughters of Shetland 1899-1900* (Lerwick 1991) pp. 69 180
17. SA4/523/2 Disposition by Mrs Barbara Hay or Cheyne to Messrs John Hardie and William Sinclair, joiners in Lerwick August 11 1868
18. Manson Thomas, *Lerwick During the last Half Century* (Lerwick 1923) p. 139
19. SA4/523/1 April 28 1790
20. Charter by Thomas Laurenson dated February 22 1670 makes reference to the Meeting House being built by William Tyrie
21. *Shetland Advertiser* November 24 1862
22. Craven The Rev. J.B., *History of the Episcopal Church in Orkney 1688-1882* (Kirkwall 1883) p. 130

23. *Diary of the Rev. John Hunter Episcopal minister in Shetland, 1734-1745* reprinted from the Scottish Antiquary December 1891 p. 8.
24. Cant R.G., *The Medieval Churches and Chapels of Shetland* (Shetland Archaeological and Historical Society 1975) p. 19
25. From notes by Margaret Stuart Robertson
26. CS235 M31/1 Bundle of papers in S.R.O., Edinburgh.
27. SA1/3/5 Registered Sasines concerning Shetland 1674-1709
28. Information from Margaret Stuart Robertson
29. Information from A.W. Fox
30. Robertson Margaret Stuart, *Sons and Daughters of Shetland 1899-1900* (Lerwick 1991) p. 69
31. Manson Thomas, *Lerwick During the last Half Century* (Lerwick 1923) p. 6
32. Robertson Margaret Stuart, *Sons and Daughters of Shetland 1899-1900* (Lerwick 1991) pp. 69 180
33. Oral information Betty Simpson
34. Manson Thomas, *Lerwick During the last Half Century* (Lerwick 1923) p. 139
35. SA D1/619/8/3 Special edition of *Shetland News* 'The Lerwick Paving Case' July 15 1898
36. SA4/523/6 September 10 1903
37. *The People's Journal* June 23 1906
38. *The Shetland Times* July 14 1906
39. *ibid.*, June 2 1995
40. *ibid.*, December 31 2009
41. *ibid.*, June 2 1995
42. SA4/523/10
43. *The Shetland Times* June 2 1995
44. Oral information from A.W. Fox

Stout's Pier and Stout's Court
1. SA 833/29.1.1819
2. Manson Thomas, *Lerwick During the last Half Century* (Lerwick 1923) p. 140
3. The author's personal knowledge
4. Laurenson Graeme A., *Kiwi in the Shetland Scattald* (New Plymouth ND) pp. 100-106

Nice Court
1. SA November 5 1678 Sasine Laurence Williamson to William Richan
2. CS235 M31/1 Bundle of papers in S.R.O., Edinburgh.
3. Tait E.S. Reid, *A Lerwick Miscellany* (Lerwick 1955) p. 3
4. CS235 M31/1 Bundle of papers in S.R.O., Edinburgh
5. Sutherland Paul J., *Morton Lodge No. 89 250 years of a Lerwick Institution 1762-2012* (Lerwick 2012) pp. 21-22
6. *ibid.*, pp. 55-57
7. www.estateagencyshetland.co.uk/archive/1-hayfield-court
8. SA SC12/6/1856/12 September 19 1856
9. SA4/523/2 June 9 1863
10. SA4/523/3 November 25 1869

11. SA4/523/10 May 6 1943
12. The author's personal knowledge
13. *The Press and Journal* September 8 1997 Obituary for John (Jock) Hay
14. SA4/523/13 November 20 1961
15. SA4/523/13 August 9 1964
16. Related at Derick's funeral service
17. *The Press and Journal* September 8 1997 Obituary for John (Jock) Hay

Ross Court and Steamers' Store
1. Information from Margaret S. Robertson
2. Personal experience of the author and information from Diane Watt
3. SA4/523/1 March 18 1790
4. Robertson Margaret Stuart, *Sons and Daughters of Shetland 1800-1900* (Lerwick 1991) p. 165
5. SA4/523/1 July 6 1829
6. SA4/523/10 May 5 1949
7. SA4/523/11 July 12 1951
8. SA TO2/39 Minutes of meeting of Lerwick Town Council Housing Committee May 2 1957
9. SA TO1/16 Meeting of Lerwick Town Council June 11 and December 3 1963
10. SA4/523/1 July 6 1829
11. *ibid.*, August 14 1839
12. *ibid.*, November 3 1843
13. Oral information from Peter McKenzie
14. Robertson Margaret Stuart, *Sons and Daughters of Shetland 1800-1900* (Lerwick 1991) pp. 117-118
15. Manson Thomas, *Lerwick During the last Half Century* (Lerwick 1923) p. 30
16. Tait E.S. Reid, *A Lerwick Miscellany* (Lerwick 1955) pp. 39-40
17. *The Shetland News* January 29 1898 p. 5
18. Manson Thomas, *Lerwick During the last Half Century* (Lerwick 1923) p. 139
19. Personal experience of the author
20. Nicolson James R., *Lerwick Harbour* (Lerwick 1977) p. 17
21. *ibid.*, p. 14
22. *The Shetland Times* February 1 1908
23. *ibid.*, pp. 28-29.
24. SA4/523/13 January 6 1961
25. The lodberry is now owned jointly by the Smith Brothers and the author
26. Donaldson Gordon, *Northwards by Sea* (Lerwick 1978) pp. 21-22
27. Nicolson James R., *Lerwick Harbour* (Lerwick 1977) pp. 14-16
28. SA4/523/5 December 15 1897
29. *The Shetland Times* December 30 1899
30. Nicolson James R., *Lerwick Harbour* (Lerwick 1977) pp. 148-150
31. Oral information from Alex Smith

Craigie's Court and the Craigie Stane
1. Sandison William, *A Shetland Merchant's Day-Book in 1762* (Lerwick 1934) p. 24
2. *The Shetland News* March 26 1898 Article 'Old Lerwick'

3. Information from Dr Ian Tait Shetland Museum and Archives
4. SA4/523/1 April 23 1818
5. SA SC12/53/12/ Disposition and settlement by Captain John Craigie March 18 1855
6. Manson Thomas, *Lerwick During the last Half Century* (Lerwick 1923) p. 6
7. *ibid.*, p. 138
8. SA4/523/10 October 17 1946
9. Press and broadcast notice Post Office Telecommunications March 21 1975
10. *The Shetland Times* March 28 1975
11. Historic Scotland, Shetland Islands Council Lerwick Burgh 12.08.1996 9. 19
12. Information from Grant Gilfillan, SIC Property and Asset Department

The Lodberrie
1. Wonders William C., 'The Lodberries of Lerwick' *Scottish Geographical Magazine* vol. III No.2 p. 91 1995 (This article indicates that James's son, George, built the lodberry but this cannot be accurate as he was only born in 1771)
2. Disposition by Miss Adelaide Beatrice Catherine Hunter in favour of Thomas Moncrieff 1961
3. Tait E.S. Reid, *A Lerwick Miscellany* (Lerwick 1955) p. 40
4. SA AD22/1011925/26 report concerning the destruction by fire of shop at 22 Commercial Street, occupied by Frederick Irvine, Knowe, Lerwick November 30 1925; December 7 1925
5. Oral information from Erik Moncrieff
6. For a detailed history see Sinclair Douglas M., *Old Lerwick People and Places* (Lerwick 2017) pp. 65-68

Sands' Court, Raven's Court and Water Lane
1. Tait E.S. Reid, *A Lerwick Miscellany* (Lerwick 1955) p. 4
2. Robertson Margaret Stuart, *Sons and Daughters of Shetland 1800-1900* (Lerwick 1991) p. 10
3. Tait E.S. Reid, *A Lerwick Miscellany* (Lerwick 1955) p. 4
4. Oral information from Tammie Moncrieff
5. SA TO2/39 Housing Committee Minutes January 1953 to November 1961
6. *The Shetland News* March 5 1898 Article 'Old Lerwick'
7. *The New Shetlander* Yule Number 270 2014
8. Oral information from Erik Moncrieff
9. *The Shetland Times* July 1970

Chromate Lane
1. Information from Margaret Stuart Robertson
2. Manson Thomas, *Lerwick During the last Half Century* (Lerwick 1923) p. 166

Seafield Court
1. Information from Margaret Stuart Robertson
2. SA4/523/27 April 1778
3. SA4/523/1 November 20 1787

4. SA4/523/1 January 23 1836
5. SA SC12/53/7 September 2 1845
6. Manson Thomas, *Lerwick During the last Half Century* (Lerwick 1923) p. 135
7. Robertson Margaret Stuart, *Sons and Daughters of Shetland 1800-1900* (Lerwick 1991) p.230
8. SA4/523/2 October 8 1866
9. SA4/523/1 May 2 1836
10. Information from Margaret Stuart Robertson
11. SA4/523/1 December 31 1845
12. SA4/523/2 June 5 1863
13. *ibid.*, July 24 1863
14. *ibid.*, December 1 1866
15. SA4/523/9 January 2 1935
16. Personal experience of the author and oral information from Bruce Scott

Scottshall Court
1. SA4/523/1 August 4 1790
2. Robertson Margaret Stuart, *Sons and Daughters of Shetland 1800-1900* (Lerwick 1991) p. 136
3. Manson Thomas, *Lerwick During the last Half Century* (Lerwick 1923) pp. 135-136
4. *The Shetland Times* September 25 1992

Church Lane and Queens Lane
1. *The Shetland News* March 26 1898 Article 'Old Lerwick'
2. SA4/523/1 September 23 1852
3. SA D1/619/8/3 Special edition of *Shetland News* 'The Lerwick Paving Case' July 15 1898
4. *The Shetland News* March 26 1898 Article 'Old Lerwick'

Spence's Court
1. SA Instrument of Sasine dated 27.10.1671 in favour of Daniell Fraser and Christiane Sinclair his spouse
2. Manson Thomas, *Lerwick During the last Half Century* (Lerwick 1923) p. 10
3. SA Instrument of Sasine dated 24.09.1680 in favour of Henry Smyth, litster and Jean Tyre his spouse.
4. *The Shetland News* August 30 1890
5. *Shetland Advertiser* October 13 1862
6. *The Shetland News* August 8 1885
7. *The Shetland Times* March 4 1958

Crooked Lane
1. SA Instrument of Sasine dated March 9 1667 in favour of Gilbert Mouat, cordiner and Katherine Sutherland his spouse following Charter by John Neven of Lunning
2. Manson Thomas, *Lerwick During the last Half Century* (Lerwick 1923) pp. 174-175
3. *The Shetland News* August 18 1885

4. Tait E.S. Reid, *A Lerwick Miscellany* (Lerwick 1955) p. 7
5. *The Shetland Times* March 26 1881

Norna's Court
1. Tait E.S. Reid, *A Lerwick Miscellany* (Lerwick 1955) p. 7
2. Scott Sir Walter, *The Pirate* (London 1904) p. 454
3. Scott Sir Walter, *Northern Lights* ed. William F. Laughlan (Hawick 1982) pp. 26-48

Gardie Court
1. Duncan Wm. Rae, *Zetland Directory* (Aberdeen 1854)
2. *The Shetland Times* April 2 1907
3. Tait E.S. Reid, *A Lerwick Miscellany* (Lerwick 1955) p. 8
4. *The Shetland News* February 19 1942
5. SA4/523/4 May 4 1879
6. SA4/523/1 December 18 1798
7. *The Shetland News* March 6 1886
8. *ibid.*, April 2 1898 Article 'Old Lerwick'
9. *ibid.*, August 18 1885
10. SA Instrument of Sasine dated 11.03.1656 in favour of Laurence Umphray of Sand
11. *The Shetland Times* December 9 1958
12. *The Shetland News* October 21 1958

Heddell's Court
1. Sandison William, *A Shetland Merchant's Day-Book in 1762* (Lerwick 1934) p. 41
2. Grant Francis J., *The County Families of the Zetland Islands* (Lerwick 1893) p. 121
3. *The Shetland Times* April 21 1888
4. *ibid.*, January 12 1889
5. *The Shetland News* July 29 1893
6. *Mansons' Shetland Almanac* 1900
7. *The Shetland Times* December 9 1949
8. Valuation Roll Lerwick 1968-69
9. *The Shetland Times* October 15 1976
10. *ibid.*, April 6 1979
11. *ibid.*, April 14 2006
12. *ibid.*, May 14 2006

Heddell's Park
1. SA Minutes of Lerwick Town Council September 26 1955
2. Oral information from John Gray
3. SA TO2/39 Minutes of Housing Committee 6.1.53 to 20.11.61
4. Author's personal experience
5. Oral information from young folk

The Market Cross
1. SASC12/53/11/folio 67v Decreet December 21 1838. Engrossed March 11 1839
2. Manson Thomas, *Lerwick During the last Half-Century* (Lerwick 1923) p. 185
3. Sandison William, *A Shetland Merchant's Day-Book in 1762* (Lerwick 1934) pp. 41-44
4. Tait E.S. Reid, *A Lerwick Miscellany* (Lerwick 1955) p. 8
5. Manson Thomas, *Lerwick During the last Half-Century* (Lerwick 1923) p. 14
6. Tait E.S. Reid, *A Lerwick Miscellany* (Lerwick 1955) p. 42
7. *ibid.*, p.67
8. SA Commissioners of Police Minutes February 23 1871 p. 173
9. *Shetland Life* Number 83 September 1987 p. 29
10. Manson Thomas, *Lerwick During the last Half-Century* (Lerwick 1923) p. 16
11. Nicolson James R., *Lerwick Harbour* (Lerwick 1977) p. 123
12. *The New Shetlander* Simmer Issue Number 288 2019
13. *The Shetland Times* November 20 1875
14. *ibid.*, February 21 1997
15. *ibid.*, March 21 1997
16. *ibid.*, May 23 1997

Mounthooly Street
1. Tait E.S. Reid, *A Lerwick Miscellany* (Lerwick 1955) p. 8
2. Manson Thomas, *Lerwick During the last Half Century* (Lerwick 1923) p. 184
3. SA TO/11/260 Lerwick Town Council file concerning Buildings Mounthooly Street 1955-1957
4. SA/A19 Mounthooly Street Housing Scheme
5. Tait E.S. Reid, *A Lerwick Miscellany* (Lerwick 1955) p. 8
6. SA D6/294/2/ p. 306 printed notice by John Bannatyne that he has commenced work as a baker in Lerwick, November 15 1831.
7. SA4/523/1 September 13 1838
8. Robertson Margaret Stuart, *Sons and Daughters of Shetland 1800-1900* (Lerwick 1991) p. 88
9. *The Shetland News* March 8 1913
10. *Mansons' Shetland Almanac* 1894
11. *ibid.*, 1899
12. SA4/523/7 August 30 1909
13. SA4/523/8 May 29 1924
14. *The Shetland Times* February 15 1930
15. SA4/523/10 July 29 1940
16. Information from Leslie Irvine
17. *The Shetland Times* February 4 1972
18. Information from Leslie Irvine and the author's personal knowledge
19. Tait E.S. Reid, *A Lerwick Miscellany* (Lerwick 1955) p. 67
20. Manson Thomas, *Lerwick During the last Half Century* (Lerwick 1923) p. 176
21. Tait E.S. Reid, *A Lerwick Miscellany* (Lerwick 1955) p. 68
22. *ibid.*, pp. 104-105
23. *The Shetland Times* October 17 1885 and December 12 1885
24. SA TO/2/39 Lerwick Town Council Minutes
25. Oral information from Dennis Coutts

Navy Lane, Baker's Court and Wren Court
1. Tait E.S. Reid, *A Lerwick Miscellany* (Lerwick 1955) p. 9
2. Manson Thomas, *Lerwick During the last Half Century* (Lerwick 1923) p. 184
3. *The Shetland News* June 8 1907
4. Manson Thomas, *Lerwick During the last Half Century* (Lerwick 1923) p. 188
5. Tait E.S. Reid, *A Lerwick Miscellany* (Lerwick 1955) p. 9
6. Oral information from Margaret Stuart Robertson
7. SA4/325/1 December 7 1848
8. Manson Thomas, *Lerwick During the last Half Century* (Lerwick 1923) p. 188
9. Nicolson James R., *Lerwick Harbour* (Lerwick 1977) p. 15
10. Manson Thomas, *Lerwick During the last Half Century* (Lerwick 1923) p. 189
11. Disposition on the sequestrated estate of the late Gilbert Duncan in favour of James Hughson, shipmaster November 17 1847
12. *The Shetland Times* July 5 1996
13. Tait E.S. Reid, *A Lerwick Miscellany* (Lerwick 1955) p. 104
14. Manson Thomas, *Lerwick During the last Half Century* (Lerwick 1923) p. 189
15. SA TO/11/260 Lerwick Town Council file concerning Buildings Mounthooly Street 1955-1957
16. SA/A19 Mounthooly Street Housing Scheme
17. *A Century of Witness 1885-1985 Ebenezer Hall Navy Lane Lerwick* (Lerwick 1985)
18. *The Shetland News* July 19 1917

Law Lane
1. Manson Thomas, *Lerwick During the last Half Century* (Lerwick 1923) p. 193
2. SA TO/11/166 File regarding Prospect House 1963
3. *The Shetland Times* October 30 1992
4. *ibid.*, November 13 1992
5. *ibid.*, January 8 1993
6. *ibid.*, September 10 1993
7. *ibid.*, September 24 1993
8. Manson Thomas, *Lerwick During the last Half Century* (Lerwick 1923) p. 193
9. Robertson Margaret Stuart, *Sons and Daughters of Shetland 1800-1900* (Lerwick 1991) p. 193
10. Manson Thomas, *Lerwick During the last Half Century* (Lerwick 1923) p. 192
11. Disposition Mrs Helen Mill alias Tucker daughter and apparent sole heir of the said John Mill in favour of James Greig dated June 14 1813
12. Disposition by the Testamentary Trustees of the late Mrs Mary Spalding Cowie or Christie and the late Mrs Roberta Cowie or Nichols in favour of Henry Ratter Gilbertson March 1 1952
13. Robertson Margaret Stuart, *Sons and Daughters of Shetland 1800-1900* (Lerwick 1991) p. 175
14. Manson Thomas, *Lerwick During the last Half Century* (Lerwick 1923) p. 192
15. Robertson Margaret Stuart, *Sons and Daughters of Shetland 1800-1900* (Lerwick 1991) p. 175

Albert Court
1. Tait E.S. Reid, *A Lerwick Miscellany* (Lerwick 1955) p. 9
2. Manson Thomas, *Lerwick During the last Half Century* (Lerwick 1923) pp. 61-62
3. *The Shetland Times* December 28 1889 and July 12 1890
4. *ibid.,* May 7 1898
5. *ibid.,* September 5 1903
6. *ibid.,* January 9 1904
7. *ibid.,* January 19 1907
8. Manson Thomas, *Lerwick During the last Half Century* (Lerwick 1923) p. 190
9. SATO/1/16/ Minutes of Lerwick Town Council April 14 1964

Pirate Lane
1. *The Shetland News* February 5 1898 Article 'Old Lerwick'

Hangcliff Lane
1. Tait E.S. Reid, *A Lerwick Miscellany* (Lerwick 1955) pp. 58-59
2. *The Shetland Times* May 6 and August 26 1905
3. SAD1/133 Scrapbook James Shand, Broughty Ferry p. 39
4. Manson Thomas, *Lerwick During the last Half-Century* (Lerwick 1923) pp. 19-20
5. Oral information from Arnie Arcus and author's personal experience

Swallow Lane, later Bank Lane
1. Tait E.S. Reid, *A Lerwick Miscellany* (Lerwick 1955) pp. 10-11
2. *The Shetland News* March 5 1898
3. Manson Thomas, *Lerwick During the last Half Century* (Lerwick 1923) p. 202
4. Mitchell C.E., *Up-Helly-AA Tar-barrels and guizing looking back* (Lerwick 1948) p. 43
5. Manson Thomas, *Lerwick During the last Half Century* (Lerwick 1923) p. 203
6. Brown C.G., *Up-Helly-AA Custom, culture and community in Shetland* (Manchester 1998) p. 128
7. *The Shetland Times* May 16 1903
8. Report by James Charles Superintendent of Police to Police Commissioners August 15 1873
9. *The Shetland Times* July 4 1925
10. *The Shetland News* October 4 1945

Mariners' Court
1. Edmondston Thos., *An etymological glossary of the Shetland & Orkney Dialect* (Edinburgh 1866) p. 94.
2. Jakobsen Jakob, *An etymological Dictionary of the Norn Language in Shetland* Part II, Shetland Folk Society (Lerwick 1985) p. 730
3. Brown Callum G., *Up-Helly-AA, custom, culture and community in Shetland* (Manchester 1998) p. 90.
4. Mitchell C.E., *Up-Helly-AA Tar-barrels and guizing looking back* (Lerwick 1948) p. 65.
5. *ibid.,* pp. 67-68.
6. *The Shetland Times* August 28 1886

7. SA Minutes of Commissioners of Police 10 December 1886 p. 563.
8. Margaret S. Robertson, *Sons and Daughters of Shetland 1800-1900* (Lerwick 1991) p. 119.
9. Manson Thomas, *Lerwick During the last Half Century* (Lerwick 1923) p. 34
10. *The Shetland News* June 9 1888
11. Manson Thomas, *Lerwick During the last Half Century* (Lerwick 1923) p. 34
12. *The Shetland Times* 21 November, 1936
13. *Mansons' Shetland Almanac 1892*. The address of the shop is given as Lower Reform Lane.
14. Tait E.S. Reid, *A Lerwick Miscellany* (Lerwick 1955) pp. 81-87.
15. *The Shetland Times* December 29 1888

Reform Lane
1. Tait E.S. Reid, *A Lerwick Miscellany* (Lerwick 1955) p. 11
2. Manson Thomas, *Lerwick During the last Half Century* (Lerwick 1923) p. 37

Park Lane
1. Manson Thomas, *Lerwick During the last Half Century* (Lerwick 1923) p. 209

Pitt Lane
1. Tait E.S. Reid, *A Lerwick Miscellany* (Lerwick 1955) p. 12
2. SA4/523/1 October 9 1819
3. *The Shetland Times* November 18 1882
4. Manson Thomas, *Lerwick During the last Half Century* (Lerwick 1923) p. 42
5. Nicolson James R., *Lerwick Harbour* (Lerwick 1977) p. 51
6. *The Shetland Times* November 18 1882
7. *The Shetland News* May 9 2017

Kelday's Court
1. Manson Thomas, *Lerwick During the last Half Century* (Lerwick 1923) pp. 43-45
2. *The Shetland Times* March 17 1950
3. *ibid.*, May 16 1980
4. *ibid.*, January 14 1994

Quendale Lane
1. Tait E.S. Reid, *A Lerwick Miscellany* (Lerwick 1955) p. 13
2. *ibid.*, p. 69
3. SA4/523/3 November 18 1875
4. Manson Thomas, *Lerwick During the last Half Century* (Lerwick 1923) p. 212
5. Advertisement in Official Guide to Lerwick 1914
6. SA3/2/42/2 Interview with Lindsay Robertson 1983
7. Oral information from Alma Stove

Fox Lane
1. Tait E.S. Reid, *A Lerwick Miscellany* (Lerwick 1955) p. 15
2. *The Press & Journal* February 19 1969 and February 26 1973

References 209

3. SA AD22/2/3/51 March 25 1858 Precognition: Death of Peter Williamson and Family, Lerwick
4. *The Spectator* April 19 1858
5. Manson Thomas, *Lerwick During the last Half Century* (Lerwick 1923) p. 50
6. SA/4/523/1 May 18 1858
7. Information from Martin Emslie
8. Oral information from Hilda Halcrow

Pilot Place, now Pilot Lane
1. Tait E.S. Reid, *A Lerwick Miscellany* (Lerwick 1955) p. 13
2. *The Shetland News* July 30 and August 6 1887 'Old Lerwick Families'
3. Manson Thomas, *Lerwick During the last Half Century* (Lerwick 1923) p. 212

Burns Lane
1. *The Shetland News* July 30 & August 6 1887
2. SA SC12/6/1888/5
3. Manson Thomas, *Lerwick During the last Half Century* (Lerwick 1923) pp. 53-54
4. *The Shetland Times* February 23 1878

Hill Lane
1. *The Shetland Times* June 20 1931
2. *Mansons' Shetland Almanacs* 1947-51
3. Manson Thomas, *Lerwick During the last Half Century* (Lerwick 1923) pp. 217-218

Back Charlotte Lane
1. Tait E.S. Reid, *A Lerwick Miscellany* (Lerwick 1955) p. 14
2. Report by Superintendent of Police James Charles to Commissioners of Police July 18 1873

Charlotte Street
1. Tait E.S. Reid, *A Lerwick Miscellany* (Lerwick 1955) p. 14
2. *The Shetland Times* June 1922 Article 'Lerwick 1872 and After'
3. Manson Thomas, *Lerwick During the last Half Century* (Lerwick 1923) p. 69

Tollbooth Quay, Hay's Corner and the Towbooth Walk
1. Nicolson James R., *Hay & Company Merchants in Shetland* (Lerwick 1982) p. 3
2. Nicolson James R., *Lerwick Harbour* (Lerwick 1977) p. 91
3. Tait E.S. Reid, *A Lerwick Miscellany* (Lerwick 1955) p. 6

Mouat's Lodberry
1. SA4/523/1 August 1 1798
2. Manson Thomas, *Lerwick During the last Half Century* (Lerwick 1923) p. 9
3. Tait E.S. Reid, *A Lerwick Miscellany* (Lerwick 1955) p. 41
4. SA4/523/4 April 2 1885
5. SA AD22/101/1898/29 May 30 1898
6. Oral information from Jim Burgess

Clark's Court
1. SA4/523/1 September 13 1796
2. Sandison William, *A Shetland Merchant's Day-Book in 1762* (Lerwick 1934) p. 39
3. SA4/523/1 January 18 1813
4. SA4/523/1/ November 26 1834
5. *ibid.*, November 18 1856
6. SA4/2540/297
7. *The Shetland Times* December 24 1987
8. Gray Alison, *Circle of Light The history of the Catholic Church in Orkney since 1560* (Edinburgh 2000) p. 65
9. *John o' Groats Journal* March 17 1864
10. *The Shetland Times* December 14 1987
11. SA4/523/1 November 3 1870
12. Manson Thomas, *Lerwick During the last Half Century* (Lerwick 1923) p. 9
13. SA4/523/1 November 18 1873
14. Manson Thomas, *Lerwick During the last Half Century* (Lerwick 1923) p. 133
15. SA4/523/1 March 26 1879
16. Rollo D., *The History of the Orkney and Shetland Volunteers and Territorials 1791-1958* (Lerwick 1958) p. 18
17. *The Shetland Times* December 14 1896
18. SA D25/168/14
19. *The Shetland Times* December 15 1877
20. SA D25/168/14
21. *The Shetland Times* December 26 1903
22. *The Shetland News* January 11 1923
23. Report by the Council of the Shetland Literary and Scientific Society September 30 1944
24. SA CO5/2/38 ZCC Library Sub-Committee
25. *The Shetland Times* June 29 1966
26. Personal knowledge of author
27. Oral information from Aileen Robertson
28. Notes from agendas and minutes of Lerwick Club
29. Oral information from John Shearer
30. Information from Irene and Paul Rutherford
31. *The Shetland Times* March 31 2016
32. *Mansons' Shetland Almanacs*
33. Oral information from Brenda Westmoreland

Sinclair's Steps and Greig's Pier
1. Tait E.S. Reid, *A Lerwick Miscellany* (Lerwick 1955) p. 6
2. SA4/523/1 April 24 1818
3. Disposition by the Trustees for the creditors and younger children of James Ross of Quarff Lodge, Merchant, Lerwick in favour of Robert Sinclair, Merchant, Lerwick August 19 1811
4. Tait E.S. Reid, *A Lerwick Miscellany* (Lerwick 1955) p. 87
5. *The Shetland News* March 12 1898 Article 'Old Lerwick'

6. *ibid.*, March 26 1898 Article 'Old Lerwick'
7. SA4/523/1 December 24 1824
8. Tait E.S. Reid, *A Lerwick Miscellany* (Lerwick 1955) p. 41
9. Manson Thomas, *Lerwick During the last Half Century* (Lerwick 1923) p. 174
10. Tait E.S. Reid, *A Lerwick Miscellany* (Lerwick 1955) p. 7
11. SA4/523/6 April 9 1901
12. *ibid.*, May 15 1907
13. *The Shetland Times* May 7 1910
14. *ibid.*, February 28 2020

Leask's Lodberry
1. Robertson Margaret Stuart, *Sons and Daughters of Shetland 1800-1900* (Lerwick 1991) p. 143

Taylor's Steps and Taylor's Pier
1. Manson Thomas, *Lerwick During the last Half Century* (Lerwick 1923) p. 130
2. SA4/523/1 Disposition by Arthur Nicolson of Lochend in favour of Charles Ogilvy, Merchant in Lerwick November 17 1792
3. SA4/523/6 Dispositions by (No.1) Thomas Russell Stove and (No.2) Alfred Ernest Sturge Stove in favour of Peter Scott Goodlad, John James Coutts and James Mouat Goodlad December 15 1902
4. The artist was James Magnus Smith, house painter and decorator, Lyndhurst House, Fort Road, Lerwick
5. Oral information Capt. Michael Gray
6. Oral information Tammie Moncrieff

Victoria Wharf
1. Robertson Margaret Stuart, *Sons and Daughters of Shetland 1800-1900* (Lerwick 1991) p. 35
2. *ibid.*, p. 131
3. SA4/523/1 September 1 1785
4. SA Ballantyne John, Court of Session Papers Rough guide to post 1600 material relating to Shetland CS.238.B/7/59 May 14 1791
5. Manson Thomas, *Lerwick During the last Half Century* (Lerwick 1923) p. 128
6. Tait E.S. Reid, *A Lerwick Miscellany* (Lerwick 1955) p. 42
7. Manson Thomas, *Lerwick During the last Half Century* (Lerwick 1923) pp. 254-256
8. Nicolson James R., *Lerwick Harbour* (Lerwick 1977) p. 29
9. Donaldson Gordon, *Northwards by Sea* (Lerwick 1978) p. 114
10. Robson Adam, *The Saga of the Earls* (Lerwick 2002) pp. 134-147
11. Tait E.S. Reid, *A Lerwick Miscellany* (Lerwick 1955) pp. 124-125
12. Donaldson Gordon, *Northwards by Sea* (Lerwick 1978) p. 15
13. *ibid.*, pp. 147-149
14. Nicolson James R., *Lerwick Harbour* (Lerwick 1977) p. 153
15. *ibid.*, p. 170
16. Donaldson Gordon, *Northwards by Sea* (Lerwick 1978) p. 91
17. Nicolson James R., *Lerwick Harbour* (Lerwick 1987) p. 186

Trance Closs
1. Tait E.S. Reid, *A Lerwick Miscellany* (Lerwick 1955) pp. 9-10
2. *Shetland Advertiser* November 24 1862
3. SA/523/1 November 5 1793
4. *ibid.*, November 13 1793
5. *ibid.*, December 17 1836
6. SA D1/619/8/3 Special edition of *The Shetland News* 'The Lerwick Paving Case' July 15 1898
7. *The Shetland Times* September 28 1973
8. Disposition by Mr John T. Irvine in fav. of Mr Robert Robertson 11 Nov. 1833
9. Duncan Wm. Rae, *Zetland Directory* (Aberdeen 1854)
10. SA D1/619/8/3 Special edition of *The Shetland News* 'The Lerwick Paving Case' July 15 1898
11. Information from Don Leslie

Irvine Closs
1. SA4/523/1 February 7 1798
2. Tait E.S. Reid, *A Lerwick Miscellany* (Lerwick 1955) p. 42
3. Nicolson James R., *Lerwick Harbour* (Lerwick 1977) p. 63
4. *The Shetland Times* '25 years ago' February 28 1997
5. Nicolson James R., *Lerwick Harbour* (Lerwick 1977) p. 189
6. *The Shetland Times* February 18 1994

Harrison Square
1. Robertson Margaret Stuart, *Sons and Daughters of Shetland 1800-1900* (Lerwick 1991) p.70
2. Duncan Wm. Rae, *Zetland Directory* (Aberdeen 1854)
3. Manson Thomas, *Lerwick During the last Half Century* (Lerwick 1923) p. 30
4. Lerwick Census 1871
5. *The Shetland News* October 8 1904 p. 4
6. Oral information from John Evans

Lower Tait's Closs, now Reform Lane
1. Tait E.S. Reid, *A Lerwick Miscellany* (Lerwick 1955) p. 42
2. *ibid.*, pp. 83-86
3. *The Shetland Times* November 27 1875
4. Tait E.S. Reid, *A Lerwick Miscellany* (Lerwick 1955) p. 87

Angus Pier and Angus Closs
1. Robertson Margaret Stuart, *Sons and Daughters of Shetland 1800-1900* (Lerwick 1991) p. 8
2. Tait E.S. Reid, *A Lerwick Miscellany* (Lerwick 1955) p. 12

Mullay's Steps
1. Robertson Margaret Stuart, *Sons and Daughters of Shetland 1800-1900* (Lerwick 1991) p. 136

2. Manson Thomas, *Lerwick During the last Half Century* (Lerwick 1923) p. 39
3. Tait E.S. Reid, *A Lerwick Miscellany* (Lerwick 1955) p. 43

Peterson's Closs
1. Robertson Margaret Stuart, *Sons and Daughters of Shetland 1800-1900* (Lerwick 1991) p. 145
2. Tait E.S. Reid, *A Lerwick Miscellany* (Lerwick 1955) p. 11
3. *ibid.*, p. 43

Grierson's Lodberry
1. Nicolson James R., *Lerwick Harbour* (Lerwick 1977) p. 16
2. SA4/523/5 December 15 1897
3. *The Shetland Times* December 30 1899
4. Nicolson James R., *Lerwick Harbour* (Lerwick 1977) p. 186
5. *The Shetland Times* May 5 1978
6. *ibid.*, November 23 1979
7. *ibid.*, December 30 201179
8. *ibid.*, August 16 2020
9. Oral information from Peter Leask

Greig's Closs
1. Information from Erling J.F. Clausen 1980
2. Manson Thomas, *Lerwick During the last Half Century* (Lerwick 1923) p. 49
3. SA4/523/1 October 31 1843
4. Flinn Derek, *Travellers in a Bygone Shetland An Anthology* (Edinburgh 1989) p. 271
5. http://www.jgrae.co.uk/About-us/
6. *The Shetland News* June 30 1932
7. *The Shetland Times* February 11 1955
8. SA Valuation Roll Lerwick
9. *Shetland Visitor 1999*
10. Tait E.S. Reid, *A Lerwick Miscellany* (Lerwick 1955) pp. 43-44
11. Manson Thomas, *Lerwick During the last Half Century* (Lerwick 1923) p. 127

Campbell's Lane, now Campbell's Closs
1. SA4/523/1 October 31 1843
2. Manson Thomas, *Lerwick During the last Half Century* (Lerwick 1923) p. 125
3. Tait E.S. Reid, *A Lerwick Miscellany* (Lerwick 1955) p. 44

Nicolson's Closs
1. Duncan Wm. Rae, *Zetland Directory* (Aberdeen 1854)
2. Tait E.S. Reid, *A Lerwick Miscellany* (Lerwick 1955) p. 44
3. Smith Mark Ryan, *The Literature of Shetland* (Lerwick 2014) pp. 51-54
4. Manson Thomas, *Lerwick During the last Half Century* (Lerwick 1923) pp. 52-53
5. Oral information from Clive Henderson
6. SA Valuation Roll Lerwick 1988

Merran Moad's Steps
1. A case of lawburrows against Merran records her spouse as Andrew. (See footnote 5)
2. Manson Thomas, *Lerwick During the last Half Century* (Lerwick 1923) p. 220
3. *ibid.*, p. 123
4. SASC12/6/1799/16 Petition for lawburrows c. April 1799
5. Manson Thomas, *Lerwick During the last Half Century* (Lerwick 1923) p. 125
6. *ibid.*, pp.123-125

Tait's Lodberry
1. SA4/523/1 June 14 1860
2. Tait E.S. Reid, *A Lerwick Miscellany* (Lerwick 1955) pp. 44-45
3. Manson Thomas, *Lerwick During the last Half Century* (Lerwick 1923) p. 59
4. SA Valuation Roll Lerwick 1879-1880
5. *The Shetland Times* March 14 1885
6. SA1/14/2/17/ p. 5
7. SA4/523/5 December 15 1890
8. *The Shetland Times* April 25 1896
9. SABBCRS/1/8/4 Tape recording of Radio Shetland Coastal Forces Veterans May 1995
10. *The Shetland Times* May 30 1947
11. Oral information from Billy Kay
12. SA4/523/12 September 14 1956
13. *The Shetland Times* January 14 1994

Muir's Steps and Osy Anderson's Pier
1. *Mansons' Shetland Almanacs*
2. Tait E.S. Reid, *A Lerwick Miscellany* (Lerwick 1955) p. 45
3. Manson Thomas, *Lerwick During the last Half Century* (Lerwick 1923) p. 123
4. Duncan Wm. Rae, *Zetland Directory* (Aberdeen 1854)
5. Robertson Margaret Stuart, *Sons and Daughters of Shetland 1800-1900* (Lerwick 1991) p. 116
6. Manson Thomas, *Lerwick During the last Half Century* (Lerwick 1923) p. 59

Charlotte Place
1. Tait E.S. Reid, *A Lerwick Miscellany* (Lerwick 1955) pp. 45 and 137
2. Manson Thomas, *Lerwick During the last Half Century* (Lerwick 1923) p. 61
3. *The Shetland Times* June 9 1906
4. Tait E.S. Reid, *A Lerwick Miscellany* (Lerwick 1955) p. 45
5. Manson Thomas, *Lerwick During the last Half Century* (Lerwick 1923) p. 123

The North Lodberry
1. SA4/523/1 November 8 1851
2. *ibid.*, April 30 1853
3. Tait E.S. Reid, *A Lerwick Miscellany* (Lerwick 1955) p. 45
4. SA4/523/4 December 18 1884
5. Manson Thomas, *Lerwick During the last Half Century* (Lerwick 1923) p. 122

References

6. *ibid.*, p. 43
7. SA4/523/5 May 20 1890
8. SA4/523/5 June 20 1892
9. *The Shetland Times* December 28 1895
10. *ibid.*, July 3 1909
11. SA4/325/6 November 16 1900
12. *The Shetland Times* December 29 1906
13. *Aberdeen Press and Journal* January 14 1916
14. *The Shetland News* January 20 1916
15. SA4/523/7 January 24 1916
16. SA4/523/7 April 20 1917
17. *The Shetland News* June 11 1952
18. SA4/523/8 March 11 1922
19. SA4/523/8 April 2 1920
20. SA4/523/9 March 11 1932
21. SA Valuation Roll Lerwick 1977-78
22. *Aberdeen Press and Journal* June 7 1978
23. Oral information from Mary Jamieson
24. Oral information from Janet Davidge

Tod's Steps
1. Oral information, Damien Ristori
2. *The Shetland News* August 21 1919
3. Nicolson James R., *Lerwick Harbour* (Lerwick 1977) p. 64
4. *The Shetland News* June 11 1952
5. *The Shetland Times* February 18 1994
6. SA Valuation Roll Lerwick 1915-16
7. SA4/523/7 April 20 1917
8. Nicolson James R., *Lerwick Harbour* (Lerwick 1977) p. 108
9. SA4/523/8 March 11 1922
10. *The Shetland News* June 11 1952
11. Oral information from Tammy and Hamish Balfour
12. *The Shetland Times* '25 years ago' February 28 1997
13. Oral information from Anna and George Hepburn

The Esplanade
1. SA Valuation Roll Lerwick 1988-89
2. *ibid.*, 1999-2000
3. *The Shetland Times* November 18 1876
4. Nicolson James R., *Lerwick Harbour* (Lerwick 1977) pp. 22-25
5. *ibid.*, 27-28
6. *The Shetland Times* February 22 1896
7. Manson Thomas, *Lerwick During the last Half Century* (Lerwick 1923) pp. 16-17
8. Nicolson James R., *Lerwick Harbour* (Lerwick 1977) p. 63
9. Smith Charles Edward, *From The Deep Of The Sea An epic of the Arctic* (Edinburgh 1977) p. 274

10. *ibid.*, p. 272
11. *The Shetland Times* May 26 1890
12. Oral information from Diana Peterson
13. SA Valuation Roll Lerwick 1903-1904
14. Nicolson James R., *Lerwick Harbour* (Lerwick 1977) p. 65
15. *ibid.*, p. 140
16. Lodestar is a star that is used to guide the course of a ship, especially the North Star
17. Oral information from Barbara Smith
18. *The Shetland News* March 28 2015
19. *The Shetland Times* June 11 2010

Gullet's Brae
1. SA SC12/6/1858/18
2. *The Shetland Times* January 6 1877
3. SA SC D6/295/1
4. Manson Thomas, *Lerwick During the last Half-Century* (Lerwick 1923) p. 191
5. *The Shetland Times* October 1 1938
6. Mackay James A., *Island Postal History Series No. 8 SHETLAND* p. 24
7. Duncan Wm. Rae, *Zetland Directory* (Aberdeen 1854)
8. Manson Thomas, *Lerwick During the last Half-Century* (Lerwick 1923) p. 8
9. Smith Charles Edward, *From the Deep of the Sea* (Edinburgh 1977) p. 215
10. Shetland Family History Database
11. SA D1/133 Scrapbook by James Shand, Broughty Ferry p. 39

Whisky Lane
1. *Shetland Life* October 1984 p. 33
2. Mitchell C.E., *Up-Helly-AA Tar-barrels and guizing looking back* (Lerwick 1948) p. 19
3. Manson Thomas, *Lerwick During the last Half-Century* (Lerwick 1923) p. 244
4. *The Shetland Times* August 18 1877
5. Manson Thomas, *Lerwick During the last Half-Century* (Lerwick 1923) p. 137
6. *The Press & Journal* September 18 1996
7. *ibid.*, p. 245
8. *Shetland Life* October 1984 p. 33
9. *ibid.*, p.103
10. *The New Shetlander* Yule Number 1965 pp. 26-28
11. *The Shetland News* April 27 1901
12. *ibid.*, September 3 1904
13. *Shetland Life* October 1984 No. 48 pp. 33-35
14. *Mansons' Shetland Almanacs* 1923-1932
15. *The Shetland News* January 28 1932
16. Oral information from Robert L. Johnson
17. SA Valuation Rolls Lerwick 1962-82
18. Oral information from Ertie Fullerton
19. Oral information from Ian Anderson
20. *The Shetland Times* November 6 1915

21. *The Edinburgh Gazette* September 6 1938
22. Oral information from Margaret Fraser and Bertie Tait
23. *The Shetland News* January 16 2016
24. *Islesburgh House 1945-1980* (Lerwick 1980)
25. *The Shetland News* July 25 1903
26. *ibid.*, September 24 1904
27. *The Shetland Times* December 3 1904
28. *The Shetland News* March 13 1941
29. *ibid.*, December 10 1942
30. *ibid.*, February 4 1943
31. *ibid.*, August 26 1943
32. *Islesburgh House 1945-1980* (Lerwick 1980)
33. *The Shetland Times* February 22 1936
34. Jamieson Gordon M., *Shetland Buses In the 20th Century* (Cumbria 2000) p. 122 & 128
35. Oral information from Alexis Tulloch
36. *ibid.*, Catherine Hughson

INDEX

Page numbers in *italics* refer to captions.

Aberdeen Savings Bank *see* TSB
Aberdeen, William xii, 62
Abernethy, Mitchell 184
Adam, H. C. 103
Aitken, John M. 12, 187, 189
Albert Building 145, *165*, *168*
Albert Café 74
Albert Court 74–75, *74*
Albert Court House 73, 74, 75, *75*
Albert Hotel 74, 75
Albert Place 143
Albert Wharf 127
Alder Lodge 71, *183*, 184
Alexandra Building 23, 117, 128
Alexandra Wharf xv, 23, 128
Alfred, Prince 187
Allan, James H. 135
Anderson, A. T. & D. 103, *103*
Anderson, Arthur 62
Anderson Educational Institute *1*, 11, 87
Anderson, George 71, *97*
Anderson, Hosea/Osy 158–159
Anderson, Jerome J. 103
Anderson, John or Andrew 152
Anderson, John G. 173
Anderson, John R. 132
Anderson, Joseph 182
Anderson, May 71
Anderson, Peter 152, 153
Anderson Place 182
Anderson, Robert 152
Anderson, Robina 183
Anderson, Thomas 17
Anderson, Thomas J. 57, 58

Andersone, John 11
Angus, Chrissie 46
Angus Closs 140–141, *140*, *141*
Angus, Gilbert 140–141
Angus, James Stout 7–8, 46
Angus, John 141
Angus, Peter L. 46
Angus Pier 140–141
Annsbrae Court 55
Annsbrae House 117, 182
Annsbrae Place 182
Archer, G. 190
Arthur, Sir Gilbert 168
Arthur, John 168
Arthur, R. L. 165
Auld Kirk 44, 115
Auld Kirkyard *34*, 42, 43, 44, *44*

Back Baker's Closs *see* Navy Lane
Back Charlotte Lane 104, *104*, *158*
Bain, Gilbert 29, 141
Bain, James 29, 85
Bain, William C. 156
Bain's Beach 27, *28*, 29, *30*, 34, 36
Bain's Court 29–30, *29*, 32, *32*, 59
Bairnson, George L. 191, 192, 193
Baker's Closs *see* Mounthooly Street
Baker's Court 68–69, *69*, 70, 71
Baker's Well 66–67, *66*, *67*
Balfour, Tammy and Hamish 168
Bank Lane 11, 81–82, *81*, *82*, 83, 85, 150
Bank of Scotland 78, 79, 81
Bannatyne, John 64, 65

Bannatyne, Robert 64
Battery Closs *see* Navy Lane
Batty, George 119, *119*
Beresford, Vice Adm. Lord Charles 194
Betty Mann's Closs 47–48, *47*, *48*
Bewick, James 93
Birrell, Ralph 74
Birrell's Court 74–75, *74*, 75
Black, John 85
Black, Peter 65–66
Blance, Harry *97*
Blance, Mary 91
Bolt, Jessie 174
Bourmaster, Margaret 11
Bouwmeister, Mrs 147
Bowie, Albert E. R. 8
Brae Cottage 183
Brae Court 183
Braeside Court 96
Braeside House 64, 68, 71, *73*, 184
Braeview *69*, 71
Brand, Capt. William H. 68
Breiwick Road 4, 182
Brentham House 91, 196
Brentham Place 186, 196, *196*
Brevik Hospital / Brevik House 5, 127
Brunt Hoose 85, *136*, 138
Bullet Loan 182
Bult, Christiane 11
Bulwark Wharf 162
Burgess, George H. 190
Burgess, Jim 112
Burgh Road xvii, 52, 118, 182, 183
Burgoyne, Robert 156
Burns, David 100
Burns, Janet 100
Burns Lane/Closs xiv, *xiv*, 34, 59, 99–101, *99*, *100*
Burns Lodberry 100, *101*, 149
Burns, Magnus xiv, 99, 100, 149
Burns Pier 100, 149
Burns Walk 99–100, *100*, 177, 179
Byrne, C. & J. 157
Byrne, Ian 75, 145
Byrne, John 74–75
Byrne's Temperance Hotel 74

Cabrelli, Andrew 118–119, 155–156
Caldwell, I. C. & Mrs G. P. 131
Cameron, Norman O. M. 19
Campbell, Dorothea and Eliza 31
Campbell's Closs/Lane 149, *149*
Campbell's Pier 149
Candle Hoose 53, *54*
Cant, R. G. 11
Captain's, The/Erlend Cottage 65, 69, *69*, 71
Carfrae, David 22
Carter, Nick P. 157
Cassell, John 52
Chalmers, Margaret *see* Miss Chalmers Stair
Chalmers, William 9
Chapel House 55, 66, *66*, *67*
Chapel Place 30, 55, *55*, 59
Chapman, Jo 178
Charleson, Eric 163–164
Charlotte House 62, 63, 186
Charlotte Lane 104, 105, 152, 182
  see also Back Charlotte Lane
Charlotte Place xv, xvi, 160–161, *160*, *161*, *162*
  1 74, 158–159
  Commercial Road and 182
  North Lodberry fire 164
  Smith's studio 166
  Tod's property 164, *169*
Charlotte Street 104, 105, *105*, 152, 165, 182
Cheyne, Henry 17
Cheyne, Robert 87
Cheyney, Mrs Irene 93
Christie, Christina S. 65
Chromate Lane 11, 33–34, *33*, *34*, 35, 36, 43
Church Lane 42–43, *42*, *43*, *44*
  1851 population 34
  Malcolmson's house 97
  Scott's house 111
  Solotti's property 118, 119
  steps xv, 10, 11, 42
  tunnel exit 38
Church Road *43*, 111, 182
  construction 34, *34*, *42*, 43, 112, 117

Masonic Hall 44
  see also Auld Kirkyard
Clairmont Place *183*
  Alder Lodge 71, *183*, 184
Clark, Catherine 114
Clark, Mrs Elizabeth 114
Clark, Miss Hilda 18
Clark, William A. 113, 114, 117
Clark's Court/Place 113–119, *122*
Clark's Lodberry 113, 114
Cleeves, Ann 51
Clickimin Leisure Centre 96
Cockstool Shop 111
Coffee House 74
Colvin's house 161
Commercial Buildings 167
Commercial Road xv, *62*, 112, 182
  Charlotte House 62, 63, 186
Commercial Street *51*, *84*, *85*, *110*, *137*
  2 *8*
  2-8 (Copland's House) 7, *10*
  4 8
  6 7–8
  8 8, 13, 14
  9 (Old Manse) xiii, *7*, 25
  10 (Torrie's House) xiii, 9–10, *9*, *10*, *12*
    lodberry *7*, 9, 10, *12*, 14, 20, *39*
    Morton Lodge 17
  11 7, 8
  12 *9*, *10*, 11, 12, *12*, 13, 17
  13 7, 8
  14 (Mcbeath's/Sea Door) 19, 20 21, *20*, *39*
  15 7, 14
  16 21, 22, 144
  17 (Da Roost House) 9, 10–11, *10*, 14, *15*
  24 *see* Tolbooth
  25 19
  27 and **29** 19, *19*, *20*, *29*
  31 (Quendale House) 25–26, *25*, 32
  36 (Seaview Stores) 43, 111, 112
  42-44 (Faerdie-Maet) 113–114, *113*, 115, *115*, 118, 121
  48 120–121, *120*
  49 *see* Seafield Court
  52 (Anderson & Goodlad) 91, 122, 146
  53 184
  56 (Tangled) 123, 145
  58 (ICare) 123
  59 (Sinclair's Inn) 50, 108
  60-62 (Anderson & Co) *xvi*, 62, *134*, *167*
  61 (Vaila Fine Art) 167
  62-64 (High Level Music Centre) 126, 130
  65 (Smith & Co.) 42, 80
  66 (Santander) xiii, 130, *131*, 132, 133, 135
  67 (Antique and collectable shop) *43*, 65, 111, *111*, 118
  68 (Arthur Simpson) 133, *134*
  69 75
  73 95
  74-78 (Conochies) 49, *84*, 85, 121, 136–137, *137*, 138
  77-79 (Shetland Times) xiii, 114, *120*
  80 (Ninian) 85, 86, 138, 139
  82 (Aurora) 85, 86, 139, 140
  84 (R.A.M. Knitwear) xiii, 85, 140, 141, 142
  85 (Spence's Court) 45–46, *45*
  86 (Da Noost) 142, 143
  87 (Shetland Book Shop) 46, *46*
  88 143
  90-94 (J.G. Rae Ltd.) 22, 144, 146–148, *146*, 149
  93-95 (Jamieson's Knitwear) xiii, 45, *45*, 47
  96 (Loose Ends) xiv, 148, 149, 150
  97 (Island Larder) xiii, xiv, 47
  98 (The Dowry) 150, 151, *151*, 188, 190
  99 (Outdoor Trek) xiii, xiv, 49, 52, 53–54, *54*, 62
  101 52, 53
  102 (M&Co) xiv, 99, 100, *101*, *149*, 179
  103 56
  106 (Virgin Money) 99, 100, *101*, 102, 152, 153, 179
  107 (Tourist Centre) 56–58
  108 (Specsavers) 152, 154
  109 (Miller Opticians) 74
  110 (Envi) 154

111 (Shetland Soap Co.) 74, 76
112 159
113 (Wine Shop) xiii, 65, 76, 78, 130–131, *131*
114 (Universal Stores) xiv, 158, 159, *159*
116 158
116-126 *see* Charlotte Place
124 and **126** (Harry's Department Store) 165
125-127 (Red Cross) 85
141 (Nordsterna Shetland Crystal Boutique) xiii, 87, 142
143 (R.W. Bayes) 90, 142, 148, 157
153 94, 95, 144
155 (Shetland Clinical Services) 94, 95, *95*, 144, 148
157 (Aa Fired Up) 97
159 96–97
161 and **163** 100
167 (Hill House/Intersport) 102, *102*, *103*
169 147
173 (Boots UK Ltd.) xiv, 74, 159
175 (Sleeping Beauty) 118
177 (Love from Shetland) 53, 105
Bank of Scotland building 78, 79, 81
Burns Lane trance xiv, *xiv*, 99, *99*
Camera Centre 85, 133, 136
cart access 10
Chromate Lane entrance *34*
Church Road junction 43
Clark's Court/Clark's Place 113–119, *122*
Dennis Coutts' shop xiv
Esplanade junction 170, 171
Grand Hotel 92, *92*, 93, *93*, 127, 157
Greig's Walk 121, *121*
Hall's bakery 65
Hay's Corner 108, *110*
Kelday's Court 92–93
Leog Lane access 6
Lodberrie *see* Lodberrie, The
Meeting House 11
Middle Trance xiii, 138, *153*
Miss Chalmers Stair xv, 9–10, *9*, 12, 42
naming xvii

North Trance xiv, *153*
numbering xviii, 46
Ogilvy's Buildings 105, *105*, *161*
reflagging/repaving 63, 142
Roost, da (north) 83, *83*, 84
Roost, da (south) 9, 11
Royal Hotel xiv
Scottshall Court xiii, 37–38, *37*, *38*
shop windows 150
Shore route xii, xvii, *153*
South Trance xiii, xv, 130, 131, *131*, *153*
tar barrelling 81, 83–84
Tod's 164, 165, 167, 169
Towbooth Walk 108
Trance House xiii, 131–132, 133
tunnels xvii, 12, 20, 36, *36*, 37–38, 137, 141, 142, 148, 150–151, *161*
Twageos route xv, 10
widening 11, 85
Cooper, Davy 177
Cooper, Ronnie 80
Copland, James 7
Copland's Lodberry *7*, *39*
Copland's Pier ix, 7–8, *7*, *8*
Copland's Walk 8, *8*
Corner, George 11
Corothie, Mary & Harry 118
County Buildings 187
County Library 116, *117*
Coutts, Andrew 173
Coutts, Dennis xiv
Cowie, Dr John 73
Coyne, Robert 69–70
Craigie, Catherine and Elizabeth 25
Craigie, James 35
Craigie, Bailie James 25
Craigie, Capt. John 25
Craigie, Robert 35
Craigie Stane 21, 26, *26*, 27
Craigie, William 3
Craigie's Court xiii, 25
Crooked Lane 47–48, *47*, *48*, *123*
Cross Lane 182
Crystal Palace *174*, 175–177
Customs House 109

Dalziel, James 80
Daniels, James 117
Dark Trance *see* South Trance
Davidson, Robert 11
Deans, Ann 4, 146, 149
Deans, Robert 4, 125
Deans-Campbell, John 4, 5, 146, 149
Diana Fountain 129, *134*, 172–173, *172*
Dick, Andrew and William 3
Dingwall, Mr 64
Dirty Closs 34
Djunkowsky, Stephen de 114
Doig, Miss 193
Draa-well Closs *30*, 32
Drill Hall 194
Duncan, Andrew 72
Duncan, Charles G. 4
Duncan, Charles J. 94
Duncan, Gilbert 61, 68
Duncan, William Rae 184
Dundas, Frederick 62

Ebenezer Hall *69*, 71
Edmonston, Thomas 114
Elizabeth II, Queen 23, 59, 129
Ellesmere Buildings *131*, 132, *132*, *134*, *135*, 172
Ellesmere House 21
Erland Cottage *65*, 69, *69*, 71
Esplanade *xv*, *xviii*, *141*, *165*, *168*, 170–179, *171*, *172*
   Albert Building 115, *165*, *168*
   Church Road junction 43
   Commercial Street junction 170, 171
   construction x, xviii, *131*, 150, 153, 170–172, *171*, *174*
   Crystal Palace *174*, 175–177
   Diana Fountain 129, *134*, 172–173, *172*
   Ellesmere Buildings *131*, 132, *132*, *134*, *135*, 172
   Ellesmere House 21
   extension/widening 128, *164*, *169*, 177
   Grierson's Lodberry 22, *101*, *143*, 144–145, *144*, 148, *148*
   Harbour House 58, 133, *135*, 173, 175
   Harry's Department Store 163, *165*, 167

   Leask's Lodberry 122, *122*, 123
   Lizzie's Lodestar Café *172*, 173–175, *173*, *175*
   Merran Moad's Beach 153
   Seaman's Home cellar access 117
   Seaview House 43, 112, *112*, *117*
   shipping company premises 22, 144
   Taylor's Pier *122*, 123–124
   Tod's *164*, 165, 167, *168*, 169, *169*
   Victoria Buildings *134*, 135, 166–167
   see also Harrison Square; North Lodberry; Tait's Lodberry; Thule Bar; Tolbooth; Victoria Pier

Farquhar, William 113
Fields, Gracie 195
Fordyce, Charlie 93
Formby, George 195
Fort Charlotte *xii*, *105*, *170*, 179
   Anderson Place 182
   Charlotte Place named for 160
   construction xii
   customs house 97
   Meeting House use 11
   North Trance demolition xiv
   prison 109
   repair 4, 125
   road below xii, xv, xvii, 10–11, *153*, 170, 171
Foubister, John 62
Fox, Alexander W. 13
Fox, Charles James 96
Fox Lane 34, 96–97, *96*, 98, 150
Franklin, Sir and Lady John 147
Fraser, Capt. xii
Free Kirk Manse 73
Freefield 83, 156, 186
Freefield Docks 182
Freefield Lane *see* Market Street/Whisky Lane
Fullerton, Ertie 190
Furnival, Mr 168

Galloway, J. K. xiii
Ganson Brothers 163, 164, 166, 167, 195–196

Ganson, Laurence 195
Ganson, Robert (Bertie) 196
Ganson, Robert D. 163, 195, 196
Ganson, Thomas 163, 195
Ganson's Hall 163
Gardie Court 52–54, *52*, *54*, 55, 61
Gardie Lane 30, 52, *54*, 55, *55*, 59, 66
Garrick, Martin 145
Garrison Closs *see* Charlotte Street
Garrison Theatre 182, 194–195, *194*
Garthspool 83, 91, 156
Garthspool Road 74
Gas Pier *62*, 170
Gasworks 62, *62*, 63, 186, *187*
Gear, John 188, 189
Gibbs, Suzanne 91
Gibson, Richard 10, 129, 148, 175
Gifford, Charles 84, 98
Gifford, John 98
Gifford, William 98
Gilbert Tait's Closs *see* Reform Lane
Gilbertson, Henry R. 73
Gilbertson Public Park 53, *118*
Gilbertson Road 53
Gilbertson, Robert P. 52–53
Gilbertson, Thomas 52, 53
Gilbertson's Closs *see* Gardie Court
Gillie, George 7, 8
Gillie's Pier ix, 7–8, *7*, *8*
Gladstone Terrace *103*
Goodlad, Andrew 184
Goodlad, John (Johnnie Gullet) 183–185, *184*
Gordon Cottage *183*
Gordon, Jeannie 104
Goudie, Gilbert 11
Goudie, James 65
Goudie, Mrs Jessie 19
Goudie, Jim *75*
Goudie, Laurence 22
Goudie, Robert 130
Goudy, Gavin 61
Gow, John 77
Grand Hotel 92, *92*, 93, *93*, 127, 157
Grant, Francis J. 11
Grant, Robert 114

Grant, William A. 114
Gray, Elizabeth 19, 20
Gray, Gifford 71
Gray, James 57
Gray, James W. 157
Gray, Janet 19, 20
Gray, Magnus 173
Gray, Margaret 19, 20
Gray, Mona 57
Gray, William 19
Green Yairds 102
Greenfield House 34
Greenfield Place 34, 182
Greenwald, Roy 100
Greig, Mrs Ann 4
Greig, James 4, 73, 121, 146, 149
Greig, Margaret 73
Greig's Closs 146–148, *146*, *147*, 149
Greig's Hol 148
Greig's Lodberry x, *101*, 120, *122*, *143*, *144*, *148*
    Maikie Moad's Beach 149
    name change 121
    restoration 148, 170
Greig's Pier xviii, *xviii*, 120–121, *147*, 148
Greig's Walk 121, *121*
Gremista xix, 165, 169, 175
Gressy Loan 2
Grierson, Andrew 144
Grierson, Andrew J. 25, 92, 94
Grierson, James 25
Grierson's Closs *see* Quendale Lane
Grierson's Lodberry 22, *101*, *143*, 144–145, *144*, 148, *148*
Grime, Paul 129
Grindislea *183*
Grunberg, Jim 80
Gullet's Brae ix, 182, 183–185, *183*

Halcrow, Rosabelle 178
Haldane Place 30, 59
Half Closs 96
Hall, H. G. 164
Hall, William 65
Hangcliff Lane *ix*, 11, 34, *75*, 78–80, *78*, *79*
Harbour House 58, 133, *135*, 173, 175

Harbour Street 179, 188, 195, 196
Hardie, John 11
Harrison, Arthur 85
Harrison, Arthur H. 84
Harrison, G. 139
Harrison, George 85
Harrison, Gilbert 85, 136–137
Harrison Place 137
Harrison Square 85, 136–137, *136*, *137*, *139*
  Angus Closs 140
  Brunt Hoose 85, 138–139
  Irvine Place 133
  pedestrianisation 179
  Peterson's Closs 143
Harrison, William B. M. 137
Hay, Arthur J. 17, 114
Hay, Barbara 17
Hay, George H. B. 36, 170
Hay, Harry 188, 194
Hay, Hay 121
Hay, James 108
Hay, Capt. John (Jock) Westwood 16, 17–18
Hay, Miss Margaret E. 17, 108
Hay, Col. Westwood Norman 17
Hay, William xiv, 36, 42, 113, 160, 162
Hayfield Court *10*, *12*, *15*, 16–18, *18*, *20*
  1 (Hayfield Court House) *9*, *16*, 17, *17*, 18, *18*
  2 (Hayfield Court Cottage) *16*, 17, *17*, 18
  Meeting House site 11
  Stout's Court access 14
Hay's Corner 108, *110*
Hay's Lodberry *39*, 108, *108*
Hay's Pier *39*, 108, *108*, 170, 177
Heddell, Andrew xiii, 130
Heddell, Ann S. 148
Heddell, Francis 56
Heddell, James J. G. 56
Heddell's Beach 61
Heddell's Court 56–58, *56*, *58*, 61
Heddell's Park ix, xiv, 18, 30, 55, 59–60, *59*, *60*
Henderson, Elizabeth 25
Henderson, William 7

Henry, Mrs Jemima 93
Henry, Jim 142
Henry, John 36
Henry, Robert 36
Henshall, Douglas 28
Hepburn, George 93
Herning, Derick and Nina 18
Hicks, Mr 147
Hill House 102, *102*, *103*
Hill Lane 102–103, *102*
Hillhead xvi, *183*
  4 (Free Kirk Manse) 72–73
  'Da Lang Bar' *156*, 157
  Freefield and 186
  Half Closs/Braeside Court 96
  library premises 116, *117*
  North Hill Place 182
  tunnel 137
Hjempåfjaelet *69*, 71
Hoggan, G. W. 164
Holmsgarth 129, 145
Holmsgarth Road 24, 129, 145
Horne, Mr & Mrs I. 13
Howell, Mrs Theodora 8
Hughson, Captain James 69
Hunter, David G. K. 155, 156
Hunter, Willie 190

Innes, Mrs Ann 17
Innes, Peter 62
Innes's Lodberry *xvi*, 62
Irvine, Alexander C. 131, 133
Irvine, Andrew 133, 135
Irvine, Callum 178
Irvine Closs 133–135, *133*, *135*, 153
Irvine, George 65
Irvine, John T. 131, 133
Irvine, John 188
Irvine, Leslie 65, 66, 69, 73
Irvine, Margaret 4
Irvine Place 133, *133*
Irvine, Mrs Raewyn 73
Irvine, William 3, 4
Irvine's Pier/Lodberry 135
Irvinesgord *30*, *31*, 32
Islesburgh Community Centre 117

James Tait's Closs *see* Bank Lane
James, Capt. William 111
Jamieson, Andrew W. 116
Jamieson, Mrs Ann 173
Jamieson, Bretta 11
Jamieson, Charles D. 94
Jamieson, Denis 183
Jamieson, Harry 165
Jamieson, James 69
Jamieson, John 87
Jamieson, Magnus 90
Jean Kelday's House xiv
Jeannie Bult's Hoose *1*
Johnson, Andrew *97*
Johnson, John 188, 189
Johnson, John H. 8
Johnston, Frank 89
Johnston, George 19
Jones, John Paul xii

Kantersted Eventide Home 5
Kay, D. & G. 155, 156, 163, 164, 167
Kay, David 93, 163
Kay, George G. 93, 163
Kay, George T. 157
Kay, Theodore 93
Kean, Robert and Thomas 155
Kelday, Elizabeth 92
Kelday, Jean xiv
Kelday, John 92
Kelday's Court 92–93
King Erik House 116
King Harald Street 184–185, 189
King's Street xvii
Knab Road 42, 79, 182
Knowe, The *1*
Kveldsro Cottage 17
Kveldsro Gardens *12*, 15
Kveldsro House 20

Laing, A. L. 53, 190
Laing, James 78
Lang Bar *156*, 157
Laurenson, Alexander J. 190
Laurenson, Arthur 4, 103, 114
Laurenson, James 3

Laurenson, Jane I. 4
Laurenson, Laurence 102, 103
Laurenson, Robert (post-runner) 184
Laurenson, Robert ('Robbie Snuddie')
   79, *80*
Laurenson, Simon 66
Law Lane 72–73, 74
   8 *72*, 73
   14 (Windhouse/Ortolan House) 46,
   72, 73
   1851 population 34
   Braeside House 64, 68, 71, *73*, 184
   Prospect House 72, *72*, *78*, 137
Leask, Andrew 145
Leask, Charles 93, 163
Leask, John 145
Leask, Joseph 36, 90–91, 93, 122, 123, 163
Leask, Mrs Mary 174
Leask, Peter 145
Leask, Stuart 21
Leask, Capt. Thomas 90
Leask, Thomas 93, 163
Leask, Willie *68*, 70, *70*
Leask's Closs *see* Pitt Lane
Leask's Dock 91
Leask's Lodberry 122, *122*, 123
Lederer, Peter 58
Leog xii, *1*, 3–6, *3*, *4*, *5*, *6*
Lerwick Combination Poorhouse 127
Lerwick Hotel 183
Leslie, George 131–132, *131*, 164, 172
Leslie, John R. 132
Leys, Chrissie *75*
Lightsom Buoy 178, *178*
Linklater, James 27, 148
Linklater, Robert xiv, 159
Linklater's Pier *see* Osy Anderson's Pier
Lizzie's Lodestar Café *172*, 173–175,
   173, *175*
Lochend House xiii, 29, 32, 33, *33*, *34*, 36
Lochend's Closs 33
Lodberrie, The 27–28, *27*, *28*, *29*, *39*, *108*
   loading from 32
   slaughterhouse under 187–188
   spelling x
Loeterbagh, Dr Petrus 147–148

London Road 182
Longmuir, George 116
Lounge, The 73, 74, *74*, 75, *75*
Lovers Loan/Lane 1, *1*, 3, 4, 182
Lower Park Lane 140–141, *140*
Lower Tait's Closs 138–139, *138*
Lystina House 153

Ma family 157
Mcbeath, Andrew 20
Mcbeath's Lodberry/Sea Door 19, 20–21, *20*, *39*
Macfadyen, William 154
MacGregor, Bill 175
McKay, Hugh 84, 85
McKenzie, Mr & Mrs Peter 21
McKinlay, William 19
McMaster, George *97*
Maconachie, James 61
McWhirter, Mrs. J. A. 148
Maikie Moad's Beach 149
Main Street xvii
Malcolmson, James 138
Malcolmson, William 97
Mann, Betty 48
Manson, Alan 71
Manson, Annie 173
Manson, Dr T. Mortimer Y. 38
Manson, Thomas 188, 189
Manson's Closs *see* Fox Lane
Mariners' Court 81, 83–85, 86, 138
Market Cross xii, 61–63, *61*, *62*, *63*, 81, *156*, 165
Market Cross Well 62
Market Green 187–188
Market House 195, 196, *196*
Market Place 188
Market Street/Whisky Lane 25, 163, 182, 186–196, *186*, *193*
Marnoch, Sylvester 157
Masonic Hall 44, 115
Masonic Lodge *44*
Meeting House 11
Merran Moad's Beach 153
Merran Moad's Steps 152–153, *152*, 157
Merrylee, Miss 67

Methodist Church and Manse *183*
Middle Trance xiii, 138, *153*
Mill, Rev. John 113
Millan, Bruce 129
Millie, Bessie 49–50
Milne, Robert xii
Miss Chalmers Stair xv, 9–10, *9*, 12, 42
Miss Heddell's burn 61
Mitchell, Mr 81
Mitchell, Janet 3
Mitchell, John 3
Moad, Maikie 149
Moad, Merran 152–153
Moffat, James 188, 189
Moffatt, Capt. Commandant 194
Moltzau, Arne P. 58, 165
Moncrieff, Erik 28
Moncrieff, Thomas x, 28, 29
Morrison, Hector 85
Morrison, John 125–126
Morrison, Mrs Margaret 65
Morrison's Pier 21, 125–126
  see also Victoria Wharf
Morton, Earl of 1, 9
Mouat, Alexander H. 162–163
Mouat, Harry J. 167, 168
Mouat, Henry 166, 167, 190
Mouat, James 111, 162, 190
Mouat, John 157
Mouat, Laurence and Janet 16–17
Mouat, Marion 152–153
Mouat, Peter 162
Mouat, Richard 76
Mouat, Robert 76
Mouat, Stephen V. 12
Mouat, Thomas 76–77
Mouat, William 162
Mouat, William, of Garth 19, 50
Mouat, William ('Tarry Wumple') 76–77, 130
Mouat's Lodberry 111–112
Mounthooly Place 30, 59, *59*, *60*
Mounthooly Street 59, 64–67, *64*, *65*, *67*, *69*, 182
  1851 population 34
  burn 61

Commercial Street cart access 10
   housing scheme 71
   Law Lane access 73
   streetlights 69
Mowbray, John 90
Mowbray's Closs *see* Pitt Lane
Mowbray's Houses 90
Muir, Mrs Barbara 163
Muir, Thomas 158
Muir's Steps 158, *158*, 160
Mullay, John 11
Mullay, Robert 142
Mullay's Pier 142, 143
Mullay's Steps *136*, 142, *142*
Murray, John 11, 37
Murray's Closs *see* Scottshall Court
Murray's Hol 37, *37*
Murray's Lodberry 11–13, *12*, *13*, *37*, *39*
Mushy Park 60
Myrtle Hall 81, 82, *82*

Navy Cottage 68, 71, *183*
Navy Lane 34, 64, *64*, *65*, 68–71, *68*, *69*, *71*
New Pier *see* Stout's Pier/Wharf
Nice, Arthur 16
Nice, Barbara Ann 17
Nice Court *see* Hayfield Court
Nice, James 16
Nice, Thomas 16, 17
Nicol, Alexander 49
Nicol's Court *see* Norna's Court
Nicolson, Andrew 85
Nicolson, Andrew 150
Nicolson, Arthur 4, 29
Nicolson, Laurence J. 150
Nicolson, William 3–4
Nicolson's Closs 150–151, *150*
Norna's Court xiv, 48, 49–51, *49*, 77
Norrie, Mary 80, *80*
Nort Kirk Closs *see* Queens Lane
North Hill Place 182
North Lodberry xv, xvi, *143*, *154*, *160*, 162–165, *162*, *163*, *167*
   Ganson Bros. premises 163, 164, 166, 167, 195
   see also William Ross's North Lodberry

North Ness 182
North Pier *see* Osy Anderson's Pier
North Trance xiv, *153*

O'Brien, Mr and Mrs 114
Ogilvy, Charles xiv, 14, 36, 61, 122
Ogilvy, Charlotte 45
Ogilvy, James 138
Ogilvy, Thomas 105
Ogilvy's Buildings 105, *105*, *161*
Old Cemetery, Knab Road 79, 182
Old Manse xiii, *7*, 25
Old Tolbooth *see* Tolbooth
Ollason, Charles 121
Ollason, Robert 94–95
Ollason's Pier *see* Greig's Pier
Ortolan House/Windhouse 46, *72*, 73
Osy Anderson's Pier 158–159

Park Lane 76, 81, 87–89, *87*, *88*
   see also Lower Park Lane
Park Lane Community Garden 88–89, *89*, 91, *91*
Parker, Mr 161
Parker's Pier 161
Parkfield 194
Paton, R. 110
Peterson, Gilbert 142, 143
Peterson's Closs 143, *143*
Peterson's Pier 142, 143
Peterson's Place 143
Petrie, Capt. John W. 68–69
Petrie, P. E. 74
Pilot Lane/Place 98, *98*, 99
Pirate Lane 51, 74, *75*, 76–77, *76*, *77*
Pitt Lane 90–91, *90*, *91*
   1851 population 34
   Grand Hotel Bar advert *93*
   Leask property in 122
   Park Lane and 88, 89, *91*
   tunnel 137
Pitt, William 90, 91, 96
Post Office 109, *109*, *117*, 121, 122, 173, 184
Priest, Brian 175
Prospect House 72, *72*, *78*, 137
Queens Hotel 35, *36*, *117*

development 36
Murray's Lodberry 12, 37, *37*
sea damage 108, *109*
Queens Lane 10, 43–44, *43*, *44*, 48, 59
Sinclair's Steps 120, *120*
Queens Place 30, 48, *48*, 55, 59
Quendale House 25–26, *25*, 32
Quendale Lane 34, 94–95, *94*, *95*, 96, 144, *149*

Ratter, Alexander R. S. 115, 116, *116*
Ratter, Baabie 104
Ratter, Gilbert 190
Ratter, Lizzie 116, 117
Raven's Court xiii, 29, *29*, 30–31, *30*, *31*, 32, *32*
Redder, Mrs Jean xiv
Reform Lane *xvii*, xviii, 86, *86*, 182, 195
1851 population 34
Harrison Place 137
Lower Tait's Closs 138–139, *138*
Mariner's Court and 83, 84, 85
Park Lane and *87*, 88
Reid, Margaret and Dougal 191
Richan, William 16
Richmond, Harvey 93
Ridland, Robert and Abel 186
Roadside Hut 184
Robert Cheyne's Closs *see* Park Lane
Robertson, Alistair 130–131
Robertson, Bertie 194
Robertson, Bailie John 27
Robertson, John ('John o da Trance') xiii, 131, 132
Robertson, John R. 95
Robertson, John W. 12
Robertson, Laurence 65
Robertson, Molly 119
Robertson, Robert 131, 132
Robertson, Walter *118*, 119
Robertson, William 53
Robertson's Lodberry *see* Lodberrie, The
Roost, da (north) 83, *83*, 84
Roost, da (south) 9, 11
Roost Hoose 9, 10–11, *10*, 14, *15*
Rosegarth *183*

Ross, Alexander 187
Ross, Barbara 36
Ross Court xiii, 19–22, *19*, *20*
Ross, John 19
Ross, William 19
North Lodberry 19, 21–22, *21*, 26, *39*
South Lodberry 20, *20*, *39*
Royal Bank of Scotland 45, 120
Royal Hotel xiv, 74
Russell, Arthur 65

St Barnaby's/St Barnabas chapel 11
St Columba's Church 55
St Magnus Scottish Episcopal Church 182
St Olaf Street 116, 184
St Olaf's Hall 55
St Ringan's Church 116, 188
St Sunniva Street 194
Salmon, Fred 164
Sandison, Alexander 188
Sandison, Andrew 89
Sandison, William 10
Sands' Court xiii, 29–30
Sands, Rev. James 29
Scalloway Road 182, 183, *183*, 184, 185
Scarfa Taing 12
Schoor, Mrs Catherine 163
Scollay, Ann 17
Scollay, Arthur 10
Scollay, Issobel 16
Scollay, Patrick 9
Scollay, Robert 10
Scollay, Samuel 10, 17
Scott, Elizabeth 11, 37
Scott, John 50
Scott, Robert 37
Scott, Tavish 129
Scott, Walter 37, 111
Scott, Sir Walter 49–50, 77
Scottshall Court xiii, 37–38, *37*, *38*
Sea Door 19, 20–21, *20*
Seafield Court xiii, 17, *33*, *34*, 35–36, *35*, 91
entrance 38, *38*
tunnel 36, *36*
Yates's home 33, 35–36

Seaman's Home 43, 114, 115, *115*, 116, 117, *117*
Seaview House 43, 112, *112*, *117*
Seaview Stores 43, 111, 112
Seaview Vaults 155, *155*, *163*
Seawinds/Sea Winds xiii, 33, *33*, *34*
Sheriff's Closs *see* Law Lane
Shetland Book Shop 46, *46*
Shetland Library 116, *117*, 188
Shetland South Atlantic Whaler Memorial 177–178, *177*
Shewan, John P. 117
Shore, the xii, xvii, *153*
Sievwright, Peter 64, 68, 73
Sievwright, William 73
Simpson, Alex 189
Sinclair, Bruce 36
Sinclair, James 10, 11, 160
Sinclair, James 65
Sinclair, James 95
Sinclair, Jane 183
Sinclair, John 120
Sinclair, L. A. 95
Sinclair, Leslie *97*
Sinclair, Lily 190
Sinclair, Margaret 11
Sinclair, Nicol 113
Sinclair, Robbie 12
Sinclair, Robert 120
Sinclair, Robert 190
Sinclair, William 11, 120
Sinclair's Beach *115*, 120, *120*, *122*, 173
Sinclair's Inn 50
Sinclair's Lodberry *see* Greig's Lodberry
Sinclair's Pier *see* Greig's Pier
Sinclair's Steps 120–121, *120*, *121*
Skae, Dr 191
Skipper's Court 65, 68–69, *69*, 70, 71
Slaughterhouse Road 188
Small Boat Harbour *24*, 108, *176*, 177
Smith, Andrew 53, 121
Smith, Mrs Barbara 174
Smith, Dr Charles E. 173
Smith, Frederic 173
Smith, James S. 105
Smith, John 150

Smith, Laurence 22
Smith, Mathew 16
Smith, Peter 8
Smith, Ross 166
Smith, Tom 95
Solotti, Alex 118, *118*
South End *xvi*, 39, *167*
South Hill Place 182, 183
South Kirk Closs *see* Church Lane
South Road 183
South Trance xiii, xv, 130, 131, *131*, *153*
Spence, Balfour 45
Spence, Charles 71
Spence, Colin 21
Spence, Elizabeth 46
Spence, Gilbert 34
Spence, James R. 17, 45, 46
Spence, Jane 34
Spence, John 73, 148
Spence, Robert A. 73
Spence, Robert Niven 73
Spence, Dr William 34
Spence's Court 45–46, *45*, *46*
Steamers' Stores 21–24, *21*, *23*, 26, *39*, 129
Stebbagrinds' House 35
Steep Closs *see* Hangcliff Lane
Stevenson, Gordon *ix*
Stevenson, Robert 50
Stewart, Earl Patrick 50
Stewart, Mr and Mrs T. 65
Stone Block, the 61
Stoot's Hoose 92–93
Stout, Barbara 10, 11
Stout, Charles 146, 148
Stout, John 36
Stout, Queenie 148
Stout, Robert 11, 14
Stout, Sir Robert 15
Stout, Thomas 92
Stout's Court xv, 7, 9, 14–15, *15*, 92, 118
Stout's Pier/Wharf 8, 14–15, *14*, *39*
Stove, Alfred 150
Stove, Laurence 150
Stove, Thomas 150
Stove, Tom 95
Strong, Thomas 42

Strong's Court 43
Strong's House *1*
Summerside House 189
Sutherland, Maj. James xii, xiv
Sutherland, John R. 63
Sutherland's Closs *see* Fox Lane
Swallow Lane *see* Bank Lane
Swanson, Stanley 75, *75*

Tait, Alex and George 193
Tait, Bertie 194
Tait, Cecil 58
Tait, E. S. Reid 85, 116, 121, 139, 141
Tait, George R. 154, 155, 157, 187
Tait, Gilbert 86, 138, 139
Tait, James 81, 149
Tait, John 22
Tait, Richard 86
Tait, Robert W. 191, 192, 193–194
Tait, Mrs Robert W. 193
Tait, Willie 177
Tait's Lodberry 86, *101*, 138–139, *143*,
    154–157, *154*, 158, *160*, *162*
    as Thule Bar 119, 155, *155*, 157, *157*, 165
Tait's Pier 86, 138, 139
Tait's Place 138, 155, 157, *157*
Tarry Wumple's Closs *see* Pirate Lane
Taylor, William and Remmy 123
Taylor's Pier *122*, 123–124
Taylor's Steps *48*, 123–124, *123*, *124*
Thatch Lane/Thatch House Lane *see*
    Back Charlotte Lane
Thomason, Edward 195
Thoms, Sheriff G. H. 126, 127, 171
Thomson, Magnus 98
Thomson, Robert 154–155
Thule Bar *101*, 119, 154, 155, *155*, 157,
    157, 165
Tirl Grind 1
Tod, J. & J. 135, 164, *164*, 165, 166–169,
    168, *169*, 190
Tod's Steps 160, 166–169, *166*, *169*
Tolbooth *42*, *108*, 109–110, *109*, 111,
    112, *115*, *117*, 170
    library and news room 109, 114–115
    Morton Lodge in 17, 109

Scott's visit 50
Towbooth Walk 108
Tolbooth Quay *see* Hay's Pier
Torrie, Barbara 4
Torrie, Patrick 4, 10
Torrie's Lodberry *7*, 9, 10, *12*, 14, 20, *39*
Towbooth Walk 108
Town Hall 4, 25, *103*, 117, 153, 187, 189
Trance Closs 130–132, *130*
Trance House xiii, 131–132
TSB 132, 133, 135, *135*, 153, 167
Tulloch, Catherine L. 5
Tulloch, William 4, 5
Tullock, Thomas 184
Turnbull, Rev. 50
Twageos xv, *1*, 2, *2*, 10, 50
Twageos House 1–2, *1*, 9
Twageos Road 1
Tyrie, William 11

Umphrey, Mary C. E. 121
Union Bank Lane *see* Bank Lane

Valle, Emanuelle 118
Vance, James 11
Vettese, Alfred 119, 156
Victoria Buildings *134*, 135, 166–167
Victoria Pier *22*, *23*, *24*, *126*, *128*, 129,
    129, 145
    car park 24
    development 21, 22, 23, 126–127, *127*,
        128, 171
    Diana Fountain 172–173
    gas lamp post 62
    K boot landmark 124, *124*
    Lizzie's Lodestar Cafe 173
Victoria Wharf 125–129, *125*
    development 21, 170, *171*, 172
    Robertsons' properties 131–132
    see also Morrison's Pier

Walker, John 114
Water Lane xiii, 29, *29*, *30*, *31*, 32, *32*
Waterloo Road 182, 183
Watts, Patricia 165
Westmoreland, Brenda 119

Whisky Lane/Market Street 25, 163, 182, 186–196, *186*, *193*
White, J. R. 54
White, John 156
Widows Homes 1, *1*
Wilkins, Mr and Mrs Neil 93
William Gray's House 19
William Ross's North Lodberry 19, 21–22, *21*, 26, *39*
William Ross's South Lodberry 20, *20*, *39*
Williamson, Daniel R. 111–112
Williamson, Frank 65
Williamson, Laurence 16
Williamson, Mitchell H. 190
Williamson, Peter 97
Williamson, William 65
Willowbrae 104
Wills, John 18
Wills, Jonathan 91
Wilson, Mrs Elizabeth 174
Windhouse/Ortolan House 46, *72*, *73*
Wren Court 69, *69*, 71
Wright, T. A. 190

'Yacob' 185
Yates, Francis 33, 35–36
Yates's Closs *see* Chromate Lane
Yates's Court 36
Yates's Lodberry *35*, 36, *39*
Yorston, Mr (bank agent) 184
Yorston, Catherine 16
Yorston, Mrs Elizabeth xiv
Yorston, James xiii, 130, 131
Yorston's Trance *see* South Trance

Zetland Aerated Water Company 189–194
Zetland Hotel 114